THE EUROPEAN UNION SERIE

General Editors: Neill Nugent, William E. Paterso

The European Union series provides an authoritativ
ranging from general introductory texts to definitive assessments of key institutions and
actors, issues, policies and policy processes, and the role of member states.

Books in the series are written by leading scholars in their fields and reflect the most
up-to-date research and debate. Particular attention is paid to accessibility and clear
presentation for a wide audience of students, practitioners and interested general
readers.

The series editors are **Neill Nugent**, Visiting Professor, College of Europe, Bruges and
Honorary Professor, University of Salford, UK, and **William E. Paterson**, Honorary
Professor in German and European Studies, University of Aston. Their co-editor until his
death in July 1999, **Vincent Wright**, was a Fellow of Nuffield College, Oxford University.

Feedback on the series and book proposals are always welcome and should be sent to
Steven Kennedy, Palgrave Macmillan, Houndmills, Basingstoke, Hampshire RG21 6XS,
UK, or by e-mail to s.kennedy@palgrave.com

General textbooks

Published

Desmond Dinan **Encyclopedia of the European
Union** [Rights: Europe only]
Desmond Dinan **Europe Recast: A History of
European Union** [Rights: Europe only]
Desmond Dinan **Ever Closer Union:
An Introduction to European Integration
(4th edn)** [Rights: Europe only]
Mette Eilstrup Sangiovanni (ed.) **Debates on
European Integration: A Reader**
Simon Hix and Bjørn Høyland **The Political
System of the European Union (3rd edn)**
Dirk Leuffen, Berthold Rittberger and Frank
Schimmelfennig **Differentiated Integration**
Paul Magnette **What is the European Union?
Nature and Prospects**
John McCormick **Understanding the European
Union: A Concise Introduction (5th edn)**
Brent F. Nelsen and Alexander Stubb **The
European Union: Readings on the Theory and
Practice of European Integration (3rd edn)**
[Rights: Europe only]
Neill Nugent (ed.) **European Union Enlargement**

Neill Nugent **The Government and Politics of the
European Union (7th edn)**
John Peterson and Elizabeth Bomberg
Decision-Making in the European Union
Ben Rosamond **Theories of European Integration**
Esther Versluis, Mendeltje van Keulen and Paul
Stephenson **Analyzing the European Union
Policy Process**
Hubert Zimmermann and Andreas Dür (eds) **Key
Controversies in European Integration**

Forthcoming

Laurie Buonanno and Neill Nugent **Policies and
Policy Processes of the European Union**
Magnus Ryner and Alan Cafruny **A Critical
Introduction to the European Union**
Sabine Saurugger **Theoretical Approaches to
European Integration**

Also planned

The Political Economy of European Integration

Series Standing Order (outside North America only)
ISBN 978–0–333–71695–3 hardback
ISBN 978–0–333–69352–0 paperback
Full details from www.palgrave.com

Visit Palgrave Macmillan's
EU Resource area at
www.palgrave.com/politics/eu

The major institutions and actors

Published

Renaud Dehousse **The European Court of Justice**
Justin Greenwood **Interest Representation in the European Union (3rd edn)**
Fiona Hayes-Renshaw and Helen Wallace **The Council of Ministers (2nd edn)**
Simon Hix and Christopher Lord **Political Parties in the European Union**
David Judge and David Earnshaw **The European Parliament (2nd edn)**
Neill Nugent **The European Commission**
Anne Stevens with Handley Stevens **Brussels Bureaucrats? The Administration of the European Union**

Forthcoming

Wolgang Wessels **The European Council**

The main areas of policy

Published

Michele Chang **Monetary Integration in the European Union**
Michelle Cini and Lee McGowan **Competition Policy in the European Union (2nd edn)**
Wyn Grant **The Common Agricultural Policy**
Martin Holland and Matthew Doidge **Development Policy of the European Union**
Jolyon Howorth **Security and Defence Policy in the European Union**
Johanna Kantola **Gender and the European Union**
Stephan Keukeleire and Jennifer MacNaughtan **The Foreign Policy of the European Union**
Brigid Laffan **The Finances of the European Union**
Malcolm Levitt and Christopher Lord **The Political Economy of Monetary Union**
Janne Haaland Matláry **Energy Policy in the European Union**
John McCormick **Environmental Policy in the European Union**
John Peterson and Margaret Sharp **Technology Policy in the European Union**
Handley Stevens **Transport Policy in the European Union**

Forthcoming

Karen Anderson **Social Policy in the European Union**
Michael Baun and Dan Marek **Cohesion Policy in the European Union**
Hans Bruyninckz and Tom Delreux **Environmental Policy and Politics in the European Union**

Sieglinde Gstöhl and Dirk de Bievrè **The Trade Policy of the European Union**
Christian Kaunert and Sarah Leonard **Justice and Home Affairs in the European Union**
Paul Stephenson, Esther Versluis and Mendeltje van Keulen **Implementing and Evaluating Policy in the European Union**

Also planned

Political Union
The External Policies of the European Union

The member states and the Union

Published

Carlos Closa and Paul Heywood **Spain and the European Union**
Alain Guyomarch, Howard Machin and Ella Ritchie **France in the European Union**
Brigid Laffan and Jane O'Mahoney **Ireland and the European Union**

Forthcoming

Simon Bulmer and William E. Paterson **Germany and the European Union**
Andrew Geddes **Britain and the European Union**
Brigid Laffan **The European Union and its Member States**

Issues

Published

Derek Beach **The Dynamics of European Integration: Why and When European Institutions Matter**
Christina Boswell and Andrew Geddes **Migration and Mobility in the European Union**
Thomas Christiansen and Christine Reh **Constitutionalizing the European Union**
Robert Ladrech **Europeanization and National Politics**
Cécile Leconte **Understanding Euroscepticism**
Steven McGuire and Michael Smith **The European Union and the United States**
Wyn Rees **The US–EU Security Relationship: The Tensions between a European and a Global Agenda**

Forthcoming

Graham Avery **Enlarging the European Union**

Key Controversies in European Integration

Edited by

Hubert Zimmermann

and

Andreas Dür

First published 2012 by
PALGRAVE MACMILLAN

Palgrave Macmillan in the UK is an imprint of Macmillan Publishers Limited, registered in England, company number 785998, of Houndmills, Basingstoke, Hampshire RG21 6XS.

Palgrave Macmillan in the US is a division of St Martin's Press LLC, 175 Fifth Avenue, New York, NY 10010.

Palgrave Macmillan is the global academic imprint of the above companies and has companies and representatives throughout the world.

Palgrave® and Macmillan® are registered trademarks in the United States, the United Kingdom, Europe and other countries

ISBN 978–1–137–00615–8   hardback
ISBN 978–1–137–00614–1   paperback

This book is printed on paper suitable for recycling and made from fully managed and sustained forest sources. Logging, pulping and manufacturing processes are expected to conform to the environmental regulations of the country of origin.

A catalogue record for this book is available from the British Library.
A catalog record for this book is available from the Library of Congress.

10   9   8   7   6   5   4   3   2   1
21   20   19   18   17   16   15   14   13   12

Printed in China

Contents

List of Figures

List of Abbreviations

ATM	Auto-Teller Machine
CAP	Common Agricultural Policy
CEE	Central and Eastern Europe
CEEC	Central and East European countries
CESR	Committee of European Securities Regulators
CFP	Common Fisheries Policy
CSDP	Common Security and Defence Policy
CSFP	Common Foreign and Security Policy
CMO	Common Market Organization
COGECA	General Confederation of Agricultural Cooperatives
COPA	Committee of Professional Agricultural Organizations
COREPER	Committee of Permanent Representatives
DM	Deutschmark
EAW	European Arrest Warrant
EBA	European Banking Authority
EC	European Community
ECB	European Central Bank
ECHR	European Court of Human Rights
ECJ	European Court of Justice
ECOFIN	Economic and Financial Affairs Council
ECSC	European Coal and Steel Community
EDA	European Defence Agency
EEAS	European External Action Service
EEC	European Economic Community
EFSF	European Financial Stability Facility
EIB	European Investment Bank
EIOPA	European Insurance and Occupational Pensions Authority
EMS	European Monetary System
EMU	Economic and Monetary Union
EP	European Parliament
EPC	European Political Cooperation
ERDF	European Regional Development Fund
ERM	Exchange Rate Mechanism
ESDP	European Security and Defence Policy
ESF	European Social Fund
ESFS	European System of Financial Supervisors
ESMA	European Securities and Markets Authority

ESRB	European Systemic Risk Board
EU	European Union
FSAP	Financial Services Action Plan
GDP	Gross Domestic Product
GPS	Global Positioning Satellite
IGCs	Intergovernmental Conferences
IMF	International Monetary Fund
IO	International Organization
LDCs	Least Developing Countries
MEP	Member of the European Parliament
NATO	North Atlantic Treaty Organization
NGOs	Non-Governmental Organizations
NPE	Normative Power Europe
PDO	Protected Designation of Origin
PSE	Producer Support Estimate
QMV	Qualified Majority Voting
R&D	Research and Development
REACH	Registration, Evaluation, Authorization and Restriction of Chemicals
SD	Services Directive
SEA	Single European Act
SGP	Stability and Growth Pact
SPS	Single Payment Scheme
TACs	Total Allowable Catches
TCE	Constitutional Treaty
TEU	Treaty on European Union
WTD	Working Time Directive
WTO	World Trade Organization

Foreword

Judging from its title, this book seems to be an explicit response to the crisis currently engulfing the EU. However, its origins go back quite some years. The idea for it emerged during a lecture series organized in 2006/07 by Hubert Zimmermann at Cornell University. The series was entitled 'Can the EU Survive?', which seemed a quite outlandish question at the time. The lectures reflected on what appeared a serious setback for the EU: the failure of the so-called Constitutional Treaty. Whatever the significance of this failure, it demonstrated that the process of European integration had become much more controversial than anyone thought possible prior to the turn of the millennium.

The contributions in this book represent the key controversies that are now openly shaping EU policy and politics. Obviously, there are many more fundamental open or hidden controversies associated with European integration than could be included in one book or handled by one editor. Based on our successful cooperation for a special issue of the *Journal of Common Market Studies*, Andreas joined as co-editor. Pushed along relentlessly by the editors of Palgrave Macmillan's European Union series, Neill Nugent and Willie Paterson, and by its publisher, Steven Kennedy, we embarked on an apparently never-ending process of finding a format which would make the most out of the basic idea of the book. Despite the rather strict format they were asked to adhere to, we managed to recruit a superb group of EU specialists, characterized by an unusual level of diversity in many respects, for instance nationality, professional background and gender. These authors have cast aside professional caution, taking clear and often risky stances in the debates that follow.

Our sincere thanks go to the authors, to the Palgrave Macmillan team and to two anonymous reviewers who provided excellent advice. We also thank Heather Taylor from the University of Frankfurt and Gerald Lindner from the University of Salzburg for superb editorial work. Hubert Zimmermann is also grateful to the German Academic Exchange Service (DAAD) and the Cornell Institute for European Studies for their support of the Cornell lecture series.

ANDREAS DÜR
HUBERT ZIMMERMANN

Notes on the Contributors

Dirk Ahner, an economist by training, worked for the European Commission. After long service in DG Agriculture, he was Director General in DG Regional Policy of the European Commission until the end of 2011.

Karen J. Alter is Professor of Political Science and Law, Northwestern University, USA. Her scholarship investigates when and how international institutions become politically important. She has written extensively on the European Court of Justice, and its jurisdictional twin, the Andean Tribunal of Justice. Fluent in Italian, French and German, she has held many prestigious fellowships in France, Germany, and the United States.

Derek Beach is Associate Professor in the Department of Political Science at the University of Aarhus, Denmark. He is a specialist in the constitutional politics of the European Union.

Richard Bellamy is Professor of Political Science and Director of the European Institute at University College, London, UK. He has authored several monographs, edited many more and published over a hundred articles and book chapters, on subjects ranging from the history of elite theory and liberalism to studies of constitutionalism, democracy and citizenship. His work on the EU reflects and informs his broadly republican approach to these topics.

Christopher J. Bickerton is Associate Professor in International Relations at Sciences Po in Paris, France. With a doctorate from the University of Oxford, he has previously taught at Oxford and the University of Amsterdam. He has published widely on international and European politics. His forthcoming book is entitled *From Nation-States to Member States: European Integration and Social Change* (Oxford University Press).

Marco Brunazzo is Researcher at the University of Trento, Italy. His research deals with Europeanization, Regional Policy, the European Committee of the Regions, and local governance.

Eugénia da Conceição-Heldt is Professor of International Relations at the Technical University in Dresden, Germany. Her areas of expertise include the European Union, negotiation analysis, and International Political Economy. Among her most recent publications is *Negotiating*

Trade Liberalization at the WTO: Domestic Politics and Bargaining Dynamics (Palgrave Macmillan, 2011).

Vincent Della Sala is Associate Professor in the School of International Studies and Faculty of Sociology at the University of Trento, Italy.

Desmond Dinan teaches at the George Mason School of Public Policy, in Arlington, VA, USA. He is the author of numerous popular textbooks on European integration.

Andreas Dür is Professor of International Politics at the University of Salzburg, Austria. He is a specialist in trade policy and interest group politics and the author of *Protection for Exporters: Power and Discrimination in Transatlantic Trade Relations, 1930–2010* (Cornell University Press, 2010).

Rachel Epstein is Associate Professor at the Korbel School of International Studies at the University of Denver, USA. Her areas of interest include the power and limits of international organizations, foreign ownership in banking, and the evolution of military–security institutions, including the North Atlantic Treaty Organization. She is the author of *In Pursuit of Liberalism: International Institutions in Postcommunist Europe* (Johns Hopkins, 2008).

John Gillingham is University of Missouri Board of Curators Professor of History at the University of Missouri, St Louis, USA. He published prolifically on the early history of integration. In his recent, widely translated works *Design for a New Europe* (Cambridge University Press, 2006) and *European Integration, 1950–2003: Superstate or New Market Economy* (Cambridge University Press, 2003), he has criticized the direction the EU has taken.

Jörn Carsten Gottwald taught at the University of Cork in Ireland and experienced the meltdown of the Irish financial bubble first-hand. He is Professor for the Politics of East Asia at Ruhr-University Bochum in Germany.

Ann-Christina L. Knudsen is Associate Professor of European Studies at the Institute for Culture and Society, Aarhus University, Denmark, and holds a PhD in History from the European University Institute, Florence, Italy. Among her publications is *Farmers on Welfare: The Making of Europe's Common Agricultural Policy* (Cornell University Press, 2009).

Ulrike Liebert is Jean Monnet Chair for European Politics and Professor of Political Science at the University of Bremen, Germany. Her most recent books include *Multilayered Representation Across the EU* (with

T. Evas and C. Lord, Nomos, 2012) and *European Economic and Social Constitutionalism after the Treaty of Lisbon* (with D. Schiek and H. Schneider, Cambridge University Press, 2011).

Christopher Lord is Professor at ARENA's Centre for European Studies in Oslo in Norway and is a prolific contributor to the scholarly debate on the EU's democratic deficit.

Ian Manners is Professor at the Institute of Society and Globalization at Roskilde University, Denmark. He works at the nexus of critical social theory, normative political theory, European integration and the EU in global politics.

John McCormick is Jean Monnet Professor of European Union Politics at the Indianapolis campus of Indiana University, USA. His research interests currently focus on the global role of the European Union, and on the implications for the Atlantic Alliance of the foreign policies of the European Union and the United States.

Anand Menon is Professor of West European Politics in the Department of Political Science and International Studies at the University of Birmingham, UK.

Daniel Mügge teaches in Amsterdam, Netherlands. He has published numerous articles on European financial policy, and his dissertation on this topic won the ECPR's Jean Blondel prize 2008 for best European political science dissertation of the year. His current work concentrates on accounting standard setting and the role of the EU in global financial rulemaking.

Hanna Ojanen is Researcher at the Finnish Institute for International Affairs. Prior to that, she was Head of Research at the Swedish Institute of International Affairs in Stockholm. Since completing her PhD at the European University Institute in Florence, she has published widely on European security policy.

Mats Persson is the director of Open Europe, an independent think-tank which calls for radical reforms of the EU. He has written extensively on EU policy, including on the eurozone crisis, financial regulation, employment law and the EU budget. In 2011, he was selected by the Diplomatic Courier and Young Professionals in Foreign Policy as one of 99 influential international leaders under 33 years of age.

Mark A. Pollack is Jean Monnet Chair and Professor of Political Science at Temple University, USA. He has written widely on EU institutions and policymaking, and on the politics of international law.

Uwe Puetter is Professor and Jean Monnet Chair at the Department of Public Policy, Central European University, Budapest, Hungary. He is Director of the University's Center for European Union Research (CEUR). His work focuses on the changing character of intergovernmental relations in a densely integrated European Union and the related processes of institutional adjustment.

Jeremy Rabkin is Professor of Law at George Mason University in the USA and one of the prominent voices cautioning against the perils of international law in the US.

Tal Sadeh is Senior Lecturer in the Department of Political Science at Tel-Aviv University, Israel. He is the author of *Sustaining European Monetary Union: Confronting the Cost of Diversity* (Lynne Rienner, 2006) and many other publications on the euro.

Amy Verdun is Jean Monnet Chair Ad Personam and Chair of the Department of Political Science at the University of Victoria, in Victoria, BC, Canada, where she has been since 1997. She holds a PhD in Political and Social Sciences from the European University Institute in Florence, Italy (1995). She is co-editor of the *Journal of Common Market Studies*.

Jonathan White is Lecturer in European Politics at the London School of Economics and Political Science, UK. He was also at Humboldt University in Berlin as an Alexander von Humboldt research fellow. He gained his doctorate at the European University Institute (EUI) in Florence, and has been a visiting scholar at University College London and Harvard's Kennedy School of Government.

Cornelia Woll is Associate Dean for Research and Senior Research Fellow at Sciences Po Paris in France and Leader of an Otto-Hahn Junior Research Group at the Max Planck Institute for the Study of Societies in Cologne, Germany.

Introduction: Key Controversies in European Integration

In mid-2005, French and Dutch voters rejected a proposal for a European Constitution that had taken the member states of the European Union (EU) many years to negotiate. The resounding 'No' by two of the founding nations of the EU immediately gave rise to a vivid debate on the pros and cons of the European project. Had this visionary and unparalleled project in international cooperation, which promised to overcome the pattern of state rivalry characterizing Europe since the Middle Ages, come to an undignified halt? Was this the beginning of the end of an experiment which was presented by European leaders as shining example to other regions of the world? Or was the vote just a temporary lull in a continuous process of reform? Many detractors have likened the EU to a bicycle which can only work as long as it is in motion. In fact, while its designation suggested that the Constitution might be the founding document of a true Union, the rather less grandiose real purpose was to reform the governing structures of the EU. By making these both more efficient and democratic, the EU tried to correct its increasingly negative image among many elites and the general public and to get closer to its citizens. Notwithstanding many obituaries, the member states quickly resurrected the idea of an institutional reform with a less charged set-up. Now they framed it as an intergovernmental treaty which would not need to receive the uncertain consent of a fickle populace. The Treaty of Lisbon went into force on 1 December, 2009.

By this time, another crisis rocked the foundations of the EU. The consequences of the global financial crisis of 2007/2008 led to a massive rise in the indebtedness of many European governments. Countries such as Greece and Ireland were threatened with bankruptcy. Markets speculated on a potential spillover to other members of the eurozone, the 17 countries which have introduced a common currency, the euro. A breakup of the most ambitious European project since the founding of the European Community (EC) in the 1950s suddenly seemed a distinct possibility. All over Europe, openly eurosceptic parties, such as the 'True Finns' of Finland – a traditionally pro-European Northern country – gained increasing strength campaigning on the issues of Southern profligacy and increasing labour migration from Eastern EU member countries. While we do not yet know the final outcome of this latest crisis, the EU is again busy reformulating some of its fundamental

1

ground rules as a consequence. These two serious crises show that the EU should not be taken for granted. European integration is a political process which is reversible once its output turns negative and/or the political support for it vanishes. The often predicted breakup of the EU has not yet happened; but that does not mean that it will never come.

This book proceeds from the assumption that the European Union is an open-ended and strongly contested project. It is both spectacularly successful and deeply flawed, and the politics of the EU are characterized by numerous controversies which are pertinent not only to the EU itself but also illustrate many of the most salient problems of international cooperation in today's world. We tackle these controversies head on in the form of dichotomous debates. Some of the most prominent EU scholars reflect on the current and future state of the EU against the background of enlargement to 27 members, ratification of the Lisbon Treaty, and global financial crisis. The aim is to provide readers with an up-to-date account of current issues in EU politics and to enable them to take sides in one of the great debates of European politics: the future of the European Union. While most of the books that provide information on the EU describe the history, the institutions, policy areas, and protracted workings of the EU (Cini and Perez-Solorzano Borragan, 2009; Dinan, 2010; Hix and Høyland, 2011; McCormick, 2011a; McCormick, 2011b; Nugent, 2010; Wallace, Pollack and Young, 2010; Yesilada and Wood, 2010), this book is different. It focuses on the profoundly political core of the European Union. The authors represent the whole spectrum of thinking about the EU, from pro-European to openly eurosceptic perspectives. Thematic chapters address many of the most important issues in EU politics, with pairs of authors presenting diametrically opposed views on each controversy. Our aim in editing the book is to spark debate, in public and in the classroom.

Can the EU survive? a community between crisis and revival

For a long time, the EU has been taken for granted and its overall positive value has been rarely questioned. And yet, the Constitutional debacle and the euro crisis were not the first crises that rocked the Union. Already soon after the founding treaties were signed in 1957, pundits predicted a break-up of the Community during the so-called Empty Chair Crisis in the mid-1960s. The same happened during the global economic turmoil of the early 1970s when exchange rate chaos undermined economic cooperation among the member states. Later in this decade, a new European malady was diagnosed, a status of stagnation called 'eurosclerosis'. Eventually, however, member states agreed on the

Single European Act (1986), which cleared the way for a genuine common market, and on the Maastricht Treaty (1992), which foresaw the creation of a common currency.

The recurrent crises and the intense debates about the EU indicate that fundamental doubts exist whether a project that transcends national borders in an unprecedented way can survive in a world that is still dominated by states. The EU is (and has always been) a fundamentally contested political project. This fact is often obscured in textbooks that describe the convoluted history, the complicated mechanics and the confusing institutional set-up of the EU. Despite the many flaws exposed by these books, they see the EU as an unambiguously positive force in European and global history.

The idea of European integration has sparked the imagination of Europeans since the nineteenth century. It represented a response to the endless conflicts which plagued Europe for centuries and culminated in the Second World War, a tragedy that cost the life of up to 50 million Europeans. Only six years after the war had ended, however, France and Germany in 1951 set up the first European institution, the European Coal and Steel Community (ECSC). Italy, Belgium, Luxembourg and the Netherlands joined. In 1957, the six original members of the ECSC signed the Rome Treaties, establishing the European Economic Community and Euratom, an organization aimed at fostering cooperation in the field of nuclear energy. Important economic reasons sustained these organizations, above all the removal of trade barriers. Right up to the present day, however, European politicians also use the argument that integration has contributed to peace in Europe to provide legitimacy to the project. Jean-Claude Juncker, Prime Minister of Luxembourg and one of the leading politicians in EU affairs during the past decades, stated: 'Whoever doubts Europe, whoever despairs of Europe, should visit military cemeteries' (Juncker, 2008).

Additional motives have pushed the integration process: the rivalry with the Eastern bloc, demands from economic interests for better market access, the hope to catch up with the United States in terms of economic and political power, and the protection of vulnerable sectors of the European population from the vicissitudes of world markets, for instance, through the Common Agricultural Policy. Sustained economic growth and the increasing wealth of European citizens led to an almost unquestioned support of the Community and proved a big attraction for potential member countries. The United Kingdom, Denmark, Ireland, Greece, Portugal, and Spain joined during the 1970s and 1980s. After a period of economic stagnation, the Twelve embarked on a programme to fulfil the promise of the Rome Treaty to finally create a single market.

The Single European Act of 1986, the first major revision of the founding treaties, exerted a pull which hardly could have been foreseen by its proponents. European legislation (the so-called *acquis communautaire*) expanded precipitously, and European institutions such as the Commission as the sole initiator of legislation in the EU, and the European Court of Justice (ECJ) as interpreter of the treaties took on ever-expanding roles. The need for cohesion within the Community, the challenges posed by the breakdown of the Berlin Wall, and the effects of an increasingly integrated market brought more and more policy areas into the realm of European integration, among them security and defence policy. In 1992, the member states gathered in Maastricht (Netherlands) to decide on a new treaty, which consolidated previous agreements and established a three-pillar structure for the newly named European Union. Most importantly, the majority of EU members embarked on the path towards a common currency which, against many odds, became a reality on New Year's Day, 2002.

However, as the EU spread its influence over more and more policy areas, which had been the exclusive preserve of nation states, contestation grew. In June 1992, the Danish population voted against ratification of the Maastricht treaty. The EU's political establishment reacted with shock. The permissive consensus, that is the unquestioned support of the project by Europeans, which had sustained European integration since the 1950s, had ended. The term 'democratic deficit', denoting the increasing distance of citizens from EU decision-making processes and the difficulties to hold EU policymakers accountable, entered the political language. Decision makers have responded by progressively increasing the powers of the European Parliament, for example in the treaty revisions of Amsterdam (1997) and Nice (2001). Nevertheless, these moves have often looked like a zero-sum game in which increasing layers of democratic legitimacy inevitably impair the EU's ability for effective decision making. In 2004 and 2007, the former Communist countries of Eastern Europe joined, together with Cyprus and Malta, prompting predictions that an already convoluted decision-making process would now become completely unwieldy and that the still fresh political and economic stability of these countries contained the seed for major upheavals. The Union of 27, however, has continued to take decisions across all areas of the EU's competencies, and, as of 2012, Croatia is destined to become the 28th member country and five more countries, Iceland, Macedonia, Montenegro, Serbia and Turkey are official candidates at various stages of the accession process.

The scholarly debate

The incessant political debates about the EU since its founding have their reflection in the big scholarly controversies that have characterized the literature on European integration since the 1950s. The most long-standing of these was fought between intergovernmentalists and supranationalists. In 1958, Ernst Haas in his book *The Uniting of Europe*, building on the experience of the ECSC, argued that sectoral integration had an inherent expansive logic, which would lead to an ever-increasing integration among European states. Haas' argument, which has become known as neofunctionalism, was that the creation of a central authority would lead to the emergence of supranational trade associations, labour unions, and political parties that would increasingly pursue their interests at the European level. This shift in loyalty and resources away from the national state and towards the emerging centre would strengthen the central authority and facilitate further integration.

The first crisis of the integration project in the 1960s, however, encouraged advocates of the so-called intergovernmentalist school of thought, most prominently among them Stanley Hoffmann (1966). Intergovernmentalists argued that nation states would remain the key players in international politics, notwithstanding any efforts at regional integration. In fact, according to these scholars, nation states were the main obstacle to further integration; and increasing diversity among national states because of varying external and internal changes would make integration even more difficult in the future. The core normative issue behind the neofunctionalism versus intergovernmentalism debate was the question of whether the nation state would and should have a future in the twenty-first century.

Eurosclerosis in the 1970s and early 1980s meant that the scholarly debates on European integration lost much of their force. It was only the Single Market Programme in the 1980s that shifted scholars' attention back to the project of European unification. Supranationalists were quick to stress the role of the European Commission and transnational actors in giving new impetus to European integration (Sandholtz and Zysman, 1989). Reflecting the basic neofunctionalist logic, they suggested that economic integration in Europe increases the demand for rules at the European level. This demand is met by the European Commission. The supranationalist account of the revival of European integration in the 1980s was immediately challenged by a revised intergovernmentalist argument, however. Liberal intergovernmentalism, as proposed by Andrew Moravcsik (1998), argues that the steps towards further integration in the 1980s and 1990s should best be understood as a result of the convergence of member-state preferences. The Commission, according to Moravcsik, was of little help in producing this outcome. At the same time, the multilevel governance approach emerged as a kind of compromise between intergovernmentalism and supranationalism. It stresses member states' partial loss of control over the integration process, but also sees the Commission's authority circumscribed owing to the need to cooperate with the Council of Ministers and the European Parliament (Marks *et al.*, 1996).

The 1990s also saw the emergence of a new literature, less concerned with explaining the process of European integration as such, and more with capturing the dynamics of policymaking in the European Union. Much recent research has aimed at explaining legislative activity in this entity, the inner workings of the European institutions, the strategies used by interest groups in lobbying EU institutions, the adaptation of national political institutions to the process of European integration, and specific policy outcomes (Egan *et al.*, 2010). The resulting literature offers a complex picture of the EU, in which a multitude of actors try to shape policy outcomes, and their success can vary from case to case. In many respects, the problems faced by the EU and identified in this huge literature are problems which are typical for an increasingly interdependent world. They exemplify the political controversies underlying each attempt of international cooperation, regardless of whether these are the high politics of global conflicts or the supposedly low politics of international standard-setting. While eschewing the normatively charged arguments of the early years of European integration, the problems of efficiency and legitimacy identified by this literature are inseparably linked with the overall debate about the future course of the EU.

Structure and scope of this book

The EU is usually depicted as a mind-bogglingly complex political system. Only very few European citizens can claim to have an at least fair knowledge of how it works and how its major institutions, such as the Council, the Commission, the Parliament, the ECJ, the European Central Bank, and so on, interact. The Treaty of Lisbon has been widely ridiculed for the spectacular failure it represents regarding the attempt to simplify the core texts of the Union. Given the importance of the EU for global political and economic affairs, it is not surprising that numerous textbooks are on the market which attempt to describe in great detail the often cumbersome ways in which the EU works. An updated list is attached to this introduction. While it is indispensable to have an understanding of the polity and policies of the EU, the underlying politics are often not spelled out. EU institutions are responses to problems of policy coordination. Their specific forms and the pattern of interaction are also shaped by different visions and ideas about what the EU should, and should not, do. Conflict abounds, ranging from seemingly irrelevant quarrels about minuscule details of EU legislation to the grand question on whether the EU is a visionary project offering hope for future world peace or rather a historical dead-end. This book takes up these debates, moving from general debates to more specific ones.

The first chapter debates the overall value of the EU. While John Mc-Cormick defends the importance and success of the EU, John Gillingham offers a radically sceptical view of its future relevance. The debate about the EU's success is closely linked to the question on the political efficiency of the EU (Chapter 2). Desmond Dinan argues that the EU is surprisingly efficient regarding its policy output, whereas Mats Persson strongly disagrees by pointing to the EU's inability to reform even in the face of clear signals showing that some of its policies do not achieve their stated purpose. 'More Power for Brussels or Renationalization?' is the question taken up in the third chapter, with contributions from Derek Beach and Uwe Puetter. The benchmark for judging political systems is the degree of their democratic quality and their efficiency in delivering political solutions. In addition, and on a more fundamental level, they have to evoke in their citizens a certain feeling of belonging to a community united by a shared purpose.

The debate about the so-called 'democratic deficit' of the EU has generated a massive number of books and articles since the Maastricht Treaty was negotiated. Authors are sharply divided about the democratic quality of the EU polity and the two essays in Chapter 4 present the contending viewpoints. Christopher Lord argues that the Union is a democratic achievement in relation to the normal practices of international organizations, even if it is in deficit to democratic states. A successful output legitimates the transfer of sovereignty and helps member states to deal with political and economic problems which they are unable to solve alone. Richard Bellamy, by contrast, stresses the EU's democratic deficit, which is inevitable as soon as political competencies are delegated away from the national level to a supranational level that lacks the prerequisites for a truly democratic system.

Potentially problematic for an overall evaluation of the EU's democratic legitimacy is the answer to the role of law in European integration. Are binding laws promulgated by international courts possible beyond the nation-state? In Chapter 5, Karen Alter takes the stance that by giving member states and individuals the possibility to resort to legal procedures against decisions of the EU, the ECJ is a vital part of European democracy. Jeremy Rabkin disagrees. He views the ECJ as an institution that has usurped democratic decision making in the EU. The issue of a common identity is taken up in Chapter 6, with contributions by Ulrike Liebert and Jonathan White. While Liebert sees a common identity emerging, not least because of the constitutional debate, White radically doubts that a European identity can ever exist outside a small circle of highly educated and mobile elites.

Perhaps the most critical area in the current EU is European Monetary Union. Doubts about this unprecedented experiment in monetary integration continue to linger, speculation about a break-up of the eurozone is frequent, and the financial crisis has cast grave doubts on the capacity of some eurozone members to deal with the challenges posed by a common currency. In Chapter 7, Amy Verdun argues that these doubts are unfounded and that the euro is here to stay. Tal Sadeh strikes a sceptical note, pointing to the internal contradictions of the common currency. Financial markets in the EU remain highly segmented as the global financial crisis of 2007–9 amply demonstrated. Vigorous efforts have been made in the past couple of years to remedy this situation and to make the EU a global regulatory power in this area. In Chapter 8, Jörn Gottwald argues that the EU has reacted with surprising speed and efficiency to the upheaval on the markets, while Daniel Mügge thinks that these efforts have so far been ineffective.

The EU's cohesion policy is aimed at improving the conditions for sustainable growth and jobs, wellbeing, and quality of the environment in the EU regions (Chapter 9). Dirk Ahner defends the position that this policy has been successful, allowing all EU citizens, wherever they live, to benefit from the shared political project of a European space with a high degree of development, cohesion and solidarity. Vincent Della Sala and Marco Brunazzo take a less benign view, stressing the ineffectiveness of this tool. Few EU policies, however, have generated as much controversy as the reviled Common Agricultural Policy. In Chapter 10, Eugénia da Conceição-Heldt thinks that it is a colossal waste with serious effects on the environment and on developing countries, whereas Ann-Christina Knudsen points to its positive features.

Foreign Economic Policy is another area in which the impact of the EU is large but also much criticized (Chapter 11). While many analysts maintain that a common trade policy has given EU members more clout and allowed them to promote sustainable trade issues, others see the EU as bullying power which pursues tough commercial policies geared towards the interests of big business. Andreas Dür argues that lobbyists determine the external economic policies of the EU, whereas Cornelia Woll maintains that EU institutions are relatively autonomous in their decision making in this policy field. Chapter 12 takes up the question of what type of actor the EU is in international affairs. While Ian Manners conceives of the EU as a normative power, Mark Pollack criticizes this conception.

Chapter 13 assesses the EU's experience with enlargement. Rachel Epstein calls enlargement a big success that should be continued. She mainly points to the advantages that accrue to acceding states. Christopher Bickerton fears that accession to the EU has had many negative side-effects for the central and eastern European countries that joined the EU in 2004. Since the turn of the twenty-first century, the EU has also attempted to develop a military capability to supplement its economic weight. This project has been beset by difficulties: member states are unwilling to surrender sovereignty in this vital area of state activity, practical difficulties complicate the merging of different national military traditions, many member states are sceptical about the whole undertaking, and the capabilities gap *vis-à-vis* the US is massive.In the final chapter (Chapter 14), Hanna Ojanen argues that, nonetheless, a common security and defence policy is a worthwhile project, while Anand Menon thinks that it will never work properly and fail to live up to the grandiose ambitions of European politicians in this field.

Chapter 1

The European Union: Success or Failure?

Editors' introduction

Is the European Union a success or a failure? Observers' responses to this question could not be more different. For some, the EU has to be credited for creating peace and prosperity in Europe. In the early 1950s, when the origins of the current union were laid with the creation of the European Coal and Steel Community (ECSC), Europe had just emerged from the Second World War. It had seen three major wars between Germany and France in less than a century. Only five years after the end of the Second World War, the two countries agreed to pool the production of coal and steel and thus make any future wars less likely. Moreover, the shattered economies of the countries participating in the ECSC and then the European Economic Community (EEC) experienced high growth rates in the 1950s and 1960s, allowing Germany and other European countries to catch up in terms of economic strength with the United States. More recently, the success of the EU has been seen in its capacity to help accession countries in the transition to democracy. Many of the newer EU member states did not have a long tradition of democracy when entering the EU. Nevertheless, as EU members, their political systems have been stabilized with, as of 2012, no country backsliding into dictatorship.

But the EU's record is not only rosy, at least according to EU sceptics: among the many faults that they observe in the EU, its democratic deficit is clearly a key issue. They see the EU driven by an unaccountable bureaucracy, with a lack of democratic oversight, and pursuing policies far from the preferences of the citizens in the EU's member states. Rather than contributing to the wealth of the member countries, some observers perceive many of the EU's policies as stifling growth and economic competitiveness. Others view the EU's economic policies as being too 'neoliberal', undermining the welfare state of continental European countries. Both of these views have gained wide currency in the wake of the financial and sovereign debt crisis that hit Europe from 2008 onwards.

In the first of two contributions to this debate, John McCormick states that the EU is a success. He argues that the EU has contributed to peace in Europe, has allowed its member states to gain power in international affairs, and provides an institutional template that is being imitated around the world. John Gillingham strongly contests this view. He maintains that the EU has been a failure and calls for a radically reformed Union, including the abolition of the European Parliament. Several of the points raised in this pair of texts will be taken up in more detail in later chapters, notably in the debates on efficiency in Chapter 2, democracy in Chapter 4 and integration by law in Chapter 5.

1.1 Why Europe works

John McCormick

There has probably been no worse time than the present to defend the merits of the European project. It has often been declared dead, dying or doomed, but the volume of such declarations has grown to a crescendo in the wake of the eurozone crisis. We have long been told that the project was flawed, that it was elitist, that it was never sufficiently democratic, and that it has often suffered from an absence of direction and leadership. Now, it appears, the chickens have come home to roost. So persistent have been the doubts that opposition to Europe has earned its own label (euroscepticism), and there is no equivalent for supporters of the project. Whether we call them europhiles, euroenthusiasts, or pro-Europeans, their views have regularly been drowned out by the prophets of doom, whose claims have become so mainstream that an exasperated José Manuel Barroso, president of the European Commission, was moved to reflect in a February 2010 speech on the 'intellectual glamour of pessimism and constant denigration' that was doing so much harm to Europe's image.

To some extent, the EU has been a victim of circumstance. It has fallen foul of the dictum that bad news attracts more attention than good news, its problems often having the kind of dramatic qualities that make news headlines, while its successes usually evolve over a longer period of time and attract less attention. It has also fallen foul of the complexity of its own rules; the treaties are long and often confusing, its work can often seem coldly technocratic, and scholars of the EU have often made matters worse with their frequent inability to make Europe either interesting or real. The EU has also fallen foul of an identity crisis; no-one can agree on what it is or what it should become, and without such agreement it is impossible to agree on whether or not it is on the right track.

To make matters worse, most Europeans know little about how the EU works, making it difficult for them to objectively assess the claims of the critics. They often misunderstand the powers of the European institutions, which have much less independence than is widely thought and can mainly do only as much as the treaties and the governments of the member states allow. They also often misunderstand the effects of European law, the tired old jokes about regulations on the curvature of cucumbers interfering with meaningful discussion about the substantive effects of the vast majority of EU laws. There are even enduring myths about the size of the EU budget, routinely dismissed as a waste of tax-payer money when in fact it is no bigger, and no more or less wasteful, than the budget of a typical large national government department.

The bemusement of Europeans has nowhere been more clearly on show than during recent national referendums on EU treaties in France, the Netherlands and Ireland. The rejection of these treaties was widely interpreted as a rejection of Europe when in fact the results were more a reflection of the displeasure among voters with their incumbent na-tional governments, or (particularly in the case of Ireland) a function of misconceptions about the content and implications of the treaties. In the case of the French rejection of the constitutional treaty in May 2005, for example, Eurobarometer opinion polls at the time revealed that nearly three out of four French citizens either knew little about the content of the treaty or had not heard of it at all – and yet 69 per cent turned out to vote, of whom 55 per cent voted No. Three days later, in the Nether-lands, 62 per cent of those who voted rejected the treaty, and yet 47 per cent admitted that they did not have enough information with which to make a decision.

Building the EU was never going to be easy: it was a marked depar-ture from previous models of administration, and it has since been made up largely on the fly, often navigating unchartered territory. Jean Mon-net long ago warned that 'Europe would be built through crises, and … would be the sum of their solutions' (Monnet, 1978: 417). He also noted – in what became known as Monnet's Law – that 'people only accept change when they are faced with necessity, and only recognize necessity when a crisis is upon them' (Monnet, 1978: 109). This has certainly often been true of the EU, but all systems of government and administration have their problems, because they are the construct of the human mind with its many flaws; that the EU should have had so many problems is a reflection less of defects inherent in the European project than of the sheer size and audacity of that project.

Consider the alternative case of the United States, often contrasted with the EU for its successes. The US, it is often suggested, is a beacon of democracy, one of the most open and productive marketplaces in the world, a paragon of technological inventiveness, the ultimate military power, a cultural superpower, owner of the most important currency in the world, and a magnet for immigrants seeking to improve themselves. And yet its national debt is spiralling out of control, its society is fractured along racial and ideological lines, the gap between the rich and the poor is large and expanding, its political institutions are dysfunctional, its leaders appear unable to reach the compromises needed to solve its long-term problems, much of its infrastructure is in need of repair, its social security system is nearly bankrupt, and its military has had – at best – a mixed record on dealing with security threats. Gallup polls between 2008 and 2010 found that more than two-thirds of Americans viewed their country as being headed in the wrong direction, while between 55 and 81 per cent were dissatisfied with the way the country was being governed (Saad, 2011). And yet no-one seriously suggests that what the US has achieved is anything short of remarkable, or that it is on the brink of collapse, or that it is not worth supporting. That the EU has problems is, we might conclude, quite normal.

We should also note that while the EU has faced numerous crises, and has been counted out many times before, it has not only survived but has proved adept at learning from its mistakes and moving on. The eurozone crisis caps them all, to be sure, but it was also predictable; Greece should not have been allowed to join (because it did not meet the terms of entry), the European Central Bank was always going to be working with one arm tied behind its back so long as it had no power to shape fiscal policy, and it was long clear that eurozone states (even Germany) were breaking their own rules on budget deficits. It would have been surprising if the eurozone had *not* had problems; this was, after all, the first time in history that a group of advanced liberal democracies had voluntarily given up their national currencies and pooled the monetary powers that went with them. The political response to the crisis has been often confused and uncertain, but it has taught European leaders valuable lessons about the importance of taking decisive action, and the EU will likely emerge from the crisis significantly improved.

Having argued, then, that popular portrayals of the EU are often flawed, that its character and powers are widely misunderstood, and that every experiment in political organization faces problems, what is there to defend in the story of the European project? A great deal, as it happens, its benefits being found primarily in the roles of Europe as a peacemaker, as a global power, and as an institutional model.

Europe as a peacemaker

To appreciate the greatest achievement of European integration, we must first remind ourselves of its core original purpose: the European Coal and Steel Community was founded in order to encourage peace between Germany and France as a first step towards broader post-war European cooperation. Looking back from our contemporary vantage point, it is hard to imagine the antagonism, doubt and foreignness with which Europeans regarded each other in 1945, or the grim political and economic challenges that faced the region, or the uncertainties about where Europe was headed. And yet so successful has been the reconciliation of its two major continental powers that the wider notion of European states ever going to war with one another again is unthinkable. So unthinkable, indeed, that we now take peace in Europe for granted; the region is living out Kant's notion of perpetual peace, and while the credit cannot be laid entirely at the door of European integration, its role has been essential.

At the heart of its contribution lie the benefits of economic integration, and particularly of the European single market. This was a goal with which even the most hardened of eurosceptics could agree. It made sense that bringing down the barriers to the movement of people, money, goods and services would create new ties and opportunities, would encourage competition and innovation, and would discourage market-skewing quotas, tariffs, monopolies, and price differentials. This is precisely what has happened, and on an entirely voluntary basis. The task is not yet complete, but the EU today has the world's largest and wealthiest capitalist marketplace, the speed with which this was achieved can be credited almost entirely to the European project, and even if that project were to collapse tomorrow, economic integration has a life and a momentum of its own that would be near impossible to stop.

The European project has also helped promote peace through its role in reducing the insidious pressures of nationalism. Where nationalists once promoted potentially dangerous political and strategic interests, they are today more interested in what Billig (1995) describes as 'banal nationalism', associated with symbols rather than demands for self-determination. (Along the way, greater recognition of – and easier access to – the multiple national cultures of Europe has become one of the great pleasures of life in today's EU). We have seen the dual phenomena of macro-integration and micro-disintegration at work, where Europe is coming together while there has also been greater recognition of national identities. Yes, there are still nationalist tensions in parts of Europe that involve violence or the threat of violence, and yes, there are still right-wing nationalist pressures sparked by non-white immigration (and sometimes even white immigration), but nationalism no longer poses the threat to Europe that it once did.

Integration has also encouraged peace through its role in reducing state-based patriotism and promoting broader notions of citizenship and identity. We often hear the charge that Europeans have found it difficult to identify with the EU, but that is because the European project has been too narrowly defined. Thanks in large part to integration, Europeans have become less foreign to one another and have come to realize how much they have in common. There is today a distinctive European view of politics, economics and society, which goes beyond support for democracy, human rights, and free markets, and includes support for welfare liberalism, cosmopolitanism (association with universal ideas), the collective society, sustainable development, secularism, and civilian and multilateral approaches to international relations (for more details see McCormick, 2010). If Europeans were to think of the EU less as a network of institutions and a body of laws, and more as a set of common values, they would better appreciate the changes wrought by the EU and better understand the meaning of identity with Europe.

Europe as a global power

The second major achievement of the European project has been the manner in which it has allowed European states to reassert themselves in the world. This may seem a hollow claim given the EU's many well-publicized problems with foreign and security policy, or its repeated crises of leadership (or lack thereof), but if we look past the headlines and consider longer-term trends, we find substantial achievements. The EU has collectively developed a set of alternative explanations for the causes of key international problems, it offers a new set of mainly civilian and soft prescriptions for the resolution of those problems, it represents the distinctive set of values listed above, its marketplace is both large and wealthy, it is the biggest source of – and magnet for – foreign direct investment in the world, it is by far the biggest provider of official development assistance, and while the euro has had enormous problems, it is the first credible alternative to the US dollar since the latter finally displaced the pound sterling in the 1950s. In short, Europe cannot be ignored.

Prior to the Second World War, the major powers were mainly European – Britain, France, and Germany leading the way – and for better or for worse they determined the pace and direction of economic and political events. But they emerged from the war greatly weakened, and found themselves carried along on a tide of Cold War tensions over which they had little control; eastern Europe did as it was told by the Soviet Union, while western Europe relied so much on the United States for military security and economic leadership that its governments had to go along with US policies even when they disagreed; the rifts over Suez in 1956, over Vietnam in the late 1960s, over the end of the Bretton Woods system in 1971, and over the Arab-Israeli problem come to mind.

With the end of the Cold War and the removal of the Soviet hegemony, the political differences between the United States and Europe became more apparent (as, it must be said, did the initial inability of the EU to cover itself with glory on the foreign and security fronts, least of all in the Balkans). Europeans fretted about their differences with the Americans but became more willing to speak up where the two sides disagreed, the breach spilling into the open with the fallout over Iraq in 2003. We are often reminded that European governments were divided, with Britain, Spain, and Italy supporting the invasion while Germany and France were opposed, but much less is usually said about opinion polls that found 70–90 per cent opposition to the war right across Europe. Other polls taken at the same time revealed – not coincidentally – that majorities in every EU state were in favour of the EU developing foreign policies independent of the United States.

It is in none of our interests to live in a world dominated by one or two superpowers, because to do so is to risk being subjected to the assertion of their political and economic agendas. (The often idiosyncratic positions of the United States on a range of political, economic, social, and foreign policy matters are illustrative of the importance of the balance and alternatives offered by Europe.) The EU is the only effective channel through which Europeans can make their collective views heard, and it does this more often than we are led to believe. It has done it, for example, through a common trade policy in which all 27 of its states – representing 500 million of the wealthiest people in the world, and accounting for a bigger share of global imports and exports than any other trading bloc – act as one in dealings with the Americans, the Chinese, and the Indians. And, on the foreign policy front, its abilities to speak as one continue to improve, aided most recently by the redesign of the office of high representative for foreign affairs and the creation of the European External Action Service.

Europe as an institutional model

The third major achievement of the European project lies in its institutional impact: it offers the template for a new way of ordering politics, economics and society that contrasts with the deeply flawed and increasingly irrelevant model of the nation-state. In the grand sweep of history, the latter has not been with us long: the oldest states date back to the Middle Ages, but most date back no further than the mid-twentieth century. And even in that relatively short time it has been fraught with problems: states create artificial divisions among humans, they have often gone to war with one another, they regularly fail to deal with other states without building antagonistic alliances, and they often do a poor job of working with other states to address cross-border problems such as terrorism, pollution, illegal immigration, and the spread of disease. None of these charges can be levelled at the EU. It has helped Europeans rise above narrow interests, has encouraged them to coordinate their responses to shared or common problems, offers them a means of pooling knowledge and expertise and of reducing duplication and overlap, and encourages them to take a more global view of the needs of human society.

A prime example of the success of coordination is offered by the case of EU environmental policy. Many environmental problems either have common sources or are shared by multiple states, meaning that only coordinated policy responses are likely to work. Like much else that it does, the EU stumbled on to environmental policy almost by accident, realizing that different standards posed a barrier to the single market, and thus demanded a cooperative approach. EU law has since brought laggard states up to the level of progressive states, has led to the introduction of environmental standards in parts of Europe where few or none existed, and has obliged a tightening of standards in non-EU states wanting access to the European marketplace. A similar process of policy spillover has been at work in several other areas of policy:

- Competition, where the EU has developed the most stringent antimonopoly laws in the world.
- Mergers and acquisitions, where the single market has encouraged European corporations to reach across internal borders.
- Education, where efforts to ensure the mobility of qualifications has gone hand in hand with efforts to encourage educational exchanges.
- Justice and home affairs, where cross-border police and judicial cooperation has been a vital addition to the set of tools used to fight crime.
- Transport, where coordinated European investment in trans-European networks has helped build new highways and railways that have improved links within the European marketplace.

Any claims that the EU works institutionally will inevitably come up against charges that it was created by elites, that it suffers from a democratic deficit, and that its bureaucracy is insufficiently accountable (as though national bureaucracies are any different). But what we see depends on where we look. If we think of the EU as an international organization (IO), then its decision-making processes are quite normal: it is a club of member states whose interests are represented in the meeting rooms of the European Council and the Council of Ministers. But while it is clearly more than a conventional IO, it is also far from being a federal Europe, lacking the minimum defining quality of a federation: two or more levels of government with independent powers. There is no European 'government' in the conventional sense of the term, because while the major EU institutions have responsibilities (as outlined in the treaties), these are no more than what has been agreed by the member states, and they can be restricted and even reduced by the work of the member states. To say that the European institutions have too much power (a common complaint of eurosceptics) is to fundamentally misunderstand how the EU works.

The EU is best thought of as a confederation, or a union of states (see Lister, 1996). Citizens elect their state governments, who in turn represent the interests of those citizens in the European institutions (the European Parliament being the major anomaly). The cumulative interests of the member states dominate the EU decision-making process, the EU institutions are limited by what the treaties allow them to do, and the treaties have in turn been written and decided upon with the governments of the member states involved at every step. True, ordinary Europeans have not been invited in most cases to vote on new treaties, but why should they be as long as the EU is not a federal European superstate? There is an exquisite irony at play here: while the EU is criticized for being insufficiently democratic, it is also criticized for moving towards the kind of federal arrangement that would make it more democratic. The EU, it seems, is damned if it does and damned if it doesn't.

Arguably the most impressive institutional achievement of the European project has been its role – through the legal and political demands it makes of its members or aspirant members – in expanding and solidifying European liberal democracy. Indeed, the EU is the most effective force in the world today for the peaceful promotion of democracy and capitalism. It encouraged the six founding states (France, West Germany, Italy, and the Benelux states) to work together in the 1950s and 1960s, it helped encourage the transition to democracy in Greece, Spain and Portugal in the 1980s, it went on to encourage democratic and free market change in post-Cold War eastern Europe, and it continues today to spread democracy through the demands that it makes of neighbouring states that have aspirations to join the EU, and of other states that seek access to the vast European marketplace.

And if imitation is the sincerest form of flattery, then we have only to look around the world at the other experiments in regional integration that have been inspired by the European case: ASEAN in southeast Asia, ECOWAS in West Africa, the Union of South American Nations, CARICOM in the Caribbean, NAFTA in North America, and the African Union, to name just a few. Not all of them have worked as well as the EU, to be sure, but clearly others think that integration is worthy of emulation, and there is almost no state that is not involved in at least one exercise in regional integration. If the EU is wrong, then so is almost everyone else.

Conclusions

To summarize, we have three main sets of achievements that show why European integration has been a good thing, and why it merits continued support and better understanding. The first of these is peace, which Europe might have been able to achieve without regional integration, but it would have taken much longer, and who knows what paths European states would have taken if they had not been moving in the same overall direction. The second is global influence, which Europe would have been unlikely to achieve if its governments had been working independently; even Germany, France and Britain are no more than middle-level powers, and the smaller EU states would have had trouble making themselves heard. The third can be found in the institutional benefits of regional integration, which even with its problems offers many advantages over the nation-state.

In short, the European project deserves to be applauded for what it has achieved and can continue to achieve. Its history has not always been pretty, and there are many ways in which it could stand to be reformed, but its critics too often misunderstand how it works, base their judgements on short-term difficulties rather than long-term gains, and overlook the broader historical significance and pioneering nature of the remarkable experiment in which Europeans have been engaged. Europe is more peaceful, prosperous and influential than it would have been without the European Union, and the best interests of Europe and the world will not be served by undoing the achievements of integration. On the contrary, what we need now is not a return to the nation-state but both more and better integration. Europeans need each other, they have more in common than most of them realize, a strong and coordinated Europe is needed to offset the power of the United States and the rising influence of China and India, and Europeans need to rise above the here and now and look to their long-term future. That future must include the European Union.

1.2 The end of the European dream

John Gillingham

As of the beginning of 2012 it is impossible to predict whether the escalating financial crisis now shaking Europe to its foundations will result in the collapse of the Economic and Monetary Union and even of the European Union, or in its radical reform and survival. One fact is, however, indisputable. The European dream has come to an end. The present agonies culminate twenty years of successive policy failure, which has disillusioned elites and embittered publics. The EU will remain discredited for years to come.

The history of European integration has always involved more than the transnational institutions associated with Brussels. The impetus to it stems from a need to renew a civilization that nearly destroyed itself in the first half of the twentieth century. The EU would, it was hoped, guide Europe into a future political and economic federation, and restore its historic prominence in world affairs. The future would then be in its hands. The dramatic rise of China and India has not shaken this triumphalism. The present crisis surely will. At stake, after all, is the survival of the EU.

The intimate association of the EU with the idea of European renewal is due in part to a halo effect propagated and sustained by legions of academics, journalists, and publicists who have devoted careers to praising and apologizing for it. No wonder that Brussels' critics have too often been discouraged, dismissed and even ridiculed and that alternative ways to knit together Europe's nations have seldom received due consideration!

This state of affairs has begun to change during the present crisis, but fresh approaches are still called for. Past crises have sometimes catalysed original research on the EU, but none has ever called its ultimate value into question. Yet the EU is intrinsically undemocratic. Its institutions are dysfunctional. Technocratic leadership has steered it onto the rocks. The EU's great deeds belong to the past. It is now barely roadworthy.

A reform plan for the EU

This essay sketches a reform plan for the EU and, given its importance, gives attention first to the EMU. Longer-term reforms must, however, begin with the orderly phase out the Brussels apparatus and specifically the European Commission (Gillingham, 2006a). Although integration and democracy are usually spoken of in a single breath, the two are in fact incompatible. Giandomenico Majone in his recent *Europe as the Would-be World Power* argues that democracy meant little to the EU's founding father (Majone, 2009). Jean Monnet realized, according to Majone, that the public of his day was not ready to countenance the idea of European political union and could not be trusted to support it. To advance his project, Monnet thus operated by stealth and championed policies in the name of economic reform whose underlying purpose was a European federation. To this end, he staged a sequence of *faits accomplis* calculated to produce irreversible outcomes. This approach, followed also by his successors, has made it nearly impossible to un-do what already has been done. Monnet's methods have exacted a heavy toll in bad governance and faulty institutional design, maladies that very much still afflict today's EU. They have, furthermore, deprived it of democratic legitimacy and also, therefore, of sovereign power.

The European Commission was the centrepiece of Monnet's scheme. The agenda-setting power vested in this executive authority built an elitist bias into the EU, according to Majone, which henceforth stifled policy making from the bottom up and by popular consensus. Although the Commission has been forced to share power with competing governance institutions over time, it has never lost its fundamental prerogatives. The other central institutions on the Brussels scene were at first little more than theatrical sets. The European Court acquired real power only gradually. The European Parliament remains largely a talk-shop. By contrast, the younger European Council, which represents the interests of the member states, would become a standing challenge to the Commission, which was stripped of much of its power by the 'Empty Chair Crisis' of 1965 precipitated by French President de Gaulle's walk-out from Brussels. The upshot of this conflict was a twenty-year policy-making stalemate. It ended with the resurgence of the Commission under President Jacques Delors. The Brussels power struggles nonetheless still continue, with the chief antagonists being the member states as represented by the Council and the Commission, represented by its President.

What subsequently became known as the democratic deficit was, in Majone's view, from the get–go intrinsic to the integration process. It can neither be closed nor overcome. Whether this is inevitable or not as matters now stand, removal of agenda-setting authority from the Commission is the essential first step in both democratizing the EU and reorganizing its fundamental institutions. A process of devolution can thereby begin and sovereign authority be repatriated to the states.

Back in the 1980s, the late Alan Milward advanced a view quite distinct from Majone's, which has had a huge subsequent impact on historical research. He argued that the eventual EU was part and parcel of a triumphant European social democracy; that the two were complementary and their development thus went hand-in-hand in a mutually reinforcing and progressive process. Milward's thesis puts the cart before the horse: the historical roots of the welfare state run far deeper than the negotiations which led to the eventual EU (Sheehan, 2008). Britain, which provided an influential model for the European welfare state, moreover, refused to join either the ECSC or the EEC. The former, although a milestone in the history of European integration, was an operational failure. The latter is responsible for the Common Agricultural Policy – something costly, regressive, bureaucratically stultifying, and unnecessary – but also for one enduring achievement, the creation of a single customs area for the six founder members. It soon drew American capital into Europe, gave rise both to the multinational corporation and the eurodollar, and served as a powerful spur to growth in the early years of the community (Gillingham, 2003: 58f). The so-called Common Market remains the *raison d'être* of the European integration process.

The crisis of mixed economy welfare state

The monetary regime change that took place in the 1970s is what called into question the compatibility between the mixed economy welfare state and the European Community (and eventual EU). The regime change resulted from the breakdown of the world financial system designed in Bretton Woods in 1944. The system rested on a peg of major currencies to the US dollar which, bolstered by national capital controls, provided buffers that insulated domestic economies from international competition. With this buffer gone, a rapid increase of capital mobility changed the integration context; new flows of liquidity imperilled corporatist business arrangements; undercut the resistance of entrenched state bureaucracies; loosened bonds between the state, industry, commerce, and finance; and set the stage for dramatic growth of the European enterprise. What previously had been a customs union with an attached farm-subsidy programme would, in short order, become something powerful, controversial, and operational. For the first time, the EU would become a major influence in European public life (Anderson, 2009: 92f; Forsyth and Notermans, 1997: 17–68; Gillingham, 2003: 97f).

The collapse of the Bretton Woods system brought into direct confrontation two contesting principles of organization which, between them, had from the inception influenced the EU's path of development. The first of them – associated with Monnet – aimed at framing the structures of a future European state. The counterpoise to it was the gradual but steady expansion of the international market economy and its increasing influence on national development. Liberalization was intrinsic to the post-war global financial and commercial settlement, but remaining restraints on capital mobility at the same time limited its impact. Once lifted, new flows of investment eroded regulations governing trade, protecting the labour market, and providing rents to favoured national producers. Set in motion thereby was an ultimately irreversible trend. The effort to restrain it by means of a misconceived state-building policy is considered a root cause of the EU's present agonies (Gillingham, 2003: 149–79).

The monetary regime change forced the nations of Europe, regardless, down the road of neoliberalism, that is, to the adoption of measures often associated with Margaret Thatcher-like privatization, de-regulation, the encouragement of competition as well as home ownership, and the promotion of democratic stakeholder capitalism. Although such policies were often introduced under different rubrics, they found wide purchase on the Continent – especially with the governments of France, Spain, the Netherlands, and the Scandinavian countries (Gillingham, 2003: 180–227).

The crisis of the insufficiently productive and no longer affordable mixed economy welfare state – and the so-called 'European social model' – was indeed at hand. Stagflation had to be overcome and economic growth restored. The only alternatives to stimulating a vigorous market economy with Thatcherite methods were either the politically perilous one of cut backs in the public sphere or the economically scary one of currency devaluation.

A missed opportunity

The most sweeping policy initiative since the founding of the EEC in 1958, the Single European Act (SEA) of 1986 was part-and-parcel of the era of global market opening that in one form or another would last into the new millennium. SEA set a timetable for the elimination of all non-tariff barriers to trade within the union, the goal being to complete the single market. Never fully implemented, the policy was, in economic terms, only partly successful. Politically, it failed to renovate the EU. From the 1990s to the present, the state builders have held the upper hand in Brussels: the day of the economic liberals has long since passed.

Commission President Jacques Delors determined the outcome. Mrs. Thatcher may have provided the inspiration for the Single European Act (SEA), but Delors implemented it. A figure cut in the Napoleonic mould – and a titan of EU history – the three-term President dreamt of a powerful centralized European state, designed and administered along French lines, that would feature a broad array of interventionist approaches such as planning, *dirigisme*, and *grands projets;* the promotion of Euro-champions; the adoption of sectoral and industrial policy; the maintenance of close coordination between the civil and military sectors; the promotion of a single social policy for Europe; and the transference of incomes on a grand scale. No economic liberal, Delors' price for promoting SEA was acceptance of new majority voting rules, which repealed the *veto* in effect since de Gaulle's notorious 1965 walk out. He won, the national veto became largely a thing of the past, and the ambitious Commissioner had the necessary wedge with which to build up the EU and the power of the Commission within it (Gillingham, 2003: 259–302).

Delors' coup set in motion the process which led to the ratification of the Treaty of Lisbon (a reheated version of the infamous rejected European constitution), as well as to the ill-conceived introduction of the euro, the creation of the eurozone, and the installation of the European Central Bank (ECB). Together, Delors' two big policies have put the EU on a downhill slope for two decades. The constitutional debacle created a legitimacy crisis, which the EMU's failure turned into something systemic, an existential crisis.

One should, at the same time, not slight the real achievements of these years, above all the successive enlargements. The Nordic enlargement, a boon to the EU, brought in rich countries with strong traditions of good government. The accession of the other two sets of nations presented challenges which, if properly acted upon, could have provided the European Union a measure of legitimacy (Gillingham, 2006a: 184–220).

The EU, nonetheless, missed a one-time opportunity to commit itself as a matter of fundamental principle to the spread of democracy into countries blighted by dictatorship, though it did give lip-service to the ideal. Instead, under the rubric of regional policy, the EU set up political slush funds to corrupt the politicians of the Mediterranean member states, which would soon soak up no less than a quarter of overall EU revenues. The eastern enlargement was a somewhat different matter. Here significant changes were accomplished, which would not have occurred without EU intervention, even though they owed still more to the peoples of the former bloc countries. Membership in the customs union, the attendant inflow of foreign capital, and the encouragement of best-practice in legal and administrative standard -setting undeniably have had a positive impact. The nations of eastern Europe are not yet, however, full participants in the EU venture. Graft is rife, and cynicism pervasive. Poor and exposed, the far-from-affluent easterners desperately want to be a part of Europe. For them, the EU is a simple necessity.

In rich western Europe, fear of immigrants and miserly attitudes prevent EU accession for either Turkey or Ukraine. The process of expanding the union, which could have led to a less inward-turning, more ecumenical, inclusive, and tolerant Europe would prove to be a one-shot affair.

Often blamed for the present *immobilisme* of the EU, eastern enlargement may have complicated the conduct of business in Brussels, if only by dint of the numbers involved, but it has not compounded EU governance problems. These are anchored in the conflicts of western Europe, where the centre of gravity in the EU still rests. The current crisis can be traced back to the Maastricht Treaty of 1992 and obviously ante-dates the entry of the new member states.

Much ado about almost nothing

The collapse of the Soviet Union and the impending reunification of Germany set the stage for the Maastricht Treaty. It unleashed a debate between 'wideners' of the EU, spearheaded on the one hand by the British, who would have both weakened it politically and steered it in the direction of an enlarged future customs union, and 'deepeners' led on the other by Commissioner Delors and German Chancellor Helmut Kohl, who, for different reasons, wanted to strengthen its institutions before bringing in new members. Kohl was determined to slay the European fear of German domination, and was also prepared to sacrifice much money and power to this end. Delors was eager to seize a one-time opportunity to build up the European Union. In the process of de-railing the British, he conjured up an institutional nightmare.

A so-called three-pillar system of the EU – a grotesque structure wobbling on unstable compromises – derived from Maastricht. Only the first upright, the single market, could support anything. The others, Common Foreign and Security Policy and Justice and Home Affairs, were nothing but hollow tubes erected in the vague hope that they could be filled in the future by the ambitions of bureaucratic state builders. Thanks to Brussels' weird political chemistry, such empty tubes soon came to be acted upon as mandates for policy making. The attempt to provide them with content could book some successes – they led, for instance, to the Schengen agreement lifting border controls in much of the union – but set the EU off on other trajectories that would cause unnecessary trans-Atlantic bickering, inseminate misbegotten and wasteful projects, muddy up governance, and sour member-state relationships to the point of gridlock.

The first such attempt, a frenzied effort to break the diplomatic bottleneck after the 2000 Nice Council summit meeting, gave impetus to the costly, pointless ten-year campaign for a European constitution. It represents still another bid to turn policy failure into a 'beneficial crisis', in this case by creating new governance machinery allegedly designed to fix what had broken down, but in reality intended to create new opportunities for concentrating power in Brussels. The attempted *fait accompli* misfired spectacularly. The campaign on behalf of the Constitution began with much official arm-twisting to discourage ratification by referenda and proceeded, in nations where referenda were actually held, to heavy-handed interventionism, which unleashed a still mounting floodtide of public anger. The unpleasant episode cured the public of its complacent habit (the 'permissive consensus') of overlooking EU shortcomings as a necessary price to be paid for future promises.

Much of what remained of Brussels neoliberalism became the unintended casualty of the French referendum. France's vociferous *Non* voters objected specifically to the Commission's bold Services Directive (SD), whose adoption would have broken down national labour market monopolies across the community and have extended the common market to the remaining roughly two-thirds of the European economy not yet affected by the SEA. The voters' message was unmistakable: forays into liberalization would rule out future federation. Since then, few such efforts have been made, and none of them has been successful.

Popular opposition to the SD in France was doubtless genuine, but underlying it was, as also obvious in the Dutch rejection of the constitution, probably a still deeper and more widespread mistrust of unaccountable and inept rule from above. The eventual shotgun ratification of the Lisbon Treaty, a warmed over but re-named version of the former Constitution, changes little operationally but saddles the tottering Brussels structure with thick new layers of fat while hobbling it with rapidly unreeling spindles of red tape. The end result? Much ado about almost nothing.

A 'bust' from the outset

The economic side of the Maastricht settlement was of greater salience than its political counterpart. It produced the Economic and Monetary Union (EMU), an institution designed above all to advance the integration project. Its power and influence soon eclipsed that of the parent organization, the EU, whose fate remains tied to it. Under normal conditions, the European Central Bank (ECB), the authority in charge of the EMU, is autonomous and free from outside control.

The EMU was supposed to accomplish three things: in order to make the welfare state affordable and stabilize currency parities, it was to have the power to discipline spendthrift governments and end competitive devaluations; by issuing a common currency and creating a single market in stocks and bonds (as well as options and derivatives), it was to establish a Europe-wide financial community equal in strength to that of the United States; and, this task accomplished, it was meant to serve as a launch pad for federal union (Gillingham, 2006a: 63–70).

The Economic and Monetary Union (EMU) was hammered out against an atmosphere of intense political pressure, but without benefit of independent outside opinion. Many eminent economists at once spotted glaring flaws in its design. There were several of them: the eurozone did not comprise a natural customs area and was thus unsuited for a one-size-fits-all policy; the new European Central Bank (ECB) lacked the authority to make fiscal or macro-economic policy; and, for enforcement, it was limited to the application of rigid and unsuitable rules; as befit a *fait accompli*, finally, no provision was made in the TEU treaty for coping with failure. The EMU should serve as a red flag to those, who, in the vein of Andrew Moravcsik, insist that the European Union is best left in the hands of technocrats and kept out of those of electorates. Experts, not laymen, designed the institution that put the future in jeopardy (Feldstein, 1997a: 23–42; Gillingham, 2003: 269–77; Gillingham, 2006a: 63–70; Mundell, 1961).

The EMU was destined to fail from the outset. The rigid rules adopted, though not completely enforceable, had a built in deflationary bias. Two of them – the limit on the overall size of sovereign debt and on increases in rates of inflation – were, certainly, never invoked. The third, which limited budget deficits to 3 per cent of GDP, was binding yet frequently violated by member states, thereby demoralizing the virtuous among them who, to uphold EMU rules, sacrificed economic growth.

European growth rates began to fall steadily during the 'run up' to monetary union in the 1990s, and the gap between them and those of the US has widened ever since. Yet the hoped-for convergence of member-state economies did not take place; rather they have diverged. For years danger signals were ignored and blatant cheating was tolerated. The ECB could do little more about the situation than grumble. Bail-outs were specifically proscribed. The lack of 'exit' provisions made an economic downturn potentially ruinous. This, then, is the setting for Europe's present agonies.

A single financial market

The way out of this difficult situation will not be found either in Brussels or Frankfurt, the seat of the ECB. The idea of a European financial union – a single market to complement the single currency – is misconceived. Developed as the euro began to circulate, the proposed Financial Services Action Plan (FSAP) was supposed to complete the monetary union by dethroning the US dollar as the world's leading currency.

Yet FSAP was based on unrealistic premises and obsolete knowledge. The euro was not the first, but actually the second, currency to circulate throughout the union. The dollar, of course, had long been employed for financing in much of Europe and, as the incumbent international currency, would continue to be. The choice of a particular money for use in financing transactions does not, moreover, depend on the issuer but on the relative costs and risks of the deal in question as well as the availability of capital and the resources for mobilizing it. There is, in other words, no necessary connection between a single circulating currency and financial markets.

The attempt to create a single financial market soon fell hopelessly behind the fast-moving pace of change. In the ten years during which the FSAP was under discussion, the City of London's turnover increased to over 80 per cent of that of Europe as a whole. Although outside the eurozone, London also hosted by far the world's largest euro markets. It is hard to imagine the City willingly relinquishing such a strong position to outside regulators in order to promote the cause of the EU (Rachman, 2006). The EU's essentially well-intentioned effort to set up a single European financial market, in other words, had the unsought consequences of shrinking secondary stock markets in the member states, increasing the power of the City, and speeding up the internationalization of European finance along American lines. It thus drove a final nail into the coffin of the 'European financial model'. Instead of encouraging the development of stakeholder capitalism and promoting operational transparency, FSAP enhanced the market position, and boosted the profitability of shadowy non-European mega-financials armed with sophisticated methods that EU officialdom did not understand and could not properly supervise. Policy failure in such a critical arena bodes ill for the EU's future as a market regulator, indeed for the long-sought financial independence of the eurozone (Buck, 2007; Levine, 2007). The pending crisis and impending collapse makes the very notion of such a thing now sound dated.

The FSAP episode also provides an uncomfortable reminder that the *soi-disant* technical expertise of the Commission is derivative. Not an in-house product, it must be acquired second hand, and at a price, from outside sources. In this situation, lobbies are essential as providers of local knowledge. So, too, are practitioners, actual doers as opposed to armchair-bound bureaucrats; what happened in the financial field has many parallels elsewhere, in high tech and research and development generally. A reliance on outside expertise also invites agency problems. But that is only a secondary drag on efficiency.

More important still, as Majone emphasizes, is the tacit requirement that policy, in whatever field, serves the higher end of promoting the EU as integrator, a priority that reduces efficiency across the board and levies heavy direct and indirect cost, including opportunity costs (Gillingham, 2006a: 138–55; Majone, 2009). The belatedly terminated attempt of the Commission to establish a 'green' agenda, by encouraging a campaign against so-called Frankenfoods, provides an important example of the latter. The uproar delayed European entrance into the strategic growth field of genetic technology, now rapidly advancing in the rest of the world, by many years.

Still more costly to the EU, in direct terms, is chronic misallocation resulting from bad policy design, a matter which, being bound up with the convoluted institutional machinery in Brussels, requires more detailed exposition than can be provided in this brief article. The problem is not easily fixed (Bartolini, 2006: 14f; Gillingham, 2006a: 4–18, 39–55). Though often advanced as a surrogate for the genuine, democratic product, the argument for 'output legitimacy' is a bad joke.

This contribution is more about the survival of the EU than its prospects for reform. It must therefore concentrate on the former, even at risk of giving short shrift to the latter. Although the crisis now facing Europe started with the collapse of the American housing bubble on Wall Street, it will be felt longer, as well as more deeply and consequentially than in the US. The faulty design of the European Monetary Union, and the divided authority within the EU, has raised the spectre of institutional collapse.

The need for radical surgery

What next? Partial repudiation of sovereign debt – default – in the weak member states is essential to ending the present crisis. It will require administering 'haircuts' – not stylish trims but US Marine-style flat-tops – to big bondholders in France, Germany, and elsewhere. This should reduce net welfare losses over the long run. To limit growth in order to protect the (in fact long lost) prestige of the euro – the policy now in effect – is a bad trade off. Europe faces a protracted period of austerity that can only be mitigated by an unpleasant cocktail of currency depreciation and inflation.

Public discussion has just begun on the EU's future. It is by now clear, however, that new projects must to be put aside and waste reduced. Fantasies, such as planning for a European strike force, should be relegated to the potato cellar for wintering. Expensive and unrealistic schemes, such as the gigantic military super-transporter, the Airbus 400, and the EU's un-launched but already outdated GPS system, the Galileo programme, must be dropped. The EU's two giant engines of waste, CAP and regional funds, should be switched off. As a last cost-savings resort, Brussels' bureaucrats might even consider cutting their own excessive salaries and emoluments. If this can be accomplished, Europe's present plight would indeed be a 'beneficial crisis'.

To save the EMU, the euro should be re-configured as a parallel currency and circulate along with, as well as be convertible to, restored national monies (Gillingham, 2006a: 63–70). A eurozone so reorganized could capture comparative advantage and reduce the threat of the systemic shock. The decision to use either, or both, national and European issues should be left up to the individual member state. In the era of the ATM and the credit card, technical procedures for exchanging currencies are far simpler and less costly than one would suppose (Gillingham, 2006b).

The restoration of monetary sovereignty will naturally involve sharp devaluations, but so what? The economically weak member states' other option would be to remain uncompetitive and face years of recession (Poehl, 2010). Decision-making power within the EMU can be re-distributed on the basis of sole, partial, or future use of the euro without eliminating the possibility of eventual full membership for those states ready and willing to abide by its rules.

A reformed EMU could prelude a re-structured EU, something which now resembles the Holy Roman Empire more closely than any modern nation-state (Zielonka, 2006). Existing theory offers little guidance as to how the necessary changes can take place (Bartolini, 2006: 387f; Majone, 2009: 179f). The EU has obviously not evolved teleologically into a federal state as 'functionalism' once predicted; it has grown by fits and starts, usually as the result of exogenous influence. Nor is the EU the efficient culmination of optimal bargaining by member states; its gross operational failures make such a notion sound farfetched. Nor has it grown out of a happy marriage with the welfare state: the ongoing internationalization process rules this out and efforts to catheterize incontinent governments still end in ignominy.

A federal Europe, as imagined by Monnet and Delors, is no longer – if it ever was – achievable. The only escape from the present trap facing a Europe living above its means in a world dominated by Asian giants and hamstrung by a dysfunctional EU is to restore the sovereignty of democratic, and thus legitimate, nation states. Only they have the moral authority to make and enforce the tough decisions that Europe's welfare requires.

If re-built on an augmented national power, a reformed EU can survive. Some things can be salvaged. The European Court of Justice (ECJ) is perhaps the leading integration success story, but while the development over many years of European case law is an impressive accomplishment, the ECJ has not prevented the EU from increasingly operating in a realm of extra-legality or 'soft law', as it is euphemistically termed. The Court did not block the 'Special Purpose Vehicle' created expressly to administer the bank bailout forbidden by the Maastricht treaty, but this is only one trenchant recent example of the ECJ's usual refusal to subject the EU to its own laws, rules, and regulations. Although the fate of the ECJ will depend heavily on that of the rest of the EU institutions, it probably can survive as a special purpose entity, like the European Court in Strasbourg, even after the disappearance of the greater part EU executive authority. The future of European law will, however, be determined in the national courts.

The prevalent eurolegal laxity has had the dire effect of encouraging the proliferation of new 'competences' for agencies and programmes unforeseen in any EU treaty or agreement, which all too quickly get out of hand. The malignancies that result are hard to excise.

Radical surgery is needed for the remaining Brussels institutions. Having lost the power to impose or even set agendas, the Commission should be reduced to a planning staff with advisory powers. The Council should meet, albeit as a standing assembly of sovereign nations, to take up transnational issues requiring interstate action as, and only as, needed. The Parliament should be abolished (Gillingham, 2006a: 200–33; see also Anderson, 2009: 505–47).

What once was expected to centralize into a *Bundesstaat* should devolve into a *Staatenbund* of revived states. The authority of the new confederation should arise from a network of individual multinational treaties of demonstrated utility drafted to deal with specific problems. Thus reconstituted, a future EU can promote the ever-closer union that its peoples, at heart, may still want. It cannot survive in its present form. The publics are fed up, and their political leaders are for the most part simply not up to the job. The European Union is a drag on adaptation to a globalizing world where power will shift to the revived civilizations of India and China. The European Union may well have to take two steps backward for every one step forward. Retrenchment and reform are, at this point, not options but necessities. Without them, the European dream will have been no more than a pipe dream.

Chapter 2

The Political Efficiency of the EU

Editors' Introduction

In 1988, German political scientist Fritz Scharpf published a seminal article (Scharpf, 1988) in which he argued that the European Union was characterized by a situation which is typical of many federal systems: it had fallen into a 'joint decision trap' in which the need for consensus and unanimous decision making among a large number of member states and many institutions at the supranational level would systematically hinder innovation and lead to sub-optimal compromise arrangements. Versions of Scharpf's critique have been part and parcel of every popular critique of the European Union ever since its foundations. From legendary French President de Gaulle's 1962 denunciation of European bureaucrats as faceless legislators, speaking in an incomprehensible 'Volapük' language, to more recent denouncements of EU regulatory policies in Europe's popular press, the efficiency of the European Union has been and is a popular target of criticism. Successive US administrations have chafed under slow decision making by Europeans. Industry associations lament the byzantine structures of EU institutions. The euro crisis of 2010/11 demonstrated only too clearly the limited enforcement capacity of the EU against rule breakers.

And yet, the European Union continues to be the major locus of common problem solving in Europe and it generates an increasing legislative output. In successive rounds of treaty revisions, European politicians have tried (and often failed) to simplify decision making and thus enhance the effectiveness of EU legislation (Finke et al., 2012). The most recent attempt was the Lisbon Treaty of 2009 which had been negotiated with a view 'to enhancing the efficiency and democratic legitimacy of the Union and to improving the coherence of its action', as stated in its preamble (Lisbon Treaty, 2009). The 2004/7 enlargement of the Union to 27 members, and the eurozone to 17 members in 2011, made such reforms inevitable. Whether they are successful is a question open to debate (see Chapter 13). It is also controversial whether the EU is worse in problem solving than countries, such as the United States with their system of checks and balances, leading to frequent gridlock between

32

Congress and US Presidents, or whether we should indeed hold the European Union to the same standards as conventional nation-states.

Desmond Dinan thinks that we should not and he considers the EU to be a surprisingly efficient organization. It has displayed a remarkable capacity for adaptation and its institutions continue to function comparatively well. Mats Persson argues that popular images of the EU as bureaucratic juggernaut are not exaggerated, given its seemingly unstoppable capacity to churn out new laws and regulations, its less than impressive record in policy fields, such as defence or agricultural policy, and its limited accountability.

Many chapters in this volume deal with the efficiency of the EU, whether it is agricultural policy (Chapter 11), financial regulation (Chapter 10) or European defence (Chapter 14).

2.1 The EU as efficient polity

Desmond Dinan

Arguing that the EU is an efficient polity seems like an uphill task. The EU is easy to caricature as 'an inefficient bureaucratic monster'. Compared to what? The EU is *sui generis*, neither a classic international organization nor a familiar nation-state. Instead, it is a unique polity that combines elements of intergovernmentalism (traditional inter-state relations) and supranationalism (shared sovereignty in various policy areas). The EU is a transnational entity with state-like attributes, notably in the judicial and legislative fields. It exists because its member states agree that the EU benefits them in ways that could not otherwise be realized. The EU enhances national welfare, broadly understood. The paradox for sovereignty-conscious countries is that by sharing cherished sovereignty in the EU they advance their national interests.

The EU enables its member states to enjoy vast economies of scale and scope in an integrated socioeconomic-political space spanning almost the entire continent of Europe. Governing such a space is a Herculean task. Any polity with twenty-seven markedly different member states and twenty-three working languages – a necessity, given that citizens have every right to understand EU decision-making procedures, rules, and regulations – is bound to be cumbersome. In view of the obvious cultural, linguistic, and organizational constraints that it faces, as well as the fact that it is democratic, the surprising thing about the EU is that it works as efficiently as it does. If looked at without ideological blinkers – free of the prejudice that supranationalism is inherently evil – and without preconceived ideas about the intrinsic inefficiency of government or dreariness of bureaucracy, the EU emerges not only as a fascinating experiment in post-national politics and policy making but also as a remarkably capable, resourceful, and resilient entity.

The European Council

At the top of the EU's institutional architecture stands the European Council, which brings together the highest political leaders of the member states (the heads of state or government), plus the Commission President. The European Council emerged in the 1970s as a crisis-management mechanism, the crisis at the time being the severe economic challenges facing European countries and the institutional sclerosis besetting the then European Community. Following the revival of European integration in the late 1980s, the European Council became the key EU decision-making body, where national leaders could reach agreement on contentious issues ranging from the budget, to enlargement, to treaty change. The fact that national leaders meet so often in the European Council, either in regularly scheduled or specially convened meetings, testifies to the pervasiveness of European integration in national political affairs and the interconnectedness of national and EU policy making.

National leaders often bring to the European Council table widely different policy preferences. Agreement is frequently difficult to reach. The leaders of France and Germany tend to predominate, which reflects a fact of life in international relations (the preponderance of the more powerful players) and the origins of European integration (the centrality of Franco-German *rapprochement*). It is not always easy for French and German leaders to reach common positions, and common Franco-German positions sometimes irritate, even alienate, other national leaders. Despite these complicated political dynamics, the European Council is adept at finding solutions to seemingly intractable problems.

The eurozone crisis of 2010/11 comes to mind. At first glance, this would seem to be an example of EU leaders behaving at their worst, dithering while the eurozone teetered on the brink of collapse. Even if the eurozone was ever in such dire straits, arguably EU leaders acted reasonably expeditiously and efficaciously, given the enormous domestic constraints that most of them faced. The point about domestic politics is essential for understanding the EU. National leaders do not operate in a vacuum when operating at the European level. They cannot agree to do things as EU leaders that are unsupportable at the national level, although their rhetoric is sometimes extravagant. German Chancellor Angela Merkel drew considerable scorn from fellow EU leaders for her initial hands-off approach to the mounting Greek sovereign debt crisis.

The Chancellor seemed stunned by the severity of Greece's situation and unaware of its implications for German creditors as well as for the stability of the eurozone. Yet Merkel was highly sensitive to domestic opinion, which grew increasingly critical of economic and monetary union and censorious of Greece. She was equally concerned about the constitutionality of a bailout, given the negative tone of recent rulings by the German Constitutional Court on EU issues.

Under the circumstances, it was impressive that the European Council decided in 2010 first to establish the (temporary) European Financial Stability Facility, then to establish the (permanent) European Stability Mechanism. As European Council President Herman Van Rompuy rightly stated 'the decisions we have taken [with respect to the crisis], constitute the biggest reform of the economic and monetary union since the euro was created' (European Council, 2011: 6). The political salience of these decisions both constrained national leaders and required action at the top of the EU executive pyramid, in the European Council. Ideally, EU leaders would have acted sooner and more decisively. But politics is the art of the possible, and most political outcomes tend to be sub-optimal. That observation is as true at the European as at the national level of governance. The ongoing response to the euro crisis, taken largely by national leaders operating in the European Council, demonstrates that the EU functions as well (or as badly) as can be expected for any political entity, especially one of its extraordinary nature.

The Council–Commission–Parliament triangle

The EU makes all kinds of decisions, such as on its composition (enlargement); financing (the budget); competence (policy scope); and institutional arrangements. Most EU decisions are of the legislative kind, taken with a view to managing a wide range of policy areas, notably agriculture, the environment, and the internal market. The legislative process involves a proposal from the Commission and co-decision by the Council of Ministers and the European Parliament (EP) in a system called the ordinary legislative procedure. The apparent complexity of the ordinary legislative procedure drives critics to distraction. Yet legislative procedures are inherently complex; they are neither simple nor easily comprehensible in any liberal-democratic polity. Given the nature of the EU, its legislative process is astonishingly efficient and productive. This was not always the case. In response to complaints about tardy decision making and the proliferation of unnecessary proposals, the EU has streamlined the legislative process in successive rounds of treaty change and internal organizational reform. The Commission now produces fewer and better quality proposals; the Council acts expeditiously and decisively through the widespread use of qualified majority voting; and the EP has refined the seemingly arcane co-decision procedure to the point that many of its own members complain that they do not have adequate opportunity to comment on legislative drafts. In other words, the problem with legislative decision making may not be that the EU is inefficient, but that it is too efficient, to the detriment of careful parliamentary scrutiny.

The Council, consisting of government ministers from the member states, meets in several formations, corresponding to the main areas of EU activity (agriculture, environment, competitiveness, and the like). This allows most government ministers, spanning the spectrum of issues covered by the EU, to conduct business in Brussels. Foreign ministers meet in two formations: General Affairs, to coordinate the work of other formations and prepare meetings of the European Council; and Foreign Affairs, to discuss the Common Foreign and Security Policy and the EU's external relations. The General Affairs and the sectoral Council formations are engaged in legislative decision making; the Foreign Affairs Council is involved in an area that is still largely intergovernmental and, given its extreme political sensitivity, remains a work in progress.

The fact that governments agree to the possibility of being outvoted in so many important policy areas is one of the distinguishing characteristics of the EU. Naturally, governments care deeply about the decision-making rules in the Council because the political stakes are so high. The system of qualified majority voting (QMV) is not as straightforward as a simple majority system (50 per cent plus one vote). Currently, the threshold for a qualified majority stands at about 73 per cent of the total number of votes around the Council table, which is the sum of votes allocated to each member states – an allocation based approximately on population size. The reason for using a qualified rather than a simple majority is to protect the interests of countries in the minority by making it more difficult for them to be outvoted. Nevertheless complaints by the more populous member states about the unfairness of the existing voting system, due to the increasing number of less-populous member states in the EU following successive rounds of enlargement, resulted in a reform of QMV in the Lisbon Treaty. Starting in 2014, most legislative decisions will require the support of at least 55 per cent of the member states (represented by their governments in the Council of Ministers), corresponding to at least 65 per cent of the EU's total population. The new system sounds more complicated than the original version of QMV, but it is more equitable.

Regardless of the modality in use, voting is the key to speedy Council decision making. The most serious political crisis in EU history broke out in 1965 when French President Charles de Gaulle withdrew his country's representatives from the Council in an effort, among other things, to halt the use of QMV. The crisis ended with the Luxembourg Compromise of 1966, a political agreement allowing national governments to prevent a Council vote from taking place whenever a 'very important' (later understood as 'vital') national interest was at stake. The subjective nature of 'very important' or 'vital' interests, and the propensity of governments to succumb to domestic pressure to claim that such an interest was indeed at stake, severely impaired Council decision making in the years ahead. Only with the Single European Act of 1986 – a major treaty change intended primarily to facilitate completion of the single European market – did governments re-commit themselves to using QMV, bringing the era of the Luxembourg Compromise effectively to an end. Thereafter, with the spread of QMV to more and more policy areas as a result of subsequent treaty reforms, the efficiency of Council decision making improved dramatically.

The Commission has an exclusive right to initiate legislation, although proposals originate in a number of ways. As in any polity, interest groups are active in promoting legislation as well as in trying to block initiatives with which they disagree. National governments are a form of interest group, often pushing the Commission to introduce particular proposals or drop others. The Commission consults a variety of outside actors, including national governments and traditional interest groups, before fashioning a legislative proposal. It is eager to improve the quality of its legislative proposal as well as increase the prospect that proposals will pass successfully through the two arms of the EU's legislative branch: the Council and the EP.

The Commission is empowered to make certain kinds of decisions on its own. These include regulations enacted under overarching, framework legislation – day-to-day executive decisions – and rulings in competition policy cases. The purpose of competition policy is to police the single market and prevent businesses and governments from getting an unfair advantage. Businesses tend to complain about anti-trust and other competition policy measures, but generally appreciate that without a vigilant watchdog the marketplace would likely be distorted to their disadvantage. In an integrated, trans-national economic space, businesses like dealing with a single competition authority. The Commission conducts competition policy fairly and swiftly (there are strict deadlines at each stage of the process). Most economic actors subject to EU competition rules view the Commission favourably, notwithstanding inevitable complaints about specific rulings (Buch-Hansen and Wigger, 2011; McGowan, 2010).

Many opponents of European integration caricature the Commission as a bloated bureaucracy full of faceless officials meddling in everyone else's affairs. In fact, the Commission is a small organization, consisting of about 35,000 staff, many of them interpreters and translators. According to the Commission, this number of staff is 'as big as the local authority of a medium-sized European city' (Commission, 2011). The twenty-seven Commissioners (one per member state) are far from faceless – each has a wide-ranging website – and the identities of Commission officials can easily be obtained. By any standard, the Commission is compact, transparent, and hard-working. Some of its internal procedures are indeed excessively bureaucratic, a result of its transnational character and of tight financial controls put in place following well-publicized cases of corruption and mismanagement in the late 1990s. Most Commission officials are capable, conscientious, and highly professional. Not least because of the prevailing climate of euroscepticism, they are careful not to act irresponsibly and exceed their authority.

The EP is another favourite target for EU-bashers. Politicians and parliamentarians (mostly the same thing in liberal-democratic systems) are generally disliked in the current climate of anti-establishmentarianism and political populism. The EP is especially unpopular because few people understand exactly what it does and how it works. As a result, the turnout in EU-wide elections for the EP, held every five years, has steadily declined since the first election took place in 1979. Most Europeans seem to view the EP as a publicly supported leisure centre for politicians who, for whatever reason, are out of favour at the national level. Unflattering coverage of the EP in the mass media tends to reinforce such a caricature.

Like most national parliaments, the EP has legislative, budgetary, and oversight responsibilities. These have increased over time, following successive rounds of treaty reform, in an effort to strengthen the EU's democratic credentials. After all, the EP is the only EU institution that is directly elected at the European level (the Council consists of governments that are directly elected at the national level), even if Europeans do not turn out in large numbers for EP elections. With more than 700 members operating in twenty-three official languages, the EP is bound to be unwieldy. Despite its size and linguistic multiplicity, the EP carries out its responsibilities remarkably efficiently. It has a powerful incentive to do so: it knows that the Council of Ministers is dubious about its capacity to perform and it wants to be taken seriously as an institutional actor. The EP also hopes that its institutional efficiency will favourably impress an inherently sceptical public.

The EP owes its success in acquiring more power and exercising it responsibly to a small but dedicated group of members in leadership positions (Judge and Earnshaw, 2008). Members of the European Parliament (MEPs) sit in trans-national political groups and on committees corresponding to the EU's areas of activities. The EP President and Vice-Presidents, together with the heads of the political groups and chairs of the committees, form a cohesive leadership cohort. The political groups are difficult to manage, given their trans-national composition and the fact that the EU does not have a government that depends for its survival on the support of a single group or a coalition of groups in the EP. Nevertheless the increasing importance of the EP, especially in the legislative arena, has greatly improved political group discipline. Going beyond ideological and political group differences, MEPs in leadership positions use every opportunity both to strengthen the EP's power and carry out the EP's responsibilities as efficiently as possible (Hix *et al.*, 2007).

In one obvious respect, the EP is intrinsically inefficient, however. Monthly plenary sessions take place in Strasbourg; the EP's secretariat is in Luxembourg; and committee meetings (as well as occasional extra plenary sessions) take place in Brussels. Having to maintain huge facilities in Brussels and Strasbourg and move every month between them – a distance of over 200 miles – is expensive, disruptive, and damaging to the EP's public image. Keenly aware of those drawbacks, the EP has been agitating to move its seat permanently to Brussels, where the Commission and the Council of Ministers are also located. But the EP is held in check by the fierce opposition of the French and Luxembourg governments, which want to maintain the *status quo* for economic and symbolic reasons. Indeed, both governments insisted on the *status quo* being written into the EU treaties, making any change extremely difficult. Many MEPs want the EP to take a stand and stay in Brussels regardless, believing that the ensuing constitutional crisis would benefit the EU, and especially EP, by generating public interest and support (Banks, 2011).

Conclusion

The EU is a highly unusual, transnational polity. It has grown dramatically in size since 2004, from fifteen to twenty-seven member states, with more waiting to join. More members mean more languages, more cultural diversity, and more socio-economic differentiation. At the same time, the policy scope of the EU has increased as well, with the original common market developing into an integrated economic area including a monetary union. Complementing the EU's socio-economic policy remit, member states have intensified cooperation in the fields of foreign policy and external security, as well as justice and home affairs.

The EU's system of governance has changed during this period of major geographical and policy expansion in an effort to satisfy the twin but sometimes competing demands of democracy and efficiency. Doubtless the EU is not as efficient as many would like it to be. It may not be as efficient as it could be, despite the constraints that it faces. But the perfect should not be the enemy of the good. Rather, we should celebrate the fact that, according to a recent academic analysis, 'the political system [of the EU] is functioning effectively in transforming inputs into outputs' (Thomson, 2011: 25).

Like any political system, the EU should strive for improvement. It has a long way to go, but deserves to be proud of how far it has come. Given the dangers posed by divided Europe before 1989 and fragmented Europe before 1945, the EU looks less like a bureaucratic monster and more like a miraculous achievement: miraculous in its relative efficiency and not only its very existence.

2.2 The EU: quick to regulate, slow to adapt

Mats Persson

Is the European Union efficient? The answer is both Yes and No. Yes, if efficiency is understood to mean the rate at which the EU introduces new rules, regulations, directives and initiatives. Yes, also, if we are referring to the ability of the EU's institutions to extend their own powers at the expense of national, regional and local bodies – albeit incrementally.

But the answer has to be No if we understand 'efficient' to mean the EU's capacity to adapt to the economic and political challenges of the modern, globalized world, or its ability to alter its policies in light of new evidence or changing economic circumstances. Alas, the EU's emphasis on process over substance often leads to sub-optimal policy outcomes.

An efficient regulator

The EU has substantial powers in the area of regulation, ranging from regulating bank break-ups to working time and driving tests. Over the last decade, the EU's rate of producing legislation has significantly increased, as shown in Figure 2.1.

In fact, the EU's opaque structure makes it practically the perfect vehicle for pushing through laws and regulations, often under the radar of public scrutiny. As Thomas Jefferson famously observed, 'democracy is cumbersome, slow and inefficient'. By having designed a system which works outside the constraints of national democratic processes, the EU

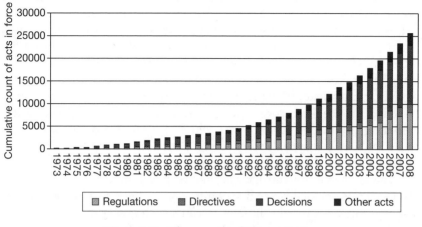

Figure 2.1 *The growth of EU regulation*

Source: EUR-Lex, Open Europe (2009).

can push through laws and measures which would otherwise have been caught by domestic opposition, most importantly national parliaments.

This tendency is both driven by, and then reinforces, the blurred line between where the EU's powers begin and where they end. Indeed, no-one is quite sure exactly how much of their sovereignty member states have transferred to Brussels; illustrated by the fact that estimates on the share of national laws now decided by the EU range from 9 per cent (House of Commons Library, 2010: 16) and 84 per cent (Deutscher Bundestag, 2005: 15).

Here, the role of the European Commission must be fully understood. The Commission combines the functions of an executive and a bureaucracy, with the sole right to initiate legislation in the European Union; crucially there are very few filters in place to ensure that the proposal is viable and corresponds to a real demand in society (Open Europe, 2010). The Commission therefore possesses agenda-setting powers enjoyed by few other public bodies. And the appetite for new regulation is substantial, stemming from a bias towards 'ever closer union'. As former Industry Commissioner, Günther Verheugen, once observed: 'There are 27 Commissioners, which means 27 Directorate-Generals. And 27 Directorate-Generals means that everyone needs to prove that they are needed by constantly producing new directives, strategies or projects. In any case the rule is: More and more, more and more, all the time' (*Der Spiegel*, 2010).

Italian academic Giandomenico Majone (2005: 39) has rightly pointed out that, 'Under the Community method only the Commission is entitled to set the legislative and policy agenda, and this monopoly allows it to pursue objectives of political integration and self-aggrandisement while pretending to solve specific policy problems – integration by stealth'.

It is true that the Commission's proposals are often subject to drawn out negotiations between EU member states and the European Parliament. As UK Deputy Prime Minister Nick Clegg once observed, 'Anything that takes 15 years to define what chocolate is, is not a model of democratic efficiency' (*The Telegraph*, 2010). But it is also true that once tabled, a proposal tends to float around Brussels until finally adopted, conjuring up images of a monster which if decapitated, quickly grows two new heads. Proposals rarely die in Brussels.

This tendency is also driven by another asset that the Commission's thousands of civil servants have at their disposal: time. Verheugen again: 'Too much is decided by civil servants... the whole development in the last ten years has brought the civil servants such power that in the meantime the most important political task of the 25 [now 27] commissioners is controlling this apparatus. There is a permanent power struggle between commissioners and high ranking bureaucrats. Some of them think: the commissioner is gone after five years and so is just a squatter' (*Süddeutsche Zeitung*, 2006).

At the end stage of the regulatory process, the implementation phase, the Commission again enjoys unusual powers in the so-called Comitology phase, where it can add elements to a law once it has already been agreed with very little input from national parliaments or even governments (Guéguen, 2010). Comitology involves special committees consisting of Commission and national experts deciding on how EU legislation should be implemented – usually behind closed doors – after the proposal has been agreed by the Council of Ministers and the European Parliament. This gives the Commission a 'second chance' to add its flavour to whatever the member states and the European Parliament have agreed. All of this makes the European Commission an 'effective' regulator.

For its part, the European Court of Justice has a tendency to rule in favour of further integration, in that it tends to reinforce the Commission's 'more Europe means more regulation' approach to legislation rather than challenging it (Burley and Mattli, 1993). In fact, the EU Treaties explicitly commit the ECJ to practice 'mutual sincere cooperation' with the other EU institutions (TEU Art. 13.2). Alec Stone Sweet (2010) has argued that the role of the ECJ and the national courts in monitoring and enforcing member-state compliance with EU law 'has provoked a steady Europeanization of national law and policymaking'.

The European Parliament could in theory shoulder the responsibility of balancing the ECJ and the Commission, but too often it acts as a cheerleader for further integration, rather than as a proper Parliament with a 'loyal' opposition scrutinizing the executive and contributing to a vibrant political debate. The European Parliament has, for example, consistently pushed for integrationist measures such as EU taxes, despite there being very little support for these amongst most electorates and governments across Europe.

But an inefficient reformer

Somewhat paradoxically, however, the tendency of the Commission, the ECJ and the EP to pursue so-called 'integration by stealth' – in turn making it 'effective' in introducing new laws – also makes the EU 'inefficient' insofar as the term is understood to mean effective in producing good, well-targeted policies. This is no small part due to the 'communitarian method' effectively favouring *process* over *content*. Although Majone comes at this from a slightly different angle, he notes that this owes to the fact that a central dilemma has never been satisfactorily addressed: 'whether European policies should be initiated in order to solve specific problems in the best possible way, or whether they are to serve, first and foremost, integration objectives' (Majone, 2005: vii). He argues that the EU's tendency of pursuing several objectives simultaneously 'tends to produce suboptimal policy outcomes'.

In practice, this means that the EU may be very good at moving in one direction – towards more regulation, deeper integration and bigger bureaucracy – but in terms of producing or changing policies in light of evidence, experience, citizens' demands or changing circumstances, the EU's 'communitarian method' simply is not fit for purpose.

There are of course areas where the EU has proven itself capable of adapting: for example the EU's competition policy, with some exceptions, has served Europe well and acted as a counterforce to national protectionist instincts that in the past have led several governments to pursue dated agendas that play well with vested sectoral interests, at the expense of wealth creation and growth. Several areas of the single market, such as some financial regulation, would fall into this category as well (but a large chunk would not).

However, in other areas the EU has struggled tremendously to produce optimal policy outcomes. Unlike national legislation, once an EU law is decided it is often set in stone, even if it proves overly burdensome or inappropriate in light of evidence and experience (Scharpf, 1988). Changing an EU law requires the re-opening and successful conclusion of negotiations with all 27 member states and the European Parliament which is very hard to achieve (and a government may even lose concessions it previously has won). New and existing EU laws can therefore continue to cause problems or generate heavy costs year after year and still be left unaddressed.

A conspicuous example is the EU's Working Time Directive (WTD), which regulates working time, rest periods and holidays across Europe. First, the very premise of centralizing regulation over working time – that is so specific to local circumstances – for 27 member states with vastly different labour market models and economic structures is not driven by best practice or common sense, but by ideology (and a desire by some member states to raise rivals' costs). The ECJ's judicial activism has since added fuel to the fire; in the so-called *SiMAP* ruling in 2000, the ECJ ruled that time spent by residents on call in a hospital or other place of work should count as full working time, even if the worker is asleep for some of that time (Sindicato, 1998). Member states have spent nearly a decade trying to come up with an alternative definition of working time and rest periods – one more in tune with the reality on the ground that will cost taxpayers less – but they have failed to do so. The most recent attempt in 2009 was blocked by the European Parliament on largely ideological grounds. Hence, despite a clear majority of member states seeing a need for revision, the Directive remains unchanged.

And the list can be extended into other policy areas as well. For example, the European Arrest Warrant, intended to ease cross-border policing for serious offences such as terrorism and organized crime, remains unreformed despite widespread evidence showing that it unnecessarily undermines civil liberties and is frequently used to hunt down suspects accused of minor crimes. A report by the EU Commission found that in the four-year period following its inception, almost 55,000 warrants were issued, and although it helped law enforcement agencies to catch some serious criminals who operated across borders, the majority were issued for minor, even trivial crimes including the theft of a bicycle or a cupboard door (*The Parliament*, 2011). Despite it being a fairly easy exercise to tweak the EAW to make it more proportionate, it remains unreformed.

Similarly, the EU still subsidises biofuels, and encourages its production under the EU renewables targets, despite plenty of evidence showing that these fuels can be counter-productive, since as much emissions are generated producing them as they save compared with traditional fuels, while their production often involves substantial environmental damage itself (Kutas *et al.*, 2007).

The biofuels targets also illustrate another problem with EU decision making: its susceptibility to companies or organizations seeking to obtain an economic gain for themselves at the expense of society as a whole, so-called rent-seeking. This works in at least two ways: first by influencing the Commission in the agenda-setting stage, in which lobbyists in Brussels can have an unusually significant impact (for reasons partly described above). And secondl by entrenching interests in the

EU's agreed policies, exacerbating the already considerable difficulties in reforming failed or questionable measures (see Chapter 11 for a debate on lobbying in the EU).

Perhaps the clearest examples of this phenomenon are the Common Agricultural Policy (CAP), which is dated and comes with a range of negative side-effects such as driving up domestic food prices, distorting markets and hurting farmers in the developing world; and the Common Fisheries Policy (CFP), which even the EU's former Fisheries Commissioner Joe Borg described as 'morally wrong' (quoted in the *Financial Times*, 2007; on CAP and CFP, see Chapter 10).While attempts at reforming CFP have a long history, the sheer length of time between identifying the problem and addressing it, as well as the ability of some member states who do relatively well out of the policy (such as Spain) to block reform, serves as a pertinent reminder of the EU's infectiveness in reforming flawed policies.

Perhaps most strangely, the European Parliament still travels between Strasbourg and Brussels every month, at an annual cost of €180 million to the European taxpayer, while emitting 20,000 tons of carbon, as estimated by the *www.oneseat.eu* campaign organized by many EU officials and MEPs.This is due to French insistence for keeping the Strasbourg location. The President of the European Parliament Jerzy Buzek defended the arrangement by comparing the Strasbourg seat to a 'monarchical symbol', while a recent attempt by MEPs to scrap one of the monthly Strasbourg sessions was compared by the French government to a 'knife-attack' and it threatened to take the European Parliament to Court. The two-seat system is a running PR disaster for the EU – and a massive waste of resources – and yet it remains in place. The EP's two-seat Parliament illustrates how the EU often puts unhealthy emphasis on symbols, process and institutions, rather than focusing all its efforts on producing effective policies that citizens actually have asked for.

Is the EU too unwieldy to succeed in the twenty-first century?

The phenomenon described above is one major reason which has led even senior European politicians to conclude that the EU is simply too unwieldy and too diverse to adapt to and compete in the twenty-first century. Former French Prime Minister Edouard Balladur gave a stark example of this pessimism when he said in 2010 that, 'Europe at 27 is doomed to confusion and failure. It suffers from problems that the Lisbon Treaty has failed to correct. Lack of authority: the 1950s structure, with the [European] Parliament, the Commission and the European Council, is too heavy. We will witness conflicts between the

Parliament-Commission duo and the European Council in the future...
Lack of coherence: the 27 member states have very different social and
juridical regimes' (*Le Monde*, 2010; own translation).

The eurozone crisis of 2010–11 is perhaps the most critical example of how the EU's 'one-size-fits-all' framework tends to foster sub-
optimal policy outcomes – in this case, a single monetary policy for a
set of economies that are structurally very diverse. Greece, for example,
should clearly not have joined the euro, given that it simply was not in
a financial position to share currency with stronger countries, such as
Germany and the Netherlands. However, there was so much political
momentum for closer union that it signed up. In a significant way, the
crisis has discredited the notion of 'ever closer union', espoused by Jean
Monnet and propelled forwards by successive generations of political
elites (Browne and Persson, 2011).

The communitarian method works when applied to complex regulations or institutions. However, the eurozone crisis is about key decisions
on spending and taxation – which strike at the heart of national democracy – meaning that national preferences and positions will block effective reform of the single currency. As a consequence, the single currency
remains unreformed, and the eurozone crisis remains a major threat to
Europe's economic growth. This is not necessarily an argument in favour of the eurozone pursuing more integration – which may be necessary to compensate for the huge economic divergences that exist within
the monetary union – but a stark reminder of how the EU's guiding
principles of 'ever closer union' and one-size-fits-all have failed to produce a well-functioning and an effective Union.

The EU's inefficiency in terms of policy output is perhaps most conspicuous in the area of foreign affairs. For years, European leaders have
talked a good game on the need for the EU to speak with 'a single voice'
and become a more efficient global player. The Lisbon Treaty was meant
to give the EU a 'foreign minister' and an 'external action service', which,
according to the plans, were meant to multiply Europe's influence on the
global stage. However, since 2009 when the Treaty entered into force,
we have been reminded time and again that the EU's processes, institutions and bureaucracies cannot magically replace 27 individual foreign
policies. As with the single currency, the communitarian method may
give the EU the tools to pursue 'integration by stealth' in the areas of
regulation and law, but in foreign policy, substance is king. Put simply, the method is wholly unsuitable for rapidly responding to challenges arising around the world. This is because the national interests of
27 member states have to be amalgamated, so as not to prejudice any of
their divergent interests in wider international affairs.

As Belgian Foreign Minister Steven Vanackere said about the EU's response to the various popular uprisings across North Africa and the Middle East in 2011: 'In the absence of a central player that reacts, makes analyses and conclusions quickly, it is the Germans today, the French tomorrow or the English who partially take up this role...The result is centrifugal, not centripetal' (*Le Soir* ,2011). The events surrounding the 'Arab Spring', in particular, demonstrate the need for fast and flexible decision making, something the EU's bureaucratic machinery is not suited to – though the EU did manage to reach a common position at the early stages of the Libya conflict for example. Former British diplomat Charles Crawford has used the laws of physics to illustrate that momentum in foreign policy is often achieved by increasing 'velocity', and not 'mass'. He argues that: 'The key point about an EU Foreign Policy is that it certainly adds heavy Mass (lots of countries intoning the same thing), but it significantly reduces Velocity (i.e. the speed with which positions are formulated and then the nimbleness of actual real-life responses and associated resource deployments). The result is uncertain and often much reduced impact' (Crawford, 2009).

The failure to both agree and subsequently implement a common position at the EU level is widely evidenced by the lack of a coherent policy towards Cuba, the Middle East peace process, or even pressing issues on its door step, such as Kosovo or relations with Russia.

Such reasoning reflects a more general conclusion about the nature of EU policy making: in areas where mass matters, such as enlargement and creating a single market for trade, the EU is efficient – in the positive sense of the word. However, in combination with the opaque 'community method', mass makes the EU inefficient in some of the very areas where it urgently needs reform, but efficient in areas that, frankly, should be left to member states.

Chapter 3

More Powers for Brussels or Renationalization?

Editors' Introduction

One question has been at the forefront of research on the EU ever since its creation: would there be a steady shift of authority away from member states and towards the supranational institutions or would member states retain or even claim back their powers? The neofunctionalist theory of European integration was the first response given to this question: its proponents expected that national actors would increasingly shift their loyalties and expectations away from the national level and towards the new centre set up in Brussels (Haas, 1958). It did not take long for intergovernmentalists to respond that national governments would not be willing to give up their control of the speed and direction of integration (Hoffmann, 1966). The debate gained particularly broad attention with the acceleration of the process of European integration in the late 1980s, this time pitting supranationalists (Sandholtz and Zysman, 1989) against liberal intergovernmentalists (Moravcsik, 1998).

Real-world events have not offered clear-cut support for either of the two extreme positions. Observers were still bemoaning eurosclerosis in the 1980s, when the EU's member countries agreed on the completion of the single market, a project that led to a period of exceptional supranational activism. The amount of legislation passed by the EU institutions radically increased at that time. Only few years later, governments agreed upon Economic and Monetary Union (EMU), effectively delegating monetary policy – a core competence of the nation state – to the European level. But just when events seemed to spell victory for supranationalism, intergovernmentalism came back with a vengeance. Voters rejected the Treaty of Maastricht (1992) in a referendum in Denmark, requiring the Danish government to negotiate a series of opt-outs in areas such as monetary union, security and defence policy, and justice and home affairs. More recent events have followed a similar pattern. In 2003 and 2004, first a convention and then an intergovernmental conference discussed a treaty text that was supposed to become something close to a constitution for Europe. Voters in France and the Netherlands, however, rejected the resulting treaty, forcing governments to draw up the less ambitious Treaty of Lisbon (2007). The position of President of the European Council that was created by this treaty has been seen as contributing to the Commission's 'loss of strategic clout' in the EU (Emmanouilidis, 2011: 183–4).

The following two texts, while focusing on the changes introduced in the Treaty of Lisbon, reflect this long-standing controversy between intergovernmentalism and supranationalism. Derek Beach questions the often-stated position that recent events in the EU signal a renationalization of competences and a return to intergovernmentalism in EU decision making. He argues first that an increasing number of policy areas are dealt with at the EU level. Moreover, the new policy areas are slowly but steadily covered by the so-called community method of decision making that grants substantial influence to the supranational institutions by assigning the monopoly to initiate legislation to the European Commission and allowing the European Parliament to decide together with the Council of Ministers. Uwe Puetter, by contrast, emphasizes the growing importance of intergovernmental procedures in the EU. Even day-to-day policy making, according to him, is increasingly dominated by intergovernmental routines that establish a new intergovernmental method of decision making. The question of more powers to Brussels or renationalization, taken up in this chapter, is of major relevance to the controversies tackled in Chapter 1 (is the EU a success or a failure?) and Chapter 4 (how democratic is the EU?).

3.1 A stronger, more supranational Union

Derek Beach

Are we witnessing a transformation of the EU from a strong supranational institution into a weaker Union dominated by governments? This contribution analyses developments in the past two decades, investigating whether we have seen a shift in power from the EU to member state governments. Is there a shift in the EU towards a new, more intergovernmental Union? The argument in this text is that what we are seeing is actually the gradual strengthening of the supranational character of the Union, following a typical trajectory. When a policy area is first included as part of the EU, decision making is intergovernmental, but over time the rules are gradually made more supranational, until the policy area is fully within the supranational community method.

Like most aspects of the EU, any discussion of who governs is complicated. Here it is important to note that there are two lines of conflict that are typical in federal-like political systems – *within* levels of

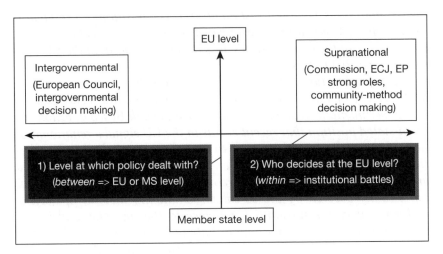

Figure 3.1   *Lines of conflict between levels,*
and within levels, of authority in the EU

authority and *between* levels of authority. In the US federal political system, there is the constant theme of federal powers versus states rights (between levels), while at the same time the three branches of authority and decision making within the federal government jockey for power and position (within levels). The main conflicts in the EU fall along these same lines, and are illustrated in Figure 3.1.

First, at which level are policies dealt with? Is policy making exclusively at the 'federal' (EU) level, a shared competence, or reserved to member states? This dimension can be thought of in terms of more or less Europe. Second, who governs *within* the EU level of authority? This dimension is primarily related to the conflict between intergovernmental institutions (European Council) and supranational institutions (European Commission, European Parliament).

This contribution deals first with conflicts on the first dimension, investigating whether we are witnessing a scaling back of the policies dealt with at the EU level. Are member states reasserting themselves, adopting national solutions instead of EU measures? This chapter contends that the core of the Union is remarkably strong, with the Treaty of Lisbon the most recent of numerous steps towards a stronger Europe.

Regarding the second dimension, are we witnessing a more intergovernmental Union, or are supranational institutions maintaining and/or increasing their powers? The argument here is that developments in the past two decades actually indicate a strengthening of the Union's supranational dimension, although the strengthening of the role of the European Council marks an attempt by governments to reassert themselves in governance of the most sensitive and high-level discussion in the EU in issues such as economic governance. Yet when dealing with daily policy making, intergovernmentalism has for the most part been a transitory phenomenon, with the final outcome for the governance of areas such as freedom, security and justice using the community method.

Conflicts between levels – a renationalization of powers to the member states?

Are we witnessing a scaling back of the policies dealt with at the EU level, with member states reasserting themselves, adopting national solutions instead of EU measures? Based upon empirical developments in the past two decades, the answer to these questions is that there is a remarkably stable core of policy competences at the EU level dealing with the single market and flanking policies related to the free movement of persons, capital, goods and services. Furthermore, while the core areas of the national welfare state are only peripherally impacted by the EU, a series of treaty reforms have substantially increased the scope of policy making at the EU level in flanking areas, for example through common immigration and asylum policies within the so-called area of freedom, security and justice.

The single market is the flagship of European integration, creating enormous economic benefits for EU member states that act as a strong centripetal force binding the EU together into a web of mutual gains. Commission experts have, for example, estimated that the single market in 2006 was responsible for an increase of EU gross domestic product by 2.2 per cent and in the level of EU employment by 1.3 per cent (Ilzkovitz *et al.*, 2007: 56).

There are few indications that this legislative core of policy areas dealt with at the EU level is under attack by national governments. Indeed, the last decade has seen considerable legislative activity at the EU level, adopting far-reaching EU rules such as the services directive dealing with removing barriers to the free movement of services, and the REACH directive regulating chemicals and their safe use. For example, 2010 saw extensive legislative activity extending the regulation of financial services at the EU level (Buckley and Howarth, 2011; Chapter 8, this volume), illustrating that the EU is still seen as a key tool for tackling cross-border challenges by EU governments.

A counter-argument often raised is that EU rules do not really matter if they have no real effect upon government behaviour, for example when governments do not comply with EU rules that run counter to their national interests. However, there is a remarkably high level of compliance by governments with EU law. The number of complaints and infringements filed by the Commission against governments fell steadily throughout the 2000s (European Commission, 2009). Furthermore, there has been a notable decrease in the number of directives that have not been transposed on time by national authorities by 2009, with the average number of directives not transposed in a timely manner down from 3.6 per cent in 2004 to 0.7 per cent in 2009 (ibid). In addition, it can be noted that EU legislation often grants national authorities extensive autonomy in implementation, enabling governments to 'comply' with relatively low costs in many instances (Franchino, 2007).

There have also been isolated instances where governments have flouted EU rules; most spectacularly when France and Germany violated the rules of the euro's Stability and Growth Pact by running budget deficits that exceeded the 3 per cent maximum. This infringement resulted in the undermining of the rules holding the eurozone together and therefore is often cited as evidence that the EU is in crisis. Yet the reality is that after the eurozone crisis started, both France and Germany have actually accepted that new strong enforcement procedures that would also bind them have to be introduced. Therefore, to avoid future incidences such as this, a legislative package is being adopted that will strengthen the enforcement of the excessive deficit procedure (COM(2010) 0522). It can therefore be concluded that instances of non-compliance are the exceptions to the general pattern of compliance with rules in the EU.

Beyond this stable core of EU policies dealing with the single market, the story of the last two decades has been a steady increase in the scope of policy competences dealt with at the EU level through successive rounds of treaty reform. The Maastricht Treaty created an Economic and Monetary Union (EMU) that led to the adoption of the euro, while introducing new policy areas, such as education where the EU could supplement national policy making. The Treaty of Amsterdam moved policy making on a range of policy areas relating to justice and home affairs to the EU level, and increased the powers of the EU in issues such as environmental protection. More recently, the Treaty of Lisbon increased the scope of EU policy making further, for example by inserting a call to promote measures for combating climate change (see Craig, 2010; Piris, 2010).

In conclusion, there are few indications that we are witnessing a shift of authority from the EU level back to national governments – it is basically a myth with scant empirical basis. Even in policy areas where there was momentum towards renationalization, such as the Common Agricultural Policy, there has been little devolution of powers to national authorities. A primary reason for the lack of devolution of policy areas in the EU to the national level is that it requires changes to the treaty, adopted by governments unanimously; an impossible hurdle when governments such as Belgium and Italy are staunch supporters of a more federal EU.

In this regard, it is useful to compare developments in the EU with the US in order to see what a major shift between levels of political authority actually looks like. In the US there has been a push since the election of Ronald Reagan as President in 1980 for a 'devolution revolution', which would transfer significant political authority from the federal to the state level. While Reagan did not achieve the far-reaching shift that he envisioned, he was able to grant states significant discretion in the interpretation of national standards, thereby shifting considerable authority back to the state level (Gerston, 2006).

Compared with developments in the US, no such 'devolution revolution' is apparent in the EU. Indeed, as will be discussed below, the most likely medium- to long-term scenario is actually one of increased policy making authority at the EU level in areas of economic governance to save the euro.

Conflicts within levels – a return to intergovernmentalism at the EU level?

The second argument about a disintegrating Europe is that we have witnessed the emasculation of the supranational institutions, with a considerable shift in power to intergovernmental institutions at the cost of the Commission. Observers point to the creation of the new 'President' of the European Council as a case in point. Yet is there evidence that we are witnessing a return to intergovernmental decision making at the EU level?

The answer to this question depends upon what type of decision making is being referred to. Simplifying slightly, there is a hierarchy of decision-making levels, ranging from history-making decisions that revise the EU treaties in so-called Intergovernmental Conferences (IGCs), over the setting of the long-term direction and agenda for the EU, to the daily policy-making process. The argument here is that while we have seen a slight increase in the power of intergovernmentalism at the highest level, in the daily policy-making process there are few signs that intergovernmentalism becomes more important.

At the highest level, the revision of EU treaties has always been dominated by EU governments, although the Commission and EP have had influence at the margins (Beach, 2005; Christiansen and Reh, 2009; Moravcsik, 1998). Given the fact that EU governments are legally the 'Masters of the Treaties', anything else would be very surprising.

Regarding the setting of the long-term agenda of the EU, the three institutions that take responsibility for this are the European Council, the Commission, and the Council of Ministers. After the Lisbon Treaty, the role of agenda-setting of the European Council has been upgraded through the introduction of a permanent 'President' appointed by governments and by reducing the role of the Council of Ministers in preparing the agenda for European Council meetings.

The importance of the European Council versus the Commission depends upon the policy area and sensitivity of the particular issue. Recent years have seen the European Council play a strong leadership role in the EU's dealing with the economic crisis, and in particular the eurozone (Tallberg, 2008, Tallberg *et al.*, 2011). Yet when discussing issues where the Commission has strong powers in daily legislative matters, such as enforcement of eurozone rules, the Commission has also been able to shape the agenda. For example, in the critical matter of how the EU's framework of economic governance could be strengthened to deal with the eurozone crisis, the President of the European Council had been tasked with leading a taskforce to formulate proposals, but the Commission 'stole much of the Van Rompuy Taskforce's thunder by coming forward with a package of six legislative proposals in September 2010 – a matter of weeks before the later was due to publish its final report' (Hodson, 2011: 242).

Furthermore, the European Council is far from being a 'unitary' actor, and evidence suggests that the three biggest member states (France, Germany and the UK) set the parameters for discussion in the European Council (Tallberg, 2008: 691). Overlapping with this, after enlargement the informal G6 forum (including France, Germany, Italy, Poland, Spain and the United Kingdom) has been used by larger member states to coordinate their positions on certain issues in an attempt to ensure effective leadership in specific issues such as the fight against organized crime and other internal matters in the enlarged EU (*Financial Times*, 2006; House of Lords, 2006).

If we turn to look at the conflict within institutions in the day-to-day policy making in the Union, we do not see an expansion of intergovernmental decision making. Over the past two decades, when new policy areas have been introduced they tend to be governed by intergovernmental decision making. However, most policy areas follow a typical trajectory. New policy areas are introduced when governments believe the benefits of coordination exceed the sovereignty costs (the costs of giving up sole control over a policy area). In sensitive issues that are at the core of national sovereignty, governments such as France have traditionally wanted to ensure that they retain a strong hand in decision making, to avoid being outvoted by other governments in the Council and overruled by supranational institutions (Commission, EP, ECJ). Over time, as governments get used to taking decisions on these issues at the EU level, they become less sceptical regarding moving the policy area to the community method.

A prime example has been the trajectory of the area of freedom, security and justice that includes immigration and asylum policies, along with police and legal cooperation. This policy area was incorporated by the Treaty of Maastricht as the 'third pillar' of the EU, with decision making dominated by intergovernmentalism, with a very weak role for the Commission and no role for the EP or ECJ. The Treaty of Amsterdam moved the immigration-related parts of the policies into the community method, albeit with a five-year transition period and certain institutional safeguards to assuage governments that were still concerned about their ability to block unwanted developments. With the Lisbon Treaty, the remaining third pillar has been removed, with all of the policies governed using the community method with few restrictions. This includes the Commission right of proposal, a strong role of the EP as the ordinary legislative procedure is used, and the full extension of the jurisdiction of the ECJ to the policy area.

In this respect, the Lisbon Treaty marks a major expansion in strengthening the supranational institutions of the EU *vis-à-vis* the Council of Ministers. Beyond the introduction of the community method in the sensitive areas of the former third pillar, the Treaty also significantly expanded the powers of the supranational EP in these policy areas by extending the use of the ordinary legislative procedure. By expanding the ordinary legislative procedure, the powers of the EP are strengthened at the expense of the Council of Ministers, given that the latter has to agree upon a proposal together with the EP. The list of sensitive issues in which the ordinary legislative procedure has been extended includes agriculture and fisheries, the liberalization of services, and in external trade matters – all issues in which governments previously were unwilling to extend EP powers (Beach, 2005).

The overall picture is therefore a reduction in the use of intergovernmentalism in daily decision making, although there remain significant exceptions in areas such as foreign and security policies, and issues relating to eurozone governance. Given the sensitivity of these issues, it remains to be seen whether they also will follow the same trajectory as issues such as freedom, security and justice.

Conclusion – a stronger, more supranational Union

The conclusion based upon the preceding analysis is that the Union is far from dead. Indeed, we have seen a considerable increase in the scope of political authority at the EU level and surprising levels of compliance with EU rules despite the economic crisis. There has been a shift of political authority within the EU, with the European Council becoming increasingly predominant in the setting of the EU's long-term agenda, but at the same time the use of the community method has been expanded to include sensitive policy areas such as freedom, security and justice, while the powers of the supranational EP have increased considerably at the expense of governments within the Council of Ministers.

3.2 The new intergovernmentalism in EU governance

Uwe Puetter

It is hard to ignore the constantly growing activism at the top-level of intergovernmental decision making in European Union (EU) politics. The meetings of the European Council are at the centre of media interest. Emergency gatherings of ministers dealing with urgent economic and financial affairs or foreign policy crises have become a routine feature of EU governance. The Commission, it appears, is just one among the many voices which air ideas about Europe – in particular when it comes to the most pressing and politicized subjects. The enquiry as to what next step the EU will take is directed towards the capitals rather than the Brussels-based bureaucracy.

The Lisbon Treaty did much to reinforce this image. Key political actors are suggesting that the character of EU governance is changing. The first full-time president of the European Council, Herman Van Rompuy, speaks of a 'new institutional balance' (van Rompuy, 2011a). The German Chancellor Angela Merkel sees a 'new Union method' which describes the blending of the classic community method and an intergovernmental method of decision making (Merkel, 2010).

Is the role of the most senior representatives of member state governments – notably the presidents and prime ministers as well as the ministers for foreign and financial affairs – really becoming more important? And, why is this so? Moreover, does the new intergovernmentalism reflect a backlash in EU integration or can we conceptualize it as a dynamic and evolutionary process?

This contribution presents a two-fold argument on the evolution of the EU's institutional architecture. It argues, first, that the most fundamental institutional changes are not driven by a further supranationalization of member state competences but through a new form of intergovernmentalism, which is the prevailing mode of governance in increasingly prominent areas of EU activity such as economic governance and foreign and security policy. Second, this new form of intergovernmentalism is not understood as a rejection of or scepticism towards European integration. It rather is an alternative form of governance which prevails over the classic community method as the main mechanism of decision making. Although it is concentrated within specific policy fields, the repercussions of this institutional dynamic impact on the overall character of EU governance. The new intergovernmentalism is consolidated through particular institutional mechanisms and practical routines which ensure that member states remain in constant dialogue over policy decisions. This institutional dynamic is reflected in the transformation of the role of the European Council and the Council. Because it concentrates on the generation of consensus through political deliberation, I propose to call this dynamic deliberative intergovernmentalism (Puetter, 2012).

The integration paradox

The adoption of the Lisbon Treaty did not resolve the debate about the future of Europe in the sense of defining an endpoint of the integration process. The Treaty neither opted for a federal Europe nor for an ultimate freezing of the status quo of integration. This indecisiveness is the reflex of an integration paradox which characterizes the EU since Maastricht. The Union is confronted with the dilemma that, because of the high degree of integration it has achieved already, any further transfer of competences to the supranational level in the sense of the classic community method would *de facto* decide the question about the transition towards a federal Europe. The classic community method is defined here as the mechanism to produce legally binding decisions in areas in which the EU has been assigned the competence to do so. This mechanism thus creates supranational authority to legislate and to perform exclusive executive functions. Although member states reject the idea of a federal Europe, they have created, and this constitutes the paradox, new areas of EU activity which are of such status and importance that they shape the overall character of the integration process. This applies in particular to the fields of economic governance and foreign and security policy which have been constituted by the Maastricht Treaty.

A role for the EU in economic governance, involving budgetary policy, macro-economic stabilization and structural reform, is unavoidable since monetary policy has become a supranational competence. Yet, such a role affects a core domain of national sovereignty and so does the Union's role in foreign and security policy. Without increasingly unified EU action in this domain the Union will find it impossible to assert itself in a globalized world. This is all the more important as individual member states are rapidly losing their unilateral capacity to act. It is the paradoxical combination of a principled resistance towards a further transfer of formal decision-making capacities to the supranational level, and the increasingly strongly shared conviction that the EU needs to act collectively in the two policy fields, which informs Europe's new intergovernmentalism. In both areas, the supranational level has no, or only very limited, competences and executive functions. The success of EU policy depends on the mobilization of national resources – be they budgetary, legislative, diplomatic or military. However, as these fields are no longer run as loose forms of cooperation but are characterized by complex and expanding policy agendas, the permanent involvement of top-level representatives of the EU member states becomes inevitable.

Deliberative intergovernmentalism

The new intergovernmentalism is the dominant decision-making method in new areas of EU activity. Such a method had not existed before. It has been introduced at a time when there is a pronounced ambition to cooperate more closely rather than less. Supranational institutions largely fail to benefit from the current expansion of joint EU decision making and activity. Moreover, while it is true that existing supranational competences are not in question, the increasing importance of economic governance and foreign and security policy for the EU's internal functioning and external appearance imply that the previously established institutional balance between classic community method and intergovernmental decision making is shifting.

The new intergovernmentalism is highly routinized. A complex coordination machinery has been built up and it seems that little can stop this machinery. The regular and often intense controversies about policy decisions lead to the further refinement of this machinery, as well as more frequent interactions between the relevant actors. Again, this is explained by the underlying conviction that closer cooperation in these two fields is of key importance. In other words, contemporary decision making at the EU level is consensus-driven. The most senior representatives of the member states argue it out and collectively determine what the EU does next. This new governance method is therefore best conceptualized as *deliberative intergovernmentalism* (Puetter, 2012).

While intergovernmentalists in the past (Moravcsik, 1993) have mainly focused on the aspect of how member states exercise control over the integration process, the new intergovernmentalism at the EU level draws our attention to how political consensus between the member states is organized, so as to pool national and supranational resources more effectively in a given situation. The consensus dependency of EU policy making in economic governance and in foreign and security policy is internalized by the key actors. They endorse and actively search for institutional settings which are conducive towards consensus-oriented intergovernmental policy dialogue. Because of the significance of the relevant decisions for domestic politics and questions of national sovereignty, there is an increasing tendency to involve the heads of state or government in the finalization of decisions. These decisions are about nothing less than on what member states spend their money,and whether they send troops or revise their foreign policy towards other countries. Therefore, deliberative intergovernmentalism ,as a theory, anticipates how core EU institutions function is transformed, as these institutions need to accommodate the increased demand for intergovernmental coordination.

Intergovernmental activity is increasing as it involves questions of day-to-day decision making. This affects the roles of the European Council and the Council and how they relate to each other as well as to the Commission and the European Parliament. The European Council is required to increasingly focus on policy detail rather than on matters of strategic direction only. Much more than in the past (Hayes-Renshaw and Wallace, 2006), the Council needs to complement its role as a co-legislator with the role of a key forum for policy coordination. In the absence of procedural mechanisms for ensuring that decisions are legally binding – as in the case of the classic community method – the focus is on achieving unanimous decisions. The adaption of working methods and procedural practices are thus of key importance.

The new areas of EU activity and the repercussions for governance

The new intergovernmentalist turn in EU governance has continuously become more pronounced from the late 1990s onwards. It was first triggered by the final stages of implementing Economic and Monetary Union (EMU). In 1998, the European Council created the eurogroup as an informal forum for policy dialogue among euro area finance ministers, the Commission and the European Central Bank (ECB). Although it lacked a Treaty mandate the eurogroup soon became the key forum for policy debate on the coordination of fiscal policies, external representation and structural reform in the euro area (Puetter, 2006). The working format of the eurogroup marked the departure from the Council's focus on legislative issues and highlighted the increased demand for debate. The meetings were organized in addition to the monthly ECOFIN Council sessions. The ECOFIN Council has responsibility for economic and financial affairs.

The early stages of EMU also highlighted the growing degree of politicization of the issues surrounding the project at the domestic level.

The EU was under pressure to find responses to unemployment, social exclusion and the lack of economic reform efforts. The European Council established the practice of issue-specific gatherings on EU socio-economic governance. The meetings triggered further intergovernmental activity by the introduction of monitoring mechanisms for national policies. Instructions were issued to the Council and the Commission. These activities were given even more prominence with the so-called Lisbon Strategy and the related open method of coordination. The process implied a significant empowerment of the European Council and transformed the agenda of the institution. The idea was that through bringing together high-level political leadership, the EU would be able to steer policy change in the national domain. The open method of coordination and so-called new modes of governance, which function without the instrument of legal constraint, were introduced to the fields of employment, social inclusion and structural reform policy (Amstrong, 2010; Pochet, 2004; Trubek and Mosher, 2003). Senior expert committees, which brought together bureaucrats from national ministries, including the Commission, were set-up in all of the above areas to underpin the political coordination process (see, for example, Horvath, 2008). The reliance on intergovernmental expertise is one of the key features of the EU's new intergovernmentalism. The powerful Economic and Financial Committee composed of deputy finance ministers and high-ranking officials plays a pivotal role in coordinating national policies and EU-level decisions (Grosche and Puetter, 2008). The Commission remains a crucial actor but it does not control the bureaucratic input.

The field of foreign and security policy contributed equally strongly to the new intergovernmentalist turn and the increasing importance of the European Council. The controversies around the European responses to the disintegration of former Yugoslavia and later the disputes about the US-led invasion of Iraq were striking examples of EU coordination failure. Yet, the interest in a strengthened foreign and security policy did not decline. To the contrary, coordination mechanisms were constantly expanded. Again, it is often only at the level of the European Council that key decisions are finalized. The growing scope and ambitions of intergovernmental policy coordination was reflected by the creation of the office of the High Representative by the Amsterdam Treaty and the Political and Security Committee by the Nice Treaty. As the most senior expert committees in socio-economic governance ,the intergovernmental Political and Security Committee is at the core of the bureaucratic process leading up to political decision making. Composed of high-ranking diplomats from the member states, it meets at least twice a week to prepare decisions by ministers and oversee policy implementation by the member states and EU institutions (Duke, 2005).

The Lisbon Treaty

The changes to the EU's overall institutional architecture introduced by the Lisbon Treaty very much reflect the prevalence of Europe's new intergovernmentalism. The Treaty confirms policy coordination as the key governance method for economic governance and foreign and security policy. For example, the new provisions on foreign and security policy even explicitly rule out the possibility of legislative decisions (Article 24.1, TEU). The European Council has become a regular EU institution – a role it had already *de facto* but not *de jure*. A permanent president leads the institution. This underlines the increased relevance of the European Council and the ambition to further develop the intergovernmental dimension. The foreign ministers are no longer regular members of the European Council. The focus is on face-to-face debate among the 'heads'. The eurogroup is incorporated in the Treaty as an informal forum for euro-area dialogue. It too has a permanent president. The position of the High Representative was transformed from an external spokesperson and EU negotiator into the permanent chair of the Foreign Affairs Council – a position which combines the representation function with the management of the internal coordination process. The Lisbon Treaty ended the traditional combination of external affairs and general EU affairs as a joint responsibility of the meetings of EU foreign ministers. The creation of a separate General Affairs Council is a further reflex of the expanding coordination agenda in foreign and security affairs. Finally, the Lisbon Treaty created the European External Action Service (EEAS) as a new diplomatic system (Carta, 2012) to assist the High Representative. Again, this new bureaucratic resource follows a model which emphasizes the close integration of national resources rather than the creation of a new supranational bureaucracy. Diplomats come from previously existing Commission and Council Secretariat units as well as from the member states.

The practice of the post-Lisbon institutions confirms the reinforced emphasis on intergovernmental policy coordination. The president of the European Council has declared economic governance and external affairs the institution's key priorities; he has introduced informal and single issue sessions. The EU's responses to the global economic and financial crisis are organized at the intergovernmental level through frenetic activity by the European Council, the eurogroup and the ECOFIN Council. The European Council now holds, in addition to its regular meetings, extraordinary meetings for the heads of state and government of the euro-area countries. In external affairs the European Council's output increases steadily. It regularly intervenes in the solution of the most controversial dossiers. The evolving institutional structures such as the role of the High Representative as the chair of the Foreign Affairs Council and the EEAS enhance the EU's capacity for further increasing the coordination activity at the intergovernmental level.

Conclusion

The Lisbon Treaty further strengthens the intergovernmental dimension of EU decision making in areas not governed by the classic community method. It rejects a redistribution of supranational and member state competences to the benefit of the supranational level. More specifically, this implies that two of the most prominent fields of EU policy making – economic governance and foreign and security policy – will not become areas of supranational competence for the foreseeable future. This reluctance is informed by an integration paradox. Because of the high level of integration already achieved in the post-Maastricht EU, such a step would imply a transition towards a federal Europe – something which member states are fundamentally opposed to at present.

Yet, the Lisbon Treaty does not lack ambition to further develop EU action through strengthening intergovernmental policy coordination. It adapts key EU institutions to this challenge. Not coincidentally the partial abolition of the rotating presidency system is concentrated on the European Council, the Foreign Affairs Council and the eurogroup. This reflects the scope and complexity of the new intergovernmentalism, which emanates from two policy sectors but has far-reaching consequences for the EU's general institutional architecture.

An underlying feature of the new intergovernmentalism is its consensus orientation. The concept of deliberative intergovernmentalism helps to understand this method of EU governance as a dynamic and evolutionary one, which transforms the way how core EU institutions work. It explains how the development of economic governance and foreign and security policy areas, which are characterized by decentralized resources and the absence of supranational authority, leads to the proliferation of intergovernmental coordination mechanisms. The relevance of these policy fields for the EU's future is reflected in the way they dominate the agenda of the European Council and those of the most senior and most frequently convened Council formations. There will be even more meetings of presidents, prime ministers and ministers in the future – but not that many new competences for the Commission.

Chapter 4

How Democratic Is the EU?

Editors' introduction

Talk about the EU's democratic deficit started in the mid-1980s, in the midst of the implementation of the single market programme. The fear arose that this programme involved a step change in the integration process that would undermine democratic accountability at the member state level without providing any compensation for this loss through improved forms of democratic oversight of policy making at the EU level. The failed referendum on the Maastricht Treaty in Denmark (1992) was the first visible rejection of EU policies by an electorate. Ever since, the critics have denounced a shift in power away from national parliaments and towards national governments and the Commission, as a result of European integration (for example, Føllesdal and Hix, 2006; Weiler, 1991). The EU's decision-making rules foresee that policies are first elaborated by the Commission, a bureaucracy that is not subject to electoral control. When these policies then are debated by national governments in the Council of Ministers, a lack of transparency impedes control by national electorates. Moreover, the critics argue that the only directly elected institution at the European level, the European Parliament, lacks the powers to counter-balance the Commission and Council in the decision-making process.

Several counter-arguments have been made to this critical assessment of the EU's democracy (for example, Majone, 1998; Moravcsik, 2002). For one, it is argued that the policies decided upon by the EU are mainly of a regulatory nature, that is, they do not create distributional concerns. In this view, regulatory policies improve the economic wellbeing of all citizens and thus do not require democratic input to be considered legitimate. Others have posited that the EU's institutional structure is much more benign than portrayed by the critics. Since national parliaments directly control national governments, and national governments are the dominant actors in the EU's decision-making process, citizens continue to control EU policies. Proponents of this view also stress the increasing powers that have been conferred on the European Parliament, to the detriment of the Commission and the Council, in a series of treaty revisions starting with the Treaty of Maastricht.

In this volume, Richard Bellamy and Christopher Lord take up this debate. Bellamy criticizes the EU's record as a democratic political system, mainly stressing the lack of a European demos. *Lord defends the EU's democratic credentials, arguing that public control of the EU while limited is still useful. The two texts take up issues that have been introduced in Chapter 1, but also relate to Chapter 2 on the political efficiency of the EU, Chapter 5 on the role of the European Court of Justice in the process of European integration, and Chapter 6 on a European identity.*

4.1 The inevitability of a democratic deficit

Richard Bellamy

Abraham Lincoln famously defined democracy as 'government of the people, by the people, for the people'. In many respects, the key debates over the EU's democratic deficit can be categorized in terms of which of these three elements they focus on. Thus, the traditional debate has centred on whether the weaknesses of government 'by' the people at the EU level reflect the absence 'of' a European people with a shared identity and interests capable of ruling itself, or the absence of appropriate institutions with suitable powers through (or 'by') which such a people might rule. This discussion has given rise in turn to a second debate alleging that for the highly technical and limited policy areas covered by the EU, government 'for' the people need not involve government 'by' the people at all. Responsible and reasonable administration suffices. So long as the EU delivers policies that benefit all in an efficient, effective and equitable way, no deficit exists. The sections that follow will explore each of these debates in turn.

Democracy 'of' and 'by' the people: 'no *demos*' vs *demos* creation

The 'traditional' debate regarding the EU's democratic deficit can be characterized as being between those that deny the EU possesses a people, thereby making government 'of' the people 'by' itself an illusion at best – what Joseph Weiler has termed the 'no *demos*' thesis (Weiler, 1995: 225), and those who believe that the presence of the requisite democratic institutions will bring a *demos* into being, rendering a government 'of' the people possible through facilitating government 'by' the people' (Hix, 2008). By and large, these two positions have talked past each other.

Those commentators who emphasize the lack of a pan-European *demos* argue that strengthening the democratic credentials of EU institutions – particularly the European Parliament – will deepen rather than lessen the democratic deficit. Unless the citizens of the various member states possess a sense of belonging to a single European people, who share certain common values and collective purposes, then a pan-European democracy will not produce a system of popular self-rule, whereby a people rules itself. Rather, it will be the means whereby certain peoples rule over other peoples (Abromeit, 1998: 32). Because even the tightest-knit societies contain disagreements, democracy generally involves majority rule rather than rule by unanimity. However, the legitimacy of majority rule rests on both majority and minority sharing sufficient interests and values for majority tyranny to be unlikely. To be legitimate, majority rule must not be the rule of one section of society over another, so much as what 'most of the people' in a society believe is in the general interest. When ethnic, cultural, social or other divisions prove so deep that they consistently take precedence over any sense of commonality, then majority rule and democracy break down – as Belgium's recurring difficulties in forming a government due to the deep and persistent divisions between the French and Flemish sections of the country vividly illustrates. Proponents of the 'no *demos*' thesis argue that in the context of the EU, democracy as rule 'by' the people likewise proves unworkable. So long as citizens feel more French, British, German and so on than European, they will regard rule by a pan-European majority as illegitimate as the French Belgians would view government by a predominantly Flemish majority.

Those inclining towards the 'no *demos*' thesis favour the continuing intergovernmental features of EU policy making and the requirement for a consensus among the member states on key issues. These processes ensure all the European peoples agree to any EU level policy. By contrast, they see the increased use of even qualified majority voting (QMV) within the Council of Ministers and the enhanced powers of the European Parliament under the co-decision procedure as inappropriate uses of the democratic method. However, many advocates of improving the democratic quality of the EU's institutions contend such initiatives will bring about a European *demos* and improve the average citizen's attachment to the Union. They believe that popular disaffection and lack of identification with Europe stems from the European peoples' frustration at the limited opportunities available for them to have a democratic say in EU affairs as a people, not from these small steps in that direction (Hix,2008). So, what is a socio-cultural constraint on any true EU level democracy for the first group of scholars, becomes a product of the failure to create an EU democracy for the second group.

Prima facie the evidence supporting the 'no *demos*' thesis is undeniable and consistent over time. For example, Eurobarometer surveys consistently indicate that less than 10 per cent of EU citizens have a strong sense of EU identity, with only around 50 per cent feeling even a weak attachment – and that strongly secondary to their local and national ties. Although a bare majority of European citizens believe their country has benefited from membership, only 3 per cent of citizens generally view themselves as 'Europeans' pure and simple, with a mere 7 per cent regarding a European identity as more important than their national one. By contrast, approximately 40 per cent describe themselves as possessing a national identity only and 47 per cent place nationality first and Europeanness second. Indeed, though 91 per cent of these citizens usually declare themselves attached to their country and 86 per cent to their locality, only 53 per cent feel attached to the EU (figures drawn from Eurobarometer, 2004, and Eurobarometer, 2007, with few changes in this regard since the 1990s, for example, compare Eurobarometer, 1990, where 51 per cent of those polled say they never feel European).

These comparatively low levels of identification with the EU appear confirmed by the figures for actual participation in EU politics. Average turn out in elections for the European Parliament runs at below 50 per cent and in many countries is as low as 25 per cent. One might expect identification with the EU to be higher among those who had moved for work or other purposes to another EU country to their own. However, the figures are even lower for EU citizens resident in another member state and exercising their right to vote in EU level elections. According to a Commission study of 2002, the proportion of non-national EU citizens even bothering to register to vote ranges from a mere 9 per cent in Greece and Portugal to just 54.2 per cent in Austria.

Those advocating strengthening EU level democracy counter that Europeans have more in common politically than 'no *demos*' arguments allow. For example, much the same left–right divide exists in all the member states, allowing ideological groupings within the European Parliament to be formed reasonably easily (Hix, 2008). There is also evidence that debates about EU matters within each of the member states follow parallel lines to a considerable extent (Risse, 2010). Likewise, they note that the member states share similar constitutional and democratic principles. For example, all are signatories of the European Convention of Human Rights, to which the EU itself is expected to accede, while Lisbon incorporated the Charter of Fundamental Rights of the European Union into the Treaty. Consequently, they surmise that little stands in the way of a genuinely pan-European politics based on majority rule. They suggest that identification with, and participation in, EU politics would increase if the European Parliament had the positive power to elect Commissioners from among MEPs and propose EU legislation, rather than simply the negative power to vet member state nominees to the Commission, sack the Commission en masse and amend or reject Commission legislative proposals. Citizens would then feel their vote counted and elections would be fought on European issues by trans-European political parties rather than being second order domestic elections fought by national parties on predominantly national issues (Hix, 2008). However, the EU has steadily increased its competences and the European Parliament its powers over the past 50 years. Yet, identification with the EU and political participation has declined in tandem with each increase in the European Parliament's power. Thus, turn out in EU elections has steadily fallen from the high of 61.99 per cent in 1979 to the low of 43 per cent in 2009. Meanwhile, European Parliament elections continue to be 'second order' and fought on domestic rather than European issues – usually the record of the incumbent government.

Notwithstanding the similarities in political culture, the dominant trend within all the member states has been towards a greater devolution of self-government downwards towards national minorities rather than upwards to supranational institutions. National and cultural sentiments have increased in political salience rather than diminished and been replaced by post-national or pan-European attachments. First, language matters. There is no pan-European media or public sphere, despite the growth of English as a lingua franca of the educated classes of most European countries. Even in well-established multilingual states, such as Switzerland or Belgium, central government is weak with regional government strong and growing stronger, and organized increasingly on linguistic lines. Second, size matters. A citizen rarely influences the outcome by his or her vote alone even in local elections. However, within a vast electorate, where the centre of power lies hundreds of miles away, one person's vote risks being worth so little that no individual would feel engaged at all. Finally, language and size also map on to common interests and political values. The more people share in both the way policies affect them and their reasoning about them, the more legitimate and easier majoritarian decision making becomes. There are fewer dangers of permanent or intense minorities. An equal share in the voting process is more likely to yield decisions that show citizens equal concern and respect precisely because they share common concerns and norms. Yet, the larger the state, the more socially, economically and culturally diverse it will be, with fewer common interests and values, with collective decision making consequently harder and more prone to majority tyranny.

Even if the citizens of all the member states share certain abstract principles, such as human rights, they value them in diverse ways and weigh and implement them differently. They have different penal and welfare systems, give different priorities to education, health and defence spending and so on. There may be a number of areas where they either have an interest in supporting a common market or in promoting collective goods, such as a clean environment. But even in these areas controversial issues abound because a common policy may have a differential impact on different countries – a point that has been revealed in a dramatic way by the eurocrisis. Hence, national representation continues to remain important within the EU decision-making process. These features all stand in the way of a majoritarian system for the EU. For example, the politicians of solvent states have clearly felt they lack the domestic democratic support needed to undertake a bold and potentially redistributive EU level policy to help the debtor states within the eurozone. However, others have argued that none of this necessarily matters – democracy can be 'for' the people without being 'of' or 'by' them. We now turn to these arguments.

Democracy 'for' the people: regulatory and deliberative

This 'new' debate is associated with Andrew Moravcsik (2002) and Giandomenico Majone (1998), though certain elements were first introduced by Fritz Scharpf (1999). Scharpf argued that it is not always the case that popular rule, or democracy 'by' the people, generates policies that are in the public interest, or democracy 'for' the people. As liberals have long feared, tyrannous majorities and powerful minorities can distort the democratic agenda so that democracy fails to favour the people as a whole.

On the one hand, majorities may oppress minorities because of misinformed prejudice, blind passion, self interest, or myopia. Minorities may also be ignored through being too small or insufficiently concentrated for their voice to register. On the other hand, powerful minorities can gain unfair advantages by exploiting their wealth or influence. They may be important donors to political campaigns, or a major employer in a key constituency, or own a large share of the media. Some over-powerful minorities may be the swing voters in a crucial marginal constituency. These two types of distortion result in passion, ignorance or selfishness undermining a reasoned and impartial appraisal of policy. The solution has been to depoliticize certain key policy areas which are deemed to be particularly important or especially susceptible to these kinds of distortion, limiting 'input' democracy 'by' the people so as to provide a more effective democratic 'output' that delivers rule 'for' the people. While counter-majoritarian mechanisms, such as constitutional courts, have been the traditional means for guarding against majority tyranny, non-majoritarian mechanisms, such as independent expert regulatory bodies and ombudsmen, have become increasingly deployed to guard against powerful minorities.

Such mechanisms are familiar within the domestic politics of all the member states. The view of Majone and Moravcsik is that so long as the EU operates in areas where 'output' democracy offers a more effective and efficient mechanism for rule 'for' the people than rule 'by' the people, the EU's democratic deficit can be viewed as a myth. The so-called shortcomings of EU democracy simply reflect the sort of constraints on majoritarian democracy that are familiar within states. The federal arrangements typical of most large and diverse states, such as the United States, usually mix majoritarian, counter-majoritarian and non-majoritarian mechanisms – such as an elected President, a constitutional court, a senate that equally represents the constituent units regardless of their population, and a central bank – in an effort to balance unity with diversity in the making of federal policy. The EU does much the same, with the majoritarian element considerably more constrained than in most federal systems to reflect its limited competences. In particular, the EU's economic policies are regulative rather than redistributive. They seek solutions that are Pareto-optimal – that is, which make everyone better off and nobody worse off. Being both highly technical and win–win, they are of low electoral salience. Sufficient democratic accountability is provided by the dual oversight of the European Parliament, on the one side, and the Council of Ministers, on the other. The main concern is how far the EU is moving beyond policies for which such arrangements are suited. Whilst Scharpf (2009) now fears the line may have been breached, Moravcsik (2002) feels that it is simply a matter of preventing over-enthusiastic europhiles pushing the boundaries of the EU beyond what most European citizens desire – hence the rejection of the proposed Constitutional Treaty.

This thesis has attracted much criticism (Bellamy, 2010; Føllesdal and Hix, 2006). For a start, many doubt that such matters are 'purely' technical or even if they can be viewed as subject to an expert consensus. Even very technical questions can raise normative issues of the kind that regularly and reasonably divide political parties and electorates. They are also likely to involve a number of broad assumptions about future human behaviour and risks that are largely unknowable, and that again are matters on which citizens often legitimately disagree. We know, for example, that differing economic theories and divergent best guesses about how the world economy is going frequently lead economic advisors to central banks to diverge in their views on interest rate increases or decreases. Given that such decisions can have huge impacts on those subject to them, as the current eurocrisis reveals, a good case can be mounted for allowing citizens some influence over them. In the member states, the presence of a strong public sphere and a degree of majoritarian political control over appointments to such bodies by national politicians ensures some popular accountability exists, at least to sustained national trends in public opinion. But, as we saw, no such European public sphere exists within the EU. As a result, democracy 'for' the people is far more detached from democracy 'by' the people compared to the member states.

Meanwhile, such bodies are subject to distortions of their own. Constraining access to them may make them more susceptible to regulatory capture by powerful interests, thereby heightening the risk of distortion by a minority. For example, devolving the setting of interest rates to central banks can insulate from public scrutiny the neo-monetarist content of orthodox monetary policy choices by presenting them as the product of 'sound' economic management. Yet, such choices may serve financial institutions better than the economy at large and be overly skewed to serve their interests. Moreover, similar effects arise from the counter-majoritarian influence of the European Court of Justice. For example, the constitutionalization of market freedoms through its judgments– often prompted by the large corporations which, given the cost of bringing cases, are the most likely to go to court – has in a number of cases steadily eroded the majoritarian decisions of national parliaments that have sought 'public interest' restrictions on the marketization of key services. Likewise, the supermajorities *de facto* required by co-decision by the European Parliament and the Council of Ministers, even with the rarely used qualified majority voting (QMV), mean that decision making controlled by that venue favours the *status quo* and established vested interests.

Some have argued that the democratic credentials of these forms of governance can be improved through direct consultation with citizens and transnational civil society groups. They have also emphasized the deliberative qualities of these depoliticized bodies (Joerges and Neyer, 1997). However, such selective consultation, often with unaccountable groups that are invariably part-funded by the EU or with commercial lobbyists, tends to reinforce rather than overcome the dangers stemming from special interests to which such mechanisms are susceptible. Likewise, if the decision is not one that can be decided on technicalities alone, as is often the case, a deliberative consensus is as likely to be the product of 'group' think or skilful manipulation by the chair or others, as a reasoned convergence on the best possible position. Thus, even in the restricted competences of the EU, there can be no substitute for conventional rule 'by' the people and so the EU continues to suffer from a democratic deficit. These problems, though, are greatly amplified by the eurocrisis. As former advocates of this approach have argued, monetary policy is not a purely technocratic matter and it is doubtful that a common policy can be imposed across the very diverse economies of the eurozone unless there is some pan-European democratic support and control for redistributory rather than the solely regulatory policies currently on offer (Majone, 2011).

Conclusion

The EU has major difficulties in providing government 'of' and 'by' the people. Although many of its policies are 'for' most of the peoples much of the time they cannot be guaranteed to be so and will invariably damage some minority interests. As such, they require democratic legitimation of a kind the EU seems unable to provide. A number of theorists have tried to rethink EU democracy as demoi-cracy – government of, by and for the various peoples of Europe (Nicolaïdis, 2003). They praise the complexity of the EU – its multiple levels of government and its compound systems of representation – for bringing together the regional, national, transnational and supranational interests of citizens. However, if this complexity renders the EU system a better representative 'of' the people, it also makes government 'by' and 'for' the people less likely to obtain. The more complex a system, the easier it is for minorities to block measures that majorities favour and the harder it is to know who is responsible for what and to hold them to account – hence the difficulties in framing policies that might benefit the eurozone as a whole but involve predictable transfers from certain member states to other member states. A European democratic deficit of some kind seems inevitable, therefore, the price of the EU's many benefits – though one that presently risks becoming too costly for many citizens to be willing to pay.

4.2 A democratic achievement, not just a democratic deficit

Christopher Lord

Democracy requires a state. Democracy requires a people. The European Union has neither. Yet, each of what I argue here are the three defining elements of democratic rule – namely, public control with political equality and justification – is to be found in some measure in the Union's own internal arena. Let me be clear. I am not making a panglossian claim that all is for the best in the best of all possible worlds. I merely want to suggest that the Union's 'democratic surplus' over international organizations needs to be identified, as well as its 'deficit' to the democratic state. Whilst this is not a particularly original argument, I aim to make it in an original way.

Amongst the questions that can be asked about democracy and the European Union are: how democratic is it? How democratic can it be? And ought it to be democratically controlled? As I hope to show as I go along, these questions are too interconnected to be answered other than simultaneously. For starters it is unclear whether it makes sense to ask 'how democratic is the EU?' if there is no reason why it ought to be democratic (Lord, 2004). In the view of some, there may even be a lot to be said for a European Union that is not democratically controlled. After all there are some decisions that we might justifiably put beyond democratic politics, amongst them so-called Pareto-improving decisions, which depend more on the use of expertise to identify uncontroversial benefits than on political competition over values that are contentious or redistributive. So, the argument goes, why not make a virtue of the unsuitability of the European Union for democratic politics and make it a repository for decisions where democracy could even get in the way of realizing what we can all agree are mutual gains? (Majone, 2005).

I doubt that debate about a democratic deficit in the European Union can be shut down so easily. To me it seems neither here nor there whether the Union's decisions are value neutral. Quite regardless of whether they are value neutral or contested, Union decisions need to be democratically controlled simply because they have the force of law. Individuals need to be able to control as equals the making, amendment and administration of any laws by which they are bound, if they are to be regarded as morally autonomous persons of equal value (Habermas, 1996: 67; Rawls, 1993: 38).

Now such a view of democracy is plainly challenging. Consider the conditions that may be individually necessary and collectively sufficient to realize it. They might plausibly include all the following: (a) freedoms of speech and association;(b) free and fair elections; (c) appointment of the legislature and leading executive positions by popular vote; (d) a form of political competition that offers voters choices relevant to the control of the political system; (e) a civil society in which all groups have equal opportunity to organize to influence the polity; (f) a public sphere in which all opinions have equal access to public debate, and (g) a defined *Demos*; or, in other words, agreement on who should have votes and voice in the making of decisions binding on all.

Let's now make a further assumption: namely that 'ought implies can', or, at least, it does if we want to avoid being utopian. From this point of view, any debate on whether there is a democratic deficit in the EU cannot just depend on ideals of democracy. It also requires us to take a view on how those ideals can be realized at European level, assuming that we want to continue with some kind of EU at all. Perhaps the key challenge of feasibility is this: the demanding list of conditions set out in the previous paragraph may be difficult to achieve simultaneously without certain attributes of statehood. The capacity of the state to concentrate power, resources and legal enforcement has been useful in all kinds of ways to democracy: in ensuring that the decisions of democratic majorities are carried out; in guaranteeing rights needed for democracy; in drawing the boundaries of defined political communities; in motivating voters and elites to participate in democratic competition for the control of an entity which can manifestly affect their needs and values.

So is the EU able to achieve all of this, even though it is not a state, and even though its publics seem limited in their willingness to associate together at the European level as a single democratic people? In what follows, I consider three possibilities: one which would return the Union to closer democratic control by its member states; a second which would move it closer to a democratic political system in its own right; and an intermediate solution which, I argue, has already been attempted in important ways. Under that intermediate solution, the Union uses certain forms of self-limitation on the part of its own member states to develop an innovative approach to the democratic control of a multi-state structure.

View 1: member state democracies could exert more control over the Union

Many suggestions have been made for how national democracies could do more to control Union decisions. For example, more governments could be required to follow the Danish example in agreeing the positions they take in the Council of Ministers with their national parliaments. Maybe this could even be done without diminishing the Union's capacity to solve collective action problems. If there are international public goods (that is, benefits that accrue to all member states) that can be realized at the Union level, then it will always be in the interests of all member states to cooperate by consensus to secure those goods. Indeed, any decision-rule other than consensus would only encourage redistributive decision making for which several commentators argue the Union has no democratic authorization (Majone, 2005). If there are choices of value to be made – perhaps in the way in which the surplus from cooperation should be spent – then, say the defenders of national democratic control, let those questions be contested in the one arena that does meet the conditions for competitive and majoritarian democratic politics: namely, the domestic arena (see also Lord, 2011 for further discussion of this argument).

It seems to me, however, that this argument identifies a democratic deficit in the response of national democracies to the European Union, rather than a democratic deficit in the Union itself. I doubt that the main constraints on national democracies doing more to control and scrutinize the participation of their own governments in Union decisions are located at the Union level. To the contrary, it seems to me that the Union is fairly well structured for the control of its decisions by national governments and parliaments. Whilst the Commission doubtless retains significant control over the detail of proposals, the Union's overall agenda-setting powers depend on a consensus of the European Council for what the Lisbon Treaty terms 'strategic direction'. Even where the rules allow for majority voting in the Council of Ministers, most decisions are in practice taken by an overwhelming consensus of member governments. Nor is it easy to see how things could be otherwise. Given that member states lend out their enforcement structures to EU policies, the Union depends on the day-to-day cooperation of elected national governments. It, arguably, even has to allow for some 'real-time' adaptation of existing policies to shifting member state preferences through such procedures as comitology, that is, committees that oversee the implementation of EU legislation by the Commission (Sabel and Zeitlin, 2007).

View 2: the Union's own political system could be more democratic

According to a contrasting claim the EU could be made more democratic through the medium of its own political system. Thus it is arguable that it is not enough that the EU has an elected Parliament. The leadership of the executive, and not just a part of the legislature, should be elected in any fully democratic system. Those who propose such an arrangement for the Union typically invite us to take a kind of 'gamble on endogeneity': a gamble that any missing ingredients of democratic politics – such as political community or parties prepared to structure voter choice in ways relevant to the public control of the Union itself – will develop *within* institutions designed to expose more of the Union's leadership to competitive elections (Føllesdal and Hix, 2006).

Amongst difficulties with this proposal, one stands out. The leadership position which can most plausibly be directly or indirectly elected – namely, the Presidency of the Commission – is not the leader of an integrated executive. Rather, the Union has to negotiate much of its agenda and even its enforcement powers with member states. If an elected Commission Presidency is to be justified as a means of allowing the Union's policy agenda and the administration of its laws to be controlled by a competition for the people's vote, then two further things would have to change too. First, any proposals on which the Commission is elected would have, if necessary, to trump those items on the Union's agenda the Commission has agreed with a consensus of the European Council. Second the Commission would need to tighten its direction over the national administration of Union policies to the point at which it can avoid being put in the impossible position of having electoral responsibility without power. Any perception that an elected Commission President is a poorly clothed emperor would reduce the chances of it transforming voter participation in European elections or the willingness of parties to contest them on European issues.

View 3: a limited but useful form of democratic control

So far I have considered two arguments that the Union is in democratic deficit. Both attempt to take the problem of feasibility seriously. One suggests that any need for a *demos* or attributes of democratic statehood at the European level could be avoided by simply improving democratic control of the Union by its national *demoi* organized in their member states. The other predicts that greater political competition for office in the Union own political system will, of itself, stimulate the development of a democratic people willing to engage in a democratic politics with one another. Against the first view, I have argued that it identifies deficits in how national democracies have adapted to the Union, rather than deficits in the Union itself. Against the second, I have argued that it over-states the potential for political and executive centre-formation in the Union in its present form.

Yet, it seems to me that both views also have related weaknesses. The second under-estimates how far the Union remains an association of states and how far that, in turn, constrains its capacity for a democratic politics of its own. The first view, on the other hand, under-states the Union's distinctiveness as an association of states, and how that, in turn, means the Union is less constrained than other international bodies to rely only on the institutions of its component democracies for democratic politics and control.

Here my central claim is that EU member states have chosen to associate on the basis of certain qualifications to their own statehood. Thus member states mostly tolerate the supremacist claims of Union law. They pre-commit themselves to certain methods of cooperation, for example, by agreeing only to act on a proposal from the Commission in certain matters. They have, arguably, also qualified their own statehood in relation to the Union's representative system. Rather than follow the common practice of claiming a monopoly on the representation of their own publics in international bodies, member state governments typically claim that the Union is legitimated by multiple channels of representation, including a directly elected European Parliament, national parliaments and governments themselves, and arrangements for the representation of sub-national territorial units and civil society actors (see for example, Lisbon Treaty A8).

This pattern of representation is, in turn, supported by two forms of self-limitation on the part of member states. First, member states effectively commit themselves to support the Union's own representative system with certain preconditions and infrastructures needed for democracy. Democratic rights are primarily secured by national law. European elections are administered in member states. National parties aggregate and mobilize votes. Second, member states share powers at the Union level with a directly elected European Parliament which has significant powers to co-decide legislation, annual budgets and the designation of the political leadership of the European Commission (even if the European Parliament does not elect the Commission, it does have a veto on its appointment).

The first of these elements lessens the need for the Union to have the attributes of either a democratic state or people. But does the second really add value to the solution of just using national democracies to control the Union after all? Consider the values of public control, political equality and justification from which I started out.

Public control

A difficulty with relying only on national democracies to control the Union is that there is a long chain of delegation from national publics to the participation of their governments in EU decisions. This may lead to 'agency loss' or even what James Bohman describes as 'reverse agency' (2007: 70), where, instead of exercising control on behalf of their publics, national governments use international bodies to operate with greater freedom from the controls their publics normally exercise on them. Thus it is important to the role of democracy in avoiding arbitrary and unchecked forms of domination that the Union does not allow the executive branches of member state governments to control EU decisions on their own. Under the ordinary legislative procedure, much legislation has to be co-decided with a directly elected European Parliament which member state executives do not themselves control. Moreover, this check and balance does not depend for its value and effectiveness on European Parliament elections being 'about Europe'. Even assuming European elections are second-order, the European Parliament, is elected and organized along left–right lines, which correspond to the central choices of value in most European societies. Second-order elections also favour national parties of opposition, which, of all parties, are most likely to use the European Parliament's powers to check and balance the governments in the Council.

Political equality

A further problem with relying exclusively on control of the Union via national democracies is that the latter are represented in decision making via governments that are highly unequal in their bargaining power. Co-decision with the European Parliament provides something of a corrective to this by requiring the concurrent consent of a second majority which is formed more often along left–right ideological than national lines. Representatives from member states, which are weak in intergovernmental bargaining, may be mainstream in European Parliament coalition formation.

Justification

I have sketched a somewhat unheroic arrangement in which a European Parliament which contributes little to 'popular will formation' at least provides some checks and balances. But justification does not require a full-blown process of popular will formation. Mutual accountability between mutually suspicious representatives will do. Since the European Parliament specializes in accumulating expertise on EU matters, it is less likely than national parliaments to be disadvantaged by asymmetries of information in demanding and evaluating justifications for Union decisions. Moreover, absence of shared political community at the European level does not imply that European publics are without responsibility to consider the effects of their own views and behaviours on one another. After all, they participate in a Union whose shared policies have significant external effects on individuals from other member states who are often encouraged to rely on those shared policies in the formulation of their own life plans. Given that common responsibility, a European Parliament that allows representatives from across the Union to consider the effects of shared policies on one another is a desirable complement to any segmentation of debate that would be likely to follow from relying only on national democracies to scrutinize Union decisions.

Conclusion

Bohman has remarked that 'democracy is that set of institutions by which individuals are empowered as free and equal citizens to form and change the terms of their collective living together, including democracy itself' (2007: 66). Citizens can no more be said to be able to 'form and change the terms of their living together' where they lack the institutional means to solve collective action problems that deeply affect their life chances than where they have no means of exercising public control as equals over the laws that bind them. Thus the 'input' and 'output' conditions for democracy need to be solved simultaneously. Some have suggested that this implies a dilemma as much as a deficit: a dilemma in which the Union lacks the input conditions for democracy, whilst member states, acting alone, lack capacities to produce some policy outcomes their people have come to associate with self-governing peoples (Scharpf, 1999). Yet I have attempted to suggest here that the Union already has some modest achievements in lessening the predicament. It has innovated beyond what is normal for international bodies in providing elements of public control, political equality and justification through a representative system that does not depend entirely on member states.

Chapter 5

Too Much Power for the Judges?

Editors' introduction

For a long time, the European Court of Justice (ECJ), founded along with the other core EU institutions in the 1950s and seated in the tiny Duchy of Luxembourg, has operated below the radar of public consciousness. Since the 1990s, however, researchers, and increasingly also European politicians and citizens, have realized how consequential the rulings of this court are. The ECJ is now recognized as the 'most effective supranational judicial body' (Stone Sweet, 2004: 1) that ever existed. It has jurisdiction over the whole range of EU policies, with the exception of the Common Foreign and Security Policy and issues of law enforcement and internal security. The existence of an effective court is indispensable in a Community of 27 member states which often only manage to agree on vague compromises, leaving the interpretation of the details to lawyers. Convinced that strict adherence to agreed laws and rules is necessary for the functioning of a political body such as the EU, the 27 judges of the ECJ have consistently asserted the supremacy of Community law, following the landmark Costa v ENEL *ruling of 1964 (Costa v ENEL, 1964). They have not hesitated to rule against powerful member states and to pursue their own interpretation of the 'spirit' of the treaties. Member states have generally complied with their rulings. The ECJ also has emerged as indispensable actor in the EU's political system of checks and balances, often strengthening the powers of the European Parliament against the dominant executives of the Commission and Council.*

Nonetheless, the increasing activity of the Court has led to intense criticism: is the ECJ guilty of wilful judicial activism, violating the prerogatives of elected representatives? Has it pushed a specific vision of European society behind closed doors, inaccessible to popular control and democratic oversight? Can the Court legitimately rule on deeply contested interpretations of human rights and other normative concerns, given pervasive doubts about a common European identity and value system (see also Chapter 6)? Above all: can supranational law be fully legitimate in a world of national jurisdictions?

Karen Alter shows how the Court emerged as a response to the abuse of law in European history and how it evolved as a check against a new wave of authoritarianism. She argues that claims of 'judicial activism' are misplaced since the ECJ only does what it is asked to do by governments and private litigants. The Court is increasingly controversial because the issues on which it has to rule are increasingly controversial. Jeremy Rabkin argues that the ECJ is a strange creation since its character as 'court without a state' undermines the legitimacy of its rulings and impair its effectiveness. It cannot answer the most pressing issues of the European Union while it pursues its own particular vision of Europe, which is not shared by the European population.

The central role of law in a political entity such as the EU, which in its policy making relies heavily on regulatory policies, makes the debate about the power of the ECJ a core controversy in European integration. This debate further deepens the discussion in Chapter 3 on a renationalization of EU politics and on the democratic credentials of the EU (see Chapter 4).

5.1 Understanding the European Court's political power

Karen J. Alter

The European Court of Justice (ECJ), along with the European Court of Human Rights, are unusual in that they have emerged as two of the most influential international courts in history. An American landing in Europe will undoubtedly be surprised that an 'international court' has become powerful enough to exercise supreme legal authority over national law, overruling the decisions of elected governments and even of European governments acting in concert through the European Union's Council of Ministers. Equally surprising to some people is that a seemingly all-powerful ECJ seems hamstrung when it comes to helping address the many challenges facing Europe. This surprise, I will argue, is partly because people often fail to think about what a court can and cannot add to governance – national or international.

The formal history of the ECJ is certainly extraordinary. The ECJ started out as a modest institution, with limited competence to address legal questions concerning European Community law. In the 1960s, most realms of policy and politics were still decided nationally, international courts were distant entities, and it was hard to imagine that the ECJ could become an important legal and political body. This contribution explains why the ECJ has become the institution it is today. It then addresses what the ECJ can and cannot contribute to helping Europeans address their most pressing issues today. The reason to return to history is so that we can better understand the situation political leaders were trying to avoid when they created a powerful ECJ.

The European Court steps into a political vacuum

Europeans emerged from the Second World War shell-shocked. They had witnessed elected governments and 'civilized' countries commit unbelievable atrocities. These atrocities took place under the rule of law. Germans chose Adolf Hitler and Italians chose Benito Mussolini through democratic means; government officials in Germany and occupied Europe followed formal administrative procedures as they certified the documents sending innocent people to death; when official orders were challenged judges ratified that the law had been followed; and many ordinary people dutifully followed the law, reporting on fellow citizens and tacitly supporting the deportation and murder of political opponents and innocents alike. The new leaders who assumed office at the end of the Second World War were those who had been fighting against fascism and Nazism. They no longer trusted governments to do the right thing.

The task of subordinating European governments to a supranational rule of law began with the Council of Europe, which drafted a European Convention on Human Rights in 1950, creating a blueprint for a European Court of Human Rights. The European Community's Court of Justice was created as part of the European Coal and Steel Community (ECSC). Its job was to ensure that the strongest member governments did not capture the powerful High Authority, the supranational body that would oversee state compliance with ECSC rules. Smaller countries and even firms were authorized to bring to the ECJ legal challenges to High Authority actions.

The ECSC was meant to be a first step towards building a European constitutional order, one that would force European governments to work together and be bound by the rule of law. Supporters of a federalist vision for Europe expected the European Court of Justice to merge with the European Court of Human Rights, ensuring that Europe became a constitutional space governed by the rule of law (Friedrich, 1954). Then everything fell apart.

The French Parliament rejected the draft treaty for a European Defense Community in 1954, which had the effect of also ending any hope for a European Political Community. European governments did manage to agree to the Treaty of Rome, a charter to establish a common market, but then General De Gaulle assumed office in France and the entire European project came into question. De Gaulle rejected the agreed-upon roadmap for building a common market, boycotted Council of Minister negotiations and demanded that the European Community not shift to decision making by qualified majority voting. On the home front, De Gaulle also curtailed civil liberties and the rule of law with respect to his highly controversial actions in the Algerian War of Independence. De Gaulle repeatedly circumvented the French Parliament, orchestrating a referendum to change the Constitution so that the office of the President would become an elected office, thereby allowing him to become a strong democratically elected leader governing, through political maneuvering, a fractious French politics (Hoffmann, 1966). In short, in the 1960s it looked like France was returning to the path of democratic authoritarian nationalism, and effectively thwarting European integration.

We need to remember a few things at this junction. First, the architects of European integration were lawyers, diplomats, scholars and politicians who had personally suffered through the disaster that was the Second World War. Second, European integration has always been about binding the fate of European countries so that fascism could not gain a footing to spread across the continent. Third, although they are formally distinct entities, the European Union project has always been linked to the human rights project of the Council of Europe. It is linked in spirit, and in the very individuals who worked to build both projects.

The European Court of Justice stepped into multiple vacuums when it launched its legal revolution of the 1960s. The European Community was faltering as the deadlines inscribed in the Treaty of Rome passed with little progress made towards building a common market. The European Court of Human Rights was politically paralysed because so few member states agreed to its authority. It was in this context that the French judge on the ECJ authored the Court's bold rulings suggesting that the Treaty of Rome constituted a binding agreement that created obligations for European governments and rights for European citizens. In 1962 the ECJ declared the direct effect of European law in national legal orders, thereby authorizing private litigants to invoke European law in national courts (*Van Gend en Loos*, 1962). In 1964 the ECJ declared the supremacy of European law over conflicting national law (*Costa v ENEL*, 1964), and in 1977 the ECJ demanded that national judges set aside any national rules that conflicted with European Community law (ECJ 1978). The ECJ then worked to build support for its vision of the Treaty of Rome as a constitution for Europe.

Most national judges were not very impressed with the ECJ's bold claims in the 1960s. National judges had their own rules governing the relationship between national and international law. Moreover, continental lawyers generally believed that the role of judge was to apply the law to concrete cases, and that the ECJ's supremacy doctrine went beyond this limited role. But they were sympathetic to the argument that someone had to make sure that the decisions and actions of the European Commission and the Council of Ministers respected the rule of law. National judges knew that they were poorly placed to serve as guardians of the rule of law at the European level. First, national judges knew very little about technical European Community laws. Second, there were many legitimate interpretive questions about European rules, and it would undermine legal certainty and perhaps disadvantage their country's firms and citizens if judges in different countries answered these questions differently. Third, governments had set upon an important project of European integration; national judges needed to find a way to live with this political choice. At the time, it did not seem likely that the European Union would come to be the largest producer of economic rules or that European regulations and directives would end up affecting so many areas of national policy. The 'sovereignty' transferred through European integration appeared limited and small; it hardly jeopardized the ability of French, German, Dutch or Italian citizens to determine their country's fate. Since the ECJ was clearly best placed to adjudicate disputes involving European law, national judges went along, largely deferring the hard questions that would later arise.

It took years for the ECJ to build support for its vision of European law within national legal communities. A new generation of lawyers had to accept that 'community law' was different than international law, and that 'community law' was part of national law. And the ECJ had to build trust within national judiciaries by showing a willingness to respond to the concerns of national judges. This relationship of cooperation, if not always trust, is the font of the ECJ's political and legal power (Alter, 2009: Chapters 4–6). While some ECJ rulings may provoke controversy, the reasons national judges provide support for the European legal system is the same today as it was in the 1960s and 1970s.

We can now answer how the European Court became so powerful, and thus why it remains powerful today. The ECJ built relationships of support within national legal communities, and among those groups and governments that wanted to make sure that European integration did not become the victim of fickle governments. Meanwhile, governments greatly expanded their role in national economies, and they increasingly passed European laws regulating more and more domains of national policy. These expansions meant that there were more national and European level rules subject to judicial review (Maduro, 1998). Private litigants brought cases to national courts and the ECJ, thereby allowing the ECJ to develop doctrines that try to balance individual rights, states rights, and European integration (Cichowski, 2007; Stone Sweet, 2004). The rise of ECJ authority dovetailed with the rising power of supreme courts in many European countries (Stone, 1995), and the growing understanding that although supreme courts are counter-majoritarian institutions, they are also key defenders of the rule of law.

The ECJ is the keeper of European Union law. It has stepped into legal and political vacuums to weave together disparate national practices, creating bodies of law to guide European and national policy making. Many of the ECJ's judicial creations garner wide support. For example, since the European Community had very few formal rules guiding administrative procedure, the ECJ built a European equivalent of the American Administrative Procedure Act, insisting that the Commission follow certain due process procedures as the European Commission implements European policy (Lindseth, 2010). The ECJ has also built human rights doctrines to address national judicial concerns that European law, and the European political process, did not sufficiently protect the rights of individuals (De Burca, 2011).

Why is the ECJ so criticized? the challenge of governing today's Europe

Courts are just one of three branches of democratic governance, along with the executive and legislature. The power of any Supreme Court is inherently limited by the reality that courts must wait for litigants to present them with cases, at which time judges have relatively few tools at their disposition. Judges can demand compensation for violations inflicted on private litigants; they can declare illegal acts null and void; and they can offer interpretive guides for administrators, lawyers and judges. Judges cannot force governments to do things they do not want to do, but they can help define what the law requires in the hopes that citizens will care enough about the rule of law to demand that their government respects the law.

If we think about what courts can do, it becomes obvious, for example, that the ECJ could never resolve the tensions crippling the European monetary system. Nor is it able to address political problems associated with assimilating immigrants, an issue which is still addressed primarily at the national and local level. The ECJ can help develop European law as novel questions arise and it can work with national judges and administrators to create a uniform understanding of European law. The ECJ can also rule on Commission and private litigant challenges to state actions that arguably violate European law. But it can only play these roles when litigants present cases, and it can only suggest to others what they should be doing if they wish to be seen as law-abiding actors.

It is not hard to find ECJ rulings that have gone beyond what member states expected. To focus only on these rulings, however, is to forget that there are probably even more ECJ legal inventions that have been welcome. There was no European administrative law, no European human rights law, no rules demanding proportionality, the use of the least intrusive means to protect legitimate public aims, and no European rules ensuring that European law would take priority over conflicting national laws. These are, at this point, less controversial ECJ creations, but they are all part of the package of having the ECJ 'fill in' the holes of European law.

Moreover, while it is convenient to shoot the messenger, political bodies are equally responsible for enlarging the role of the ECJ in European politics. The reason the ECJ ends up developing the law is because European political bodies use a regulatory style that empowers the ECJ. Daniel Kelemen (2010) shows how eurolegalism, like its American counterpart, is actually an unintended result of a number of specific policy choices. The key choice is that policy makers empower private actors to oversee implementation and compliance with common rules. There are many reasons why European political bodies repeatedly fall back on governing through private litigant enforcement. One reason is that the goal of 'subsidiarity' – letting local officials determine the most appropriate means to comply with European rules – entails setting clear European goals but allowing significant discretion in how the goals are achieved. Another reason is that Europeans want to have a small European bureaucracy, and they also want common rules to be respected. Since the European Commission lacks sufficient resources to monitor and enforce its regulatory rules in the ever-growing number of member states, it instead sets clear European Community requirements and demands national- and firm-level transparency so that the Commission can rely on enforcement by private litigants suits raised in national courts. The result is legal suits challenging arguably illegal local practices. The ECJ, by consequence, ends up as the adjudicator of these disputes.

A third political choice is to not create central controls to the appointment process for ECJ judges. The ECJ may well be the most independent court in the world because each country gets to nominate national judges to the ECJ. While choices must be ratified by the other member states, no one country or group of countries is able to control the body of judges being nominated and appointed. The ECJ also decides cases based on panels that ECJ judges themselves randomly determine. These design features make the ECJ impossible to stack or control. Meanwhile, legislating at the European level is already so difficult that it is hard for governments to change European rules that the ECJ interprets differently than intended. This extremely high level of judicial independence is by design; small countries do not want an ECJ that large states can dominate, nor do newer member states want to let older member states say what European law requires (Alter, 2006; Kelemen, 2011).

This is not to deny, however, that serious challenges face the ECJ today. For some people, the main problem is that the ECJ over-rules democratic governments. This is an old issue, and even its latest reincarnations are not quite what the critics suggest. Recent concerns about a 'government of judges' focus on the ECJ's ruling in *Kadi v the European Council of Ministers and Commission of the European Communities* where the ECJ called into question an EU regulation that was passed by the Council of Ministers so as to implement a binding United Nations Security Council mandate. Certain governments appeared outraged that the ECJ would claim authority to question the validity of an act of the UN Security Council, which required governments to seize the assets of those who are fingered as 'supporters of terrorism' (*Kadi*, 2008). It is also true that many judges, legal scholars and civil rights proponents question whether a mystery UN committee dominated by the United States should be able to put individuals on a list that no one is then allowed to query or scrutinize. One can see the ECJ as over-reaching by questioning a decision that was overwhelmingly endorsed by Europe's democratically elected governments. Or one can see the ECJ as the guardian of European policy ensuring that all European regulations respect due process and the rule of law (De Burca, 2010). Or, one can see the ECJ as strategically acting so that the German Constitutional Court did not itself find the European Regulation inapplicable in Germany (Murkens, 2009). In fact, the *Kadi* ruling is not nearly as controversial as supporters of executive prerogatives might make it seem.

A bigger problem, in my view, is that the EU has increasingly entered into a 'no win' terrain where political decisions pit member state interests against each other. The ECJ's Laval case provides one illustration of this problem. *In Laval v the Swedish Building and Electrical Unions*, the ECJ condemned the Swedish unions' tactics of blockading all worksites of a Latvian company, Laval, that had won a construction contract to renovate a public school in Sweden. Swedish unions wanted Laval to follow the Swedish collective agreement process of negotiating labour contracts, which would have made its labour costs more equal to Swedish labour costs. The company instead made an agreement with Latvian unions. The ECJ found that the European Posted Workers Directive, which set clear minimum standards for Europe, precluded the Swedish unions from using certain tactics against firms that had followed the European procedures. The Swedish government naturally took the side of its unions, defending the Swedish tradition of collectively negotiated contracts, although in confidence Swedes will concede that it is nearly impossible for a Latvian firm to successfully navigate the opaque collective agreement process used in Sweden. The political reality was that Swedish union's tactics against a foreign company, although arguably lawful under Swedish law, were found to be excessive under European law (ECJ, 2007). This ruling, and others, have led activists and scholars to join with critics of the right in questioning whether European integration is undermining cherished national values (Joerges, 2011).

I see these 'no win' situations as a bigger problem because they can start to crack the ECJ's support basis within national legal communities and the broader public. It is increasingly hard for the European Union to create a constitutional and political balance that can satisfy new and old member states alike. The ECJ does not make the policies that these different voices protest, but the European governance style of relying on private enforcement means that it becomes the forum in which debates about the application of contested rules play out. There is no way for the ECJ to avoid these controversies. The ECJ must offer rulings in the cases that are presented to it. If the question is whether Laval gains rights and protections from the Posted Workers Directive, the answer undoubtedly is 'yes'. In other words, the problem is not the ECJ, the problem is that the base law the ECJ is asked to apply is controversial.

The European Union is an increasingly mature and heterogeneous polity. Nostalgia for the past combines with the sense that EU membership brings costs to make it politically expedient to run for office on a platform of leaving the European Union. This question of exit is perhaps more present in Europe than it is in the United States, although it is also true that Conservative politicians score points by suggesting that it is never too late to secede from the American Union. The ECJ becomes a frequent boogey man, blamed for delivering the bad news that national policies must change.

The bottom line is that a legal and political union requires constant balance. Critics from the right suggest that democratically elected governments, or perhaps international institutions like the UN and the World Trade Organization (where conveniently enough the US has a strong voice), should determine the balance. But the separation of powers gives judges a say in determining whether or not governments are adhering to the rule of law.

Conclusion

The ECJ may have started as an international court, but today it is the Constitutional Court of Europe, overseeing the balance between European integration, national rights, citizen rights, and the many international commitments that European governments must also respect.

The ECJ's constituency in this process is not the national governments, who will pander to populist sentiments. Rather, the ECJ worries about finding a legal solution that can satisfy national judges, who are also struggling to balance European integration with national constitutions in the many complex cases that citizens bring. Sometimes judicial rulings seem unfair and even wrong. And sometimes governments and politicians merely like to complain so as to push the blame on others. ECJ rulings, like the law the ECJ applies, surely cannot please everyone. But the alternative – letting governments do as they please, or turning the issue entirely over to national courts – is not a solution to this problem, especially for a continent where democratically chosen leaders have repeatedly displayed a willingness to let security concerns and national interests trump individual rights and European objectives.

5.2 The European Court of Justice: a strange institution

Jeremy Rabkin

The European Court of Justice is a very strange institution. It is strange in the literal sense that no other international court has the same formidable combination of powers. In a deeper sense, it partakes of the strangeness of its setting – the European Union, which, in its underlying political premises, is so strange that it seems other-worldly. To put the point concisely, the European Court of Justice exercises the authority of a national constitutional court – without a national government or a national constitution or anything like a cohesive nation behind it.

So this court based in Luxemburg exercises supreme legal authority from Ireland to Malta, from Sweden to Slovenia. It not only claims the authority to over-rule decisions of national governments, but also decisions of the EU's own Council of Ministers, representing the overwhelming majority of these elected governments acting in concert. In a recent ruling, for example, the ECJ invoked abstract language in the EU's Charter of Fundamental Rights to hold that insurance policies must not charge different rates to male as compared with female purchasers – over-riding a contrary provision approved by the Council of Ministers, as well as over-riding the law of nature (or at least of well-documented actuarial realities) (ECJ, 2011).

A unique international tribunal

The ECJ asserted its claim to legal supremacy as early as the 1960s. It has exercised that supremacy on an ever-wider scale since then. Though aspects of the ECJ's activity bear comparison with other courts in other settings, its combination of powers remains entirely unique for an international tribunal.

To start with, there is the power to over-ride a state's resistance to being sued. It was common practice in the nineteenth century for states to submit disputes with other states to international arbitration – but only with the consent of the states involved and only after considerable negotiation about the exact questions to be submitted to the arbitrators. The International Court of Justice (often called the 'World Court'), established under the UN Charter in 1945, still follows this traditional pattern: a state may sue another state there, but only with the consent of the other state. At the ECJ, every EU state is obligated to accept the Court's authority to decide suits brought against it. So where, for example, the ICJ hears about two or three cases a year, the ECJ handles hundreds of cases each year.

In most international organizations, states are left to settle disputes in state-to-state negotiations, so resort to arbitration is exceptional. The EU has its own free-standing enforcement arm, the European Commission, which can initiate suits against member states – even where other states would not have cared to press the claim. If states do not adhere to rulings of the ECJ, the Court can impose substantial fines for noncompliance. No other international organization has such a powerful, centralized scheme for enforcing the organization's rules. In the World Trade Organization, for example, as under the North American Free Trade Agreement, there is provision for compulsory arbitration of disputes – but no central enforcement authority to insist on arbitration when no other state wants to press the point.

Enforcement of EU law against member states is not only left to the Commission, however. The ECJ can also hear claims from private individuals or private business or advocacy organizations. Cases brought by private claimants in national courts can be 'referred' to the ECJ for rulings of relevant issues in EU law – and the national courts are then bound to implement the ruling of the ECJ. The power to reach into the international legal system of the member states is the most formidable and the most unique power of the ECJ. Decisions of the WTO's Appellate Body are said to be 'final' but they do not, in themselves, change the law of the member states: in the last resort, they simply authorize a complaining state to impose retaliatory trade sanctions on the offending state. Even decisions of the European Court of Human Rights do not, of themselves, change the law in a state found to be in violation of the European Convention on Human Rights: the Human Rights Court can only demand that the offending state pay financial compensation to the individual complainant but the government of that state must decide for itself how and in what way to change the law condemned by the Human Rights Court. By contrast, the ECJ directs national courts on the standards they should apply in their own rulings – both in the particular case and in future cases.

As far back as the 1960s, the ECJ directed national courts to uphold the Court's view of European law, even when national parliaments had laid down a contrary standard. The famous ruling in *van Gend en Loos* (1962) effectively claimed a kind of constitutional status for EU law – so that it would take priority over national legislation, even when a parliament had enacted that legislation subsequent to its endorsement of the EU treaty. In later cases, the ECJ insisted that even bureaucratic directives of the European Commission must, in this way, take priority over statutes enacted by national parliaments. Then it held that such bureaucratic directives must take priority even over national constitutions, as interpreted by national constitutional courts. The European Court of Justice claimed the status of the ultimate Supreme Court of Europe.

None of this would seem odd if the European Union were simply a federal state. The US Supreme Court does not shrink from invalidating laws enacted by states of the Union, sometimes even repudiating provisions in state constitutions to maintain the supremacy of federal law. But the original US Constitution of 1787 clearly stipulated that federal law would be 'supreme law of the land' with 'judges in every state bound thereby, anything in the constitution or laws of any state to the contrary notwithstanding'. The Treaty of Rome had no such language. Nor did any subsequent treaty, revising, extending, reinforcing the institutions of the European Community and the ultimate European Union over the next fifty years. It was only with the so-called constitutional treaty of 2004 and its slightly revised successor, the Lisbon treaty, that the 'supremacy' of European law was formally acknowledged. But the Lisbon treaty then indicated that a considerable range of expanded powers – mostly involving foreign and security policy – would be excluded from the Court's jurisdiction: the drafters of the Treaty evidently did not trust the Court to decide for itself, as is the usual practice in national courts faced with issues possibly unsuited for judicial resolution.

The composition and operating procedures of the Court also differ remarkably from supreme courts or constitutional courts in federal states. The political organs of the European Union do not select the judges who serve on the European Court of Justice. Each member state gets to send one judge. The ECJ judges then serve for the relatively short period of six-year terms, which might seem to keep them on a short leash. But the Court has, throughout its history, kept to the practice of announcing all decisions through a single opinion. Since there are no published dissenting or concurring opinions, there is no way of knowing the preferences or reservations of any particular judge, hence no way of knowing whether individual judges have tried to respect the particular concerns of their home state governments.

A powerful institution

The European Court of Justice exercises powers of a national court in a federal state – but in a system which is not actually a federal state. In many ways, that is an advantage for the court. The European Parliament has no power to challenge the court since it cannot initiate legislation or demand commissioners or members of the Council who would confront the court. Distracted national leaders do not find it easy to organize resistance to the Court. The President of the Council has not attained the sort of European-wide prominence which would be required to mobilize public opinion across the continent for a confrontation with the Court.

The ECJ is a reflection of the European integration process over which it presides – and has often pushed forward, when the Council of Ministers could not agree on forward steps. The Court has been extremely active in nullifying national laws that inhibit the free flow of goods across borders. After the 1960s, the Court's targets were not actual tariff barriers or direct import restrictions but such matters as safety or quality regulations that had the effect of favouring domestic producers. In effect, the Court ensured that the largest, most lucrative markets in the northern states would be open for all members. Advocates of free markets in the United States have expressed admiration for the ECJ's persistence in this endeavour, showing far more scepticism of national regulatory measures than the US Supreme Court shows toward measures adopted by states of the United States when they are challenged for disrupting inter-state commerce.

The ECJ's support for market liberalization has been balanced, however, by its support for European-wide measures of social regulation, either read into the treaties (as in its holdings on sex discrimination) or upheld as valid initiatives by the European Commission. In effect, the Court has struck a political balance: access to German and Dutch markets, on the one hand, support for regulatory measures favoured by the more affluent states, on the other (so that less affluent states, with lower labour costs, cannot improve their competitive advantage by also offering lower regulatory compliance costs with lax environmental or safety standards).

Some scholars view the ECJ and the Commission as serving the interests of the larger or richer states within the EU (Carrubba *et al.*, 2008: 435; Garrett, 1992: 533; Moravcsik, 1998: 482–90).Others have shown that in the landmark cases of the 1960s and 1970s, governments (including those of the larger and richer states) filed legal briefs cautioning against the stands which the Court ultimately took (Cichowski, 1998: 387 and 2004: 489; Stein, 1981: 1; Stone Sweet and Brunell, 1998: 63). The most persuasive studies of the ECJ document show that in many policy fields the Court has successfully imposed a 'judicialization' of policy making, where the Court itself – more than governments in the background – does get the last word and lawyers for contending political or commercial interests (rather than government ministers) play the principal roles (Cichowski, 2007; Kelemen, 2010; Stone Sweet, 2004).

Observers of different political persuasions may differ on whether the Court has achieved the right balance. What no one can say is that the Court simply applies established law. The Court's jurisprudence is often described as 'teleological' – meaning that it aims to fulfil a vision for the future (here, of a more integrated European-wide economy and society) rather than simply upholding the intentions of those who negotiated and endorsed the various treaties on which European law rests. National governments may not object to leaving so much initiative to the opaque deliberations of the ECJ judges, but national governments remain at the mercy of the Court's judgments.

If the Court does not necessarily serve the priorities of elected national governments, neither does it serve an abstract vision of 'rule by law' or even of 'consensus by law' or 'justice above nations'. Since the ECJ has over-ridden national parliaments and even national constitutions for the sake of liberalizing markets, it might seem logical that the Court would defer to judgments of the World Trade Organization's Appellate Body – a court which operates more openly (allowing dissenting and concurring opinions, for example) and champions market liberalization on a global scale. But the ECJ has repeatedly rejected claims to apply WTO rulings directly to EU law. It leaves the European Commission (and where necessary, the Council of Ministers) to decide how rulings of the WTO should be implemented within Europe.

Similarly, one might think the European Court of Justice would show great deference to organs of the United Nations. A number of member states, notably Italy and Germany, made explicit provision in their postwar constitutions to acknowledge the authority of the peace-enforcing mission of the United Nations. Advocates of European integration have continually warned that if European institutions falter, Europe risks return to dangerous national rivalries, so peace seems to be an overriding priority. But the European Court of Justice insisted, in 2008, that a formal resolution of the UN Security Council – regarding freezing of assets used to finance terrorism – could not be binding on European governments to the extent that it conflicted with due process guarantees in European law (*Kadi*, 2008). So the ECJ empowered itself to over-ride the constitutional norms of member states but rejected the notion that the UN Security Council could over-ride what the ECJ regarded as EU norms.

None of these decisions would be surprising for a national court outside of Europe. These rulings simply remind us that the ECJ protects its own vision of a European legal order, rather than more general claims about law. The Court itself seems to recognize that other nations may have different views – even other western nations. The question is whether enough Europeans share the Court's view of what is best for them.

Europeans have ceded vast powers to the European Union but they have not trusted it to exercise military force. They have not even trusted the EU to organize itself on the democratic parliamentary lines adopted by all the member states at home. The 2004 constitutional treaty – supposed to assure that the whole structure would finally have the full authority and legitimacy of a national constitution – had to be scaled back when decisive majorities in France and the Netherlands rejected it in open referenda. The Lisbon Treaty which superseded the constitutional treaty is (like its predecessor) far too technical and detailed – and far too evasive or elliptical on major issues – for anyone to understand (other than legal specialists).

An institution unable to solve the EU's main challenges

Currently, the Union faces great challenges. Germany does not want to make open-ended commitments to assist profligate southern states, now staggering under impossible debt burdens. The common currency may prove impossible to sustain without major adjustments in how countries tax their own citizens and arrange their national budgets. Countries that put up with ECJ redesign of their regulatory standards may be far less patient with central direction of local fiscal policies. But if there is strong political opposition to austerity policies imposed from Brussels – or new taxes to finance new bailouts – will there be as much deference to centralized regulatory policies and the Court that oversees them?

Meanwhile, many European states struggle with the reality that immigrants, particularly from Muslim countries, seem to have formed themselves into separatist enclaves, seething with resentment, hostility and threats of violence. In 2010, the German Chancellor gave a frank speech announcing that 'multiculturalism' had failed. That view was soon endorsed by similar pronouncements from the President of France and the Prime Minister of Britain. They all urged greater efforts to assimilate immigrants into a common culture. But surely these will have to be national cultures. If politicians at the national level can mobilize support for somewhat coercive (or controversial) measures designed to pressure minority communities toward more complete cultural assimilation, will the same nationalist leaders readily submit to ECJ rulings restricting their efforts?

Finally, there is the challenge of reconciling the EU with European human rights norms. To quiet background doubts about the vast powers delegated to faceless bureaucrats in Brussels, the EU has promised to become a full participant in the European Convention on Human Rights. That would subject all EU policies to the scrutiny of the European Court of Human Rights in Strasbourg. After setting itself up as superior to all other courts in Europe, will the ECJ calmly submit to direction from the ECHR? After all, many judges of the ECHR come from non-EU countries and few seem to share the ECJ's 'teleological' vision of European integration. But if the ECJ defies its rival European court, that will likely remind Europeans that European integration does not always give high priority to the individual rights of European citizens.

In the end, the ECJ reflects the situation of the EU: if the European Union comes under severe strain in coming years, the ECJ won't be able to save it. Nor can it expect to survive a break-up of the larger European project. Remote, mysterious, essentially bureaucratic, the ECJ is a mirror of the EU, itself: it can process a vast range of technical questions but is not designed to face the supreme crises that may still confront Europeans in the course of human events.

Chapter 6

Can There Be a Common European Identity?

Editors' introduction

Preoccupation with European identity emerged in parallel with concerns about the EU's alleged democratic deficit (see Chapter 4). Many political theorists see a common identity as a prerequisite for a functioning democratic political system. To the extent that democracy is defined as government 'by the people', it requires that citizens feel part of the same collective entity. The EU's member states have reacted to this perceived need for a European identity by introducing the concept of a European citizenship, which was expected to help in the creation of a political community. In a declaration attached to the Treaty of Lisbon, sixteen EU member states declared that they would use the informal EU flag, anthem ('Ode to Joy'), motto ('United in diversity') and Europe Day 'to express the sense of community of the people in the European Union'.

Despite these valiant – some say, pathetic – efforts, both the extent to which a genuine European identity has emerged and the possibility for and desirability of a common identity are deeply contested (Bruter, 2005; Cram, 2012; Fligstein, 2008; Risse, 2010). The Eurobarometer, a survey carried out on behalf of the European Commission, regularly asks respondents whether they feel that they are European citizens. In 2011, across the 27 member states of the EU, 23 per cent of respondents indicated that they 'definitely' feel that they are a citizen of the EU, with another 39 per cent picking the answer 'yes, to some extent' (Eurobarometer, 2011). In a 2010 survey, 12 per cent of respondents said that they felt 'very attached' to the EU and another 41 per cent felt 'fairly attached' (Eurobarometer, 2010a). While proponents of the view that a European identity exists use these figures to show that a majority of citizens have a feeling of belonging to the EU, doubters point to the fact that in response to the question on attachment approximately 90 per cent of respondents indicated that they were fairly or very attached to their country, city and region – which is many more than the 53 per cent that feel attached to the EU.

In the following, Ulrike Liebert argues that as a result of external challenges, European norms, discursive contestations, and citizenship practices, a European identity has indeed emerged over time. Jonathan White counters that not only are there few signs that a European identity is emerging, but that the pursuit of a European identity may even be problematic from a normative point of view. This controversy is of relevance to Chapter 1 on the success or failure of the EU and Chapter 4 on the EU's democratic deficit.

6.1 The emergence of a European identity

Ulrike Liebert

Eurocritics often blame the EU for burdening citizens with regulatory and redistributive policies without having found – or having been able to create – a robust pan-European identity that would ensure their acceptance even of unpopular and costly decisions. It is true that after several decades of EU membership, the majority of citizens continue to identify with their respective nation states and not primarily with the EU. It is also the case that, over the past decade, conflicts about EU treaty reform and ratification plus the financial as well as debt crisis of the eurozone have brought eurosceptics and anti-Europeans to the fore, exacerbating national identity politics and undermining expectations of a collective sense of belonging among the 500 million Europeans. Yet, the instances of politicizing European integration have also contributed to the formation of a distinctively contentious pattern of European identity. Assuming that collective identities are social categories of people who inevitably differ amongst themselves on the extent of their agreement and disagreement about the meanings this entails, the emergence of common patterns of identification amidst EU-Europeans results from struggles among competing political visions of the European integration project. The norms inherent in European identity will therefore not only be a question of the contents of how Europe is constructed but also of the contestations over Europe.

I argue that over the past four decades the EU has made marked progress regarding both dimensions of identity formation, that is, its contents and its contestations. From 1973 to the present, a European identity has taken shape in four different respects: First, the idea of a European identity defined by shared norms has been conceived by European foreign ministers within the context of the Cold War, namely the EC's external relations *vis-à-vis* the USSR and the USA. Second, European identity has built on the formal norms and constitutive practices that have shaped the EU's ongoing process of economic and social constitutionalization. Third, European identity has been framed as a contentious project by competing political ideas about Europe. Fourth, European identifications have evolved through transnational mobility and activities from below, namely European citizenship practices. I conclude that although the global financial crisis of 2008/9 and the 2010/11 crisis of the eurozone have threatened critical achievements of European identity formation, they may also have lent a new impetus to many Europeans' search for a European social identity capable of governing capitalist markets.

The following reconstructs the formation of European identity in four different steps. Taken together, I do not claim that these steps will empirically or should normatively lead to a uniform European identity, but, simply, that they converge towards a common framework for a contentious – and that means open - European identity.

Conceiving 'European Identity' in EC external relations

The Foreign Ministers of the then nine member states of the European Community first proclaimed the existence of a European identity that was linked to the EU in 1973. Under the threat of the world economic crisis set off by the second oil shock, they adopted the 'Document on the European Identity' (Document, 1973), characterizing European identity by shared norms of representative democracy, the rule of law, social justice and human rights, and, above all, the practical interest in achieving 'an active role of European foreign policy in world politics'. Hence, European identity was conceived of as a mechanism to achieve unity in the EC-9's external relations and as a precondition for improving its place in world affairs: 'International developments and the growing concentration of power and responsibility in the hands of a very small number of great powers mean that Europe must unite and speak increasingly with one voice if it wants to make itself heard and play its proper role in the world.' The document emphasized that the EC's external relations to other countries and international organizations were crucial for shaping Europe's identity.

As a matter of fact, little less than two decades later, this approach did indeed bear fruit. It helped to reshape fundamentally the EC's external relations and to bring the bi-polarization of Europe and the world to an end. Not only had enlargement been at the heart of the EC's identity from the founding treaty of Rome (Fierke and Wiener, 2009: 100); it is also the case that the EU's eastern enlargement was primarily driven by collective European identity. As Frank Schimmelfennig and Ulrich Sedelmeier argue, the east-central and eastern Europeans' aim 'to return to Europe' was motivated 'by their desire to cast off an "eastern" identity and to be recognized by the European Community as "one of us"' (2009: 20). The power of this idea fuelled opposition to communist regimes, helped dismantle the Berlin Wall, and, finally, drove ten newly democratizing east and east-central European countries into EU membership. In turn, eastern enlargement forced European integration – and, thus, the institutional formation of a European identity – to deepen as well. While in the past EU citizens had passively accepted European integration and allowed it to be an exclusive domain of elites, eastern enlargement becamethe trigger – and Maastricht, EMU and the Constitutional Treaty the specific mechanisms – conducive to lifting the veil from this 'permissive consensus'.

Reconfiguring 'European Identity' in the Economic and Monetary Union

The breakdown of the communist regimes of east-central Europe and the reunification of Germany provided momentum for re-constituting the European Union's economic and monetary order (Schiek *et al.*, 2011). The Maastricht Treaty (1993) transformed the 'would-be European polity' (Lindberg and Scheingold, 1970) into the 'European Economic and Monetary Union' (EMU), coupled with a thin notion of Union citizenship. Hence, for the project of a European identity, the single European currency was a uniquely important key. The euro was by no means only a technical matter facilitating economic exchanges; it was meant to also be a political symbol with relevance to citizens' everyday lives. The launch of the euro in eleven member states in 1999 was the most visible threshold towards an 'ever closer Union', but only regarding the citizens of the 'eurozone'. Yet, as Amy Verdun and Thomas Christiansen (2000) argued, the EMU relied on the creation of a set of powerful institutions with direct and executive authority in policy making, which, however, preceded the emergence of a political community in which such decisions could be grounded. As a consequence, the euro became a political symbol of European unity, collective identity, and social solidarity for some, and a scapegoat and symbol of European centralism and fraud, and forced social and cultural homogeneity for others (Liebert, 2001).

While the EMU designed at Maastricht considerably enhanced economic and monetary integration, such success neither emerged from EU treaty reforms since 2000 aimed at improving political efficiency and democratic legitimacy nor from the so-called Lisbon Agenda (2000–10) which proposed to make the EU the most dynamic and competitive knowledge-based economy in the world. The 'Treaty establishing a Constitution for Europe' was signed in 2004, but failed to attract sufficient popular support as foundation for a pan-European constitutional patriotism. The 'Reform Treaty of Lisbon' (signed in 2007, and taking effect in 2009), was another exclusively elite-led attempt at European identity formation. Accordingly, European identity is acknowledged in this latest treaty alongside national and religious identities in the EU: On the one hand, an independent European identity is aimed at promoting 'peace, security and progress in Europe and in the world' and, for that purpose, a common foreign and security policy and a common defence policy are developed for the EU. The preamble refers to 'the democratic life of the Union' and the 'Charter of Fundamental Rights' that lay out the common values, principles and goals to which the EU commits itself, its member states and the citizens. On the other hand, the Union is called to respect the equality of member states under the treaties as well as their national identities, inherent in their fundamental political and constitutional structures, including regional and local self-government. At the same time, the treaty also recognizes the identity of churches and their specific contribution to which the Union shall maintain an open, transparent and regular dialogue. However, for the project of European identity formation, while formal constitutional norms may be necessary, they will not be sufficient. What they mean for European citizens' practices will depend on how Europe is discursively framed in national contexts. It will be shaped by the contentious ways in which the EU's constitutive norms are interpreted and linked to European identity in intellectual debates on Europe (Lacroix and Nicolaïdis, 2010).

Contesting discursive European identity constructions

Admittedly, throughout the period from the Maastricht (1992) to the Laeken summit (2001), the EU's political space was fragmented by national identities, where citizens hardly communicated across national borders, rarely understood their neighbour's languages, differed in their memories of the past, and diverged on the values they cherished. After the turn of the millennium, the politicization of EU matters gradually changed this landscape. Increasingly EU policy issues – from the 2004 EU enlargement and the 2004–9 treaty reforms to the eurocrisis management – appeared on member states' public agendas at the same time, as questions of similar concern, looked at through comparable lenses, and triggering exchanges across national boundaries. They sparked the Europeanization of domestic politics and the transnationalization of political communication. Incrementally, these processes helped overcome the segmentation of national public spheres, while preserving their diversity. Prior to Laeken the main problem hampering European identity was that of the EU's lack of politicization, while post-Laeken Europeans experienced plenty of it. Part of this sea change was the birth and death of the EU's Constitutional Treaty (TCE). Aimed at a more democratic

Union of States and Citizens, it proposed bolstering European identity with proper symbols, including a flag, anthem, and the Charter of Fundamental Rights. Its popular ratification successes (in Spain and in Luxembourg) and failures (in France and the Netherlands) were, fundamentally, a matter of contentious discursive constructions of the TCE's identity project.

While the EU's constitutional development has provided European identity with a normative framework, the ensuing public debates sparked discursive contestations among competing ideas, pitting '(neo-liberal) market Europe' against 'European Social Model'; 'Christian Union' against 'secular multi-religious Europe'; 'Europe of national democracies' against 'Democratic Federal Europe' or 'cosmopolitan regional Union' (Liebert, 2010). While opponents feared a centralized European state that would loom behind the TCE to the detriment of the peoples' national and democratic identities, others put their trust in the EU's constitutive multinational democratic identity. Whereas opponents believed that the EU's new institutional architecture would harm the free play of the markets, others suspected the TCE of being a plot against 'Social Europe'. Since the idea of a foreign European identity – 'European civilian power' – either open to its neighbours and the world or defined in opposition against some other – did not take off among European mass publics, eurosceptics found ample opportunities for voicing nationalist, xenophobic, and racist stances. In sum, the public debates about the Constitutional Treaty have undeniably enriched the European identity project in terms of content as well as contentiousness (Liebert, 2007). In the following, we will look at whether, and in what respects, these patterns interact with the social practices of European citizenship.

Constructing European identity through citizenship practices

Paradoxically, albeit having introduced 'Union citizenship', the post-Maastricht blues made the erosion of the 'permissive consensus' become manifest: Public support for the EU decreased by nearly one third, protest movements mobilized against Brussels, and eurosceptic constituencies emerged in a growing number of domestic referenda on the EU. In sum: mass public attitudes indicated a lasting shift from an elite driven project to a publicly contested politics of integration. Nevertheless, attempts at bringing the EC/EU 'closer to the citizens' cannot all be said to have failed. Empirical data support this claim in three respects:

1. National identifications as such do not necessarily constitute an impediment to a common European identity, unless they are practised in an exclusive manner. During the time span 1992–2010, 'national

identity only' has oscillated between 33 per cent (1994) and 46 per cent (Eurobarometer,1996; 2010). It does not follow from these fluctuations that European identifications have necessarily experienced a bitter defeat.

2. Europeans are simultaneously citizens of their home country and of the EU. If measuring individuals' identification 'as national and EU', 'EU and national' or 'only EU' over the period 1992–2010, these figures have not stagnated at low levels but have fluctuated, in some cases weakening and in others strengthening. Despite the EU's massive enlargement, overall levels have remained surprisingly high over this time period. For instance, between 41 per cent and 48 per cent of all respondents from the EU-9 to the EU-27 believe that in the near future they will see themselves 'as national and EU', with highs in 1992, 2001 and 2005, and lows in 1997 and 2010 (Eurobarometer; 18 different reports). Over the same time period, between 9 per cent and 17 per cent of respondents reported they identify first or exclusively with the EU, with a peak in 1994, lows in 2001 and 2005, and reaching 10 per cent in 2010. It is true that several member states have seen a net decline in levels of individual identifications with the EU, namely France, Greece, Ireland and the UK. But it is also true that Swedes, Hungarian and Germans have developed higher levels of public identification with the EU, with increases from 34 per cent to 53 per cent (Hungary), 36 per cent to 50 per cent (Sweden), and 56 per cent to 60 per cent (Germany).

3. Finally, if asked whether they think of themselves not only as nationals but also as Europeans, the respondents from all EU member states who do so 'sometimes' or 'often' have increased over time, from 45 per cent (1990) to 54 per cent (2006), despite the intake of sixteen new members during this period. Over the past two decades, unprecedented numbers of new citizens have become part of the multilevel EU polity. More than 50 per cent of these 500 million inhabitants identify as 'national plus EU citizen' or 'EU plus national' or 'EU only' (Eurobarometer: 51 per cent in 2010). And roughly the same proportion of citizens 'think European' (Eurobarometer: 54 per cent in 2006), not always, but often or sometimes.

Arguably, these developments result from evolving European citizenship practices. Respondents understand the term 'citizen of the EU' to mean anyone who is, or who becomes, a citizen of any EU member state. EU citizenship is also seen as closely related to having similar rights and obligations in each member state. It is felt to encompass the freedoms within the European Single Market; that is, the rights to mobility among member states that EU citizens enjoy. If these rights are 'taken for granted' they affect how people see themselves as citizens of the EU, whether they practise the rights of working and studying in any member state or not. Increasingly more gain the personal experience of living, working or studying in another member state or of knowing other people who practice these rights (Eurobarometer, 2010b). Interestingly, the EU's eastern enlargement of 2004 has not fundamentally altered these processes, but it has intensified and accelerated some of them. After all, the citizens of the new eastern and central-eastern EU member states may not think and feel that different from people in the older EU member states. But they are definitely more mobile across borders, more aware of Union citizenship rights and practices, and, thus more disposed to Europeanize their national identifications (Góra and Mach, 2010). Finally, part and parcel of European citizenship practices is also the new politics of European civil society (Liebert and Trenz, 2010). EU-level civil society organizations act as citizens' representatives; as a consulted partner or critical watchdog and occasionally as participants in EU politics and policy making. The 'European citizens' initiative', introduced by the 2010 Lisbon Treaty, will open new windows of opportunity to that aspect.

The unfinished journey of European identity: conclusion

Many still hold that there cannot be a common European identity and that it is an illusion to expect an international organization like the EU to evolve one. This essay has provided evidence that over the course of four decades of European integration, a European identity has gradually emerged from the dynamics of the evolving European polity: in its initial phase it was conceived of as an agency for overcoming the Cold War; following that it was reshaped by the Economic and Monetary Union; subsequently, it has interacted with the project of a European constitutional treaty; and, ultimately, it has benefited from more active European citizens' and civil society practices in the Single European Market that transcend nation state borders. Therefore, more than fifty years after the Treaties of Rome, the multiple manifestations of the emerging European identity demonstrate that the conventional wisdom according to which Europeans lack a sense of community has to be reconsidered. Thomas Risse has argued this case convincingly: 'It is true that we do not observe the emergence of a uniform and shared European identity above and beyond the various national identities. Rather the available data show the Europeanization of collective local, national, gender, and other identities. Europe and the EU are integrated in people's sense of belonging.' (Risse, 2010: 5). Following him and Stråth (2010), I have reconstructed the emergence of European identity as a result of dynamic interactions between external challenges, European norms, discursive contestations, and citizenship practices.

In view of the global financial crisis of 2008/9 and the 2010/11 crisis of the eurozone, the formation of European identity seems to be far from over: Skyrocketing state debts threaten the survival of the European Economic and Monetary Union and thus, the EU-17's economic identity, symbolized by the euro. Popular dissatisfaction with the EU is rooted in perceived threats that a 'Transfer Union' will not only transfer payments to other member states in crisis but also mandate budget cuts in one's own domestic social welfare and social security system. Yet, the European identity also stands a fair chance to re-emerge empowered from these crises – which may even lend a new impetus to the Europeans' search for a European social identity capable of coping with capitalist market failures in democratically legitimate ways.

6.2 A common European identity is an illusion

Jonathan White

There is a simple idea at the heart of discussions of 'European identity'. It is that some kind of social underpinning is required for a political community to survive and prosper. The argument may be mainly empirical – that some kind of mass bond is required if a polity is to be unified, strong, and able to provide public goods, particularly in crisis moments, or it may be mainly normative – that only where such a bond exists will the polity meet the standards of legitimacy the modern world expects. Where 'identity' is present, coherence, common purpose and a disposition to solidarity are said to be forthcoming. Where it is absent, lack of direction and fatal divisions are expected to follow. Be it for empirical or normative reasons, 'identity' is posed as a polity's necessary foundation, and its absence as a reason for scepticism. As readers will know, it is in the context of exactly such hopes and doubts regarding the prospects of the EU that the question of European identity has been consistently raised.

This gives us an indication of the intended *function* of a collective identity, but what of its particular *form*? What does the term denote? A misleading question perhaps, for 'identity' is often used with little descriptive intent, instead as a casual means to reference all those 'soft' dimensions of human existence left over once the 'hard' issues of economy and institutions have been considered. When interested actors such as the European Commission speak of 'European identity', generally they are not so much referring to a clear-cut entity as gesturing vaguely towards the solution of a problem, to that elusive substance which can oil the system's parts. 'European identity' presents itself as a word which, if spoken enough times, can place distance between the EU and its critics, warding off charges that the EU faces a crisis of legitimacy (Shore, 2000; Strath, 2002). Likewise for the EU's critics, European identity and its alleged weakness is a nicely shaped stick with which to knock Brussels on the head. The concept's ambiguity can be a plus, as it inhibits closer inspection. Alternatively, when 'European identity' is used by scholars, it is often as a means to cluster a range of narrower issues and debates, projecting them as part of a larger research programme. Those studying such diverse matters as trends in European media reporting, EU public policy, institutional discourse, practices of EU citizenship, public attitudes to the EU institutions, support for European integration in principle, attitudes to fellow citizens, or commitment to a range of value orientations, have a tendency to frame their research as the study of 'European identity': presumably so as to broaden their readership, and no doubt encouraged by their publishers, for whom the term is a reliable selling point. In other words, in deployments of the phrase 'European identity', the structure of the thing described is often secondary to the political or scholarly agenda behind it. Form follows function, one could say.

To assess European identity as real or illusory requires us to suspend these doubts about its analytical worth and sketch out a sharper meaning. What might this be?

Conceiving identity

In general terms, those invoking 'European identity' apparently wish to make reference to the oneness and stability of a social grouping. Identity in this context implies a set of people united by common dispositions, and who exhibit continuity in what they share. Two variations on this idea can be distinguished, one more objectivist and one more subjectivist. Rather than as fully distinct, they are best approached as differing alloys of the same ideas, for most thinkers of identity combine elements found in both.

In the first view, identity is objectively real but subjectively renegotiated. That is to say, the common dispositions which individuals share are taken to be grounded in realities beyond their individual or collective choosing, and can never fully be cast off, even if they can be accentuated, de-accentuated and contested. So, for example, it might be said that 'Europeans' are those who share a distinctive set of Judaeo-Christian ideas which shape how they see the world, and that this holds true even if they are unaware of this fact, or if they choose to ascribe it different meanings. Despite the nod to subjective understanding, the privileged perspective is that of the observer – it is (s)he who determines the existence or absence of identity, and it is against his or her standard that the relevant individuals are assessed. In this view, people can be mistaken about their identity: they might, for instance, be 'European' without knowing it, or believe they were European when they could not be. That people may be misled in this way is well captured in the concept of 'false consciousness', which would be the standard Marxist interpretation of national identity. The challenge for all objectivist perspectives lies in how to ground the observer's knowledge. If mistakes are possible, why trust in the observer's omniscience? Why see their account as immune to the peculiarities of personal interpretation? And which observer – whose word should be taken as final? While an objectivist conception of European identity is sometimes advanced (for example, Siedentop, 2000), it is difficult to endorse with confidence. In any case, its rather rigid understanding of identity is likely to make it a blunt tool for responding to the underlying political question of governability.

In the second, more interpretivist perspective, identities stand or fall by people's willingness to express them. They cannot exist in latent form, since the sympathies which comprise them have no underlying basis beyond people's willingness to adopt and display them. Here, identity refers to reciprocal feelings of attachment, or *practices of identification* as one might call them so as to emphasize the open-endedness of the process (Brubaker and Cooper, 2000: 14). Diffuse feelings of sympathy towards others are the focal point, whether tied in with cultural attributes or, as in civic approaches such as 'constitutional patriotism', the political values ascribed to the collectivity. While the spotlight is on people's interpretations, still one generally finds a nod to objectivism in the notion that these practices of identification are supported, stabilized and given visibility by various extra-cognitive phenomena: for instance the repeated deployment of key concepts and social categories (for example, 'Europe', 'Europeans'), of narratives which build on these, and by the cultivation of symbols (such as, flags and constitutions). Importantly – a point which the language of identification brings out more clearly than identity – these latter elements (words, narratives, symbols, and so on) are resources for identification but not constitutive of it: the research object cannot be reduced to these visible manifestations. The emphasis is on meanings – on how these resources are used and interpreted.

This conception of identity, more than the first, invites empirical investigation to establish its content. For some, this necessitates the use of opinion polls – European identity is then studied as the willingness of individuals to respond favourably to questions concerning how European they feel. For others, it points to the use of qualitative research methods such as interviews, the anthropological study of everyday life situations, or the analysis of legal and political texts. (Differences of method may reflect not just differences of methodology but differences concerning whether identity is viewed as something consciously felt and susceptible to articulation, or something that exists at a tacit level and which can only emerge spontaneously.) Given that, in contrast to objectivist accounts, these practices of identification are not treated as a function of long-term historical truths, they are potentially quite unpredictable. Accordingly, some would argue the term 'identity' should be replaced with one that does not presume continuity of practice and meaning across time ('self-understanding' has been a suggested alternative); but where continuity is suspected, 'identity' would seem a valid description.

In this latter sense, then, and postponing certain further ambiguities, a common European identity would exist when people express mutual sympathies to one another as 'Europeans', and under-gird this with appeal to signs and discourses that refer to 'Europe'. (Whether such sympathies would be compatible with enduring special sympathies to fellow nationals is a matter of much debate – Duchesne, 2010.) This conception's advantage is that, to a degree, it avoids reifying 'identity' as something stable and irrevocable. One avoids the problem of 'latent' identities, and allows individuals greater scope to shape and revise the identities they ascribe to (since identity is then something which depends on their assent, rather than a fate to which they are consigned). This conception is not without its own problems – chiefly, the epistemological one of how to establish when these practices of identification are present, given they may be viewed as little more than traces in the individual brain; but also the conceptual one that the further one moves in the direction of open-ended practice the less appropriate a static term such as identity becomes. There will also be plenty of boundary problems, given the emphasis on reciprocal recognition: what does one make of those individuals who claim allegiance to a grouping yet whose membership is questioned by others? Involuntary membership is the same problem in reverse. Still, it is broadly this conception of a common European identity which presents itself as the kind worth examining for its real or illusory character.

A question remains: how many people would need to engage in these reciprocal practices of identification before they would amount to something one could feasibly call 'European identity'? What would their necessary scope be? Given the identity question tends to be posed in the light of concerns about a polity's governability, the assumption is generally that a common European identity would need to encompass all EU citizens, or at least a sizeable majority of them. In other words,

it is expected to extend widely across the inhabitants of a politically defined territory. (Note here the ambiguity of the word 'common', which
denotes both something shared and something banal, something of the
'common people'.) Yet in principle it need not be an inclusive, mass
phenomenon: one might equally conceive it as the reserve of an elite, a
form of distinction perhaps, functioning like French aristocratic culture
in the early modern period as a basis for reciprocal recognition amongst
Europe's elites. Access to European identity would be exclusive to those
of the most exquisite refinement and good taste. That the matter is seldom cast in this way is testament to the origins of the identity debate
in political concerns at least partly shaped by modern ideas of universal
citizenship and political equality.

European identity: a foolish myth?

The most defensible conception of a common European identity has
something to do, therefore, with stable and reciprocal practices of identification between all or most inhabitants of a given territorial space. Alternative conceptions are either dogmatic, incoherent, or best captured
with a different vocabulary. As we switch to the empirical question of
whether such practices of identification currently exist on a European
scale, we are confronted with largely negative findings. Despite clear
efforts by the EU institutions to cultivate them, they remain rather thin
on the ground.

The absence, or at least marginality, of something one might call European identity seems apparent however one investigates it empirically.
For those who seek its traces in Eurobarometer opinion polls, popular
willingness to declare attachment to 'Europe' and 'Europeans' generally
emerges as weak (Duchesne, 2008; Kohli, 2000). There are notable differences across countries and social groups (Fligstein, 2008), but this
merely reaffirms the absence of mass regularity of the kind 'identity'
would suggest. While there are certainly those willing to declare that
they 'feel European', how far this translates into meaningful practices
of identification away from the polling context is unclear. For those
using interview techniques, the finding tends to be that 'Europe' rarely
provokes an emotional response, instead being a point of indifference
or resignation (Duchesne *et al.*, 2010; White, 2011). Only those with
extensive factual knowledge feel themselves qualified to discuss Europe
in depth: it is a topic one *learns* (in schools, or in the financial press)
rather than an object of spontaneous affection (Gaxie *et al.*, 2010). For
scholars taking an ethnographic approach, for instance, studying the
self-understanding of mobile elites as they move across Europe in search
of jobs, romance or adventure, the finding tends to be not that they have

subsumed themselves within a European collective, but rather that they have taken modest steps towards 'de-nationalization', that is, towards freeing themselves of existing territorial ties (Favell, 2007). Researchers of border communities meanwhile report that the removal of physical barriers to movement has often been accompanied either by forms of symbolic 'rebordering' (that is, new forms of separation, for example, between the Poles and Germans of Słubice/Frankfurt-an-der-Oder), or the development of discourses of local exceptionalism (for example, consciousness as a 'border region' that transcends the usual categories of allegiance) (Asher, 2005, Meinhof, 2001). Clearly, the uncertainty regarding which research methods are best suited to studying collective identity leaves scope for those dissatisfied with a negative finding to argue that it is the method rather than the object which is faulty; still, there does seem to be a broad convergence of results across these varied approaches. In short, while changes in the self-understanding of Europeans seem to be happening, they are not generally happening under the European sign, and do not entail patterns of reciprocal identification co-extensive with a pan-European space.

Of course, it may be premature to conclude where such changes are leading. Perhaps these practices of identification will emerge. In the meantime, one option is to revise our conception of European identity in a more realist direction. Diffuse feelings of sympathy towards others as Europeans are, it might be argued, admittedly hard to discern and, in the most literal sense, European identity is illusory. Yet perhaps the idea is meaningful nonetheless. Even if individuals themselves show few signs of such an identity, and can discern no such thing when plumbing the depths of their consciousness, if they can be persuaded *others* feel such a thing, at least at critical moments, then it might exist in virtual form. As a feeling people project onto others rather than themselves, a concept they assume must have meaning even if it means little to them, 'European identity's' effect might be to encourage people to act *as though* they shared in such a thing, even when they did not. Identity might then be seen as a fiction in the strict sense, but a useful fiction. Such a position represents a third, *inter-subjective* conception of European identity. Although it is little discussed in debates on European identity, such a conception has equivalents in the theory of public opinion (for example, Noelle-Neuman, 1984). It implies an interesting and feasible research question: how far people think others subscribe to a European identity (or how far they are willing to be persuaded by such a claim). Possibly the results would mirror those found by conventional approaches, but possibly not: certainly these second-order beliefs may be more susceptible to manipulation than the brute feelings of individuals. European identity would probably not be the first collective identity to exist primarily as a dubious but widely held conviction. The famous 'permissive consensus' may be seen as founded exactly on the widespread belief that 'most people' favoured European integration and therefore 'I' will go along with it, with resistance building precisely when the beliefs of others were put in question by certain landmark referenda results.

Whether this back-door variant has purchase or not, sooner or later a normative issue arises: is a common European identity such a benevolent notion that it is worth rehabilitating even in this rather mythical fashion? Arguably at least some versions of the idea constitute not only an illusion but a dangerous illusion. First, if, as we have argued, any meaningful application of the term 'identity' requires the supposition of a stable pattern of reciprocal practices of identification encompassing all, or nearly all, members of a given realm, it points to a rather consensual image of social relations. One sees this, in particular, in those conceptions of European identity which focus on shared cultural traditions inherited from the past. Such images have little to say about the diversities and adversarialisms one associates with a pluralist political community: antagonisms are likely to be denied within the community and turned outward on the world beyond it. Identity-talk is generally a means to convince people that they are alike and that their relations are harmonious, often with the purpose of making them easier to govern. As a model of citizenship it has clear tendencies to conformism, complacency and acquiescence. Of course, defenders of the concept will say this is a misconception: that they have in mind something far more polysemic, with individuals free to disagree on what European identity means and how they will enact it. Yet the further one emphasizes fluidity and disagreement, the less reason one has to speak of identity at all. As Brubaker and Cooper put it (2000: 11), 'it is not clear why weak conceptions of "identity" are conceptions of *identity*. The everyday sense of "identity" strongly suggests at least some self-sameness over time, some persistence, something that remains identical, the same, while other things are changing. What is the point in using the term "identity" if this core meaning is expressly repudiated?'

Second, by setting the bar so high on the kind of social integration needed for a viable polity, the concept can also acquire conservative connotations, acting as a resource for those who wish to argue a population is *un*governable and that certain political initiatives must therefore never be attempted. Here again, there is a performative dimension to appeals to European identity. The notion that Europeans lack a common identity can be used to de-legitimize transfers of wealth from affluent parts of the EU to poor, or the strengthening of the European Parliament *vis-à-vis* other EU institutions. Fair enough, one might say, if reciprocal practices of identification are indeed the precondition for such initiatives. Yet such a sweeping claim can be no more than a hypothesis, and an extremely difficult one to test at that. One should be sceptical of those bearing decisive evidence in its favour. When it is observed that 'Europeans' are reluctant to see the supranationalization of taxation powers because they 'lack a sense of European identity', the listener might ask themselves whether it is not rather that there are powerful individuals who wish to prevent such an outcome, and who, rather than debate the merits of such an initiative, wish to give people a reason why it is impossible.

Beyond European identity

To criticize notions of European identity is not to underestimate the importance of the political question we began with. There are those who would rubbish the idea of European identity on the grounds that the EU institutions need nothing but the coercive force of the law to govern, and nothing but a trail of constitutional transfers of power to guarantee their legitimacy. But these are bad grounds on which to reject the notion. Social integration of one kind or another seems both empirically and normatively necessary if the EU is to persist in an acceptable form – just not the kind 'European identity' implies.

There are various ways of conceiving transnational political community without appeal to European identity. One is to emphasise the variety of perspectives people take on Europe as opposed to the singular view conjured by the term 'identity'. This type of 'narrative diversity' has been proposed as an already existing reality for Europe's intellectual elites (Lacroix and Nicolaidis, 2010), even if questions remain regarding how far it permeates European societies as a whole. Another possibility is to avoid altogether the search for a diffuse set of sympathies towards 'Europeans' in general, looking instead to non-territorial forms of subjecthood which draw together some but not all. Political categories such as Left and Right, and ideological labels such as conservatism, liberalism and socialism, are of potential relevance here (White, forthcoming). So too are social categories which evoke equivalence of experience according to occupation or socio-economic status (for example, 'public sector workers', 'farmers', 'journalists'), and the practices of cross-national comparison which may generate receptiveness to them (White, 2011). Issue-specific concerns and relations of adversarialism seem as plausible a basis for cross-national allegiances as the widely inclusive ties of European identity, and are arguably more consistent with political pluralism. Rather than an entity reified and made the target of identification, 'Europe' and its political arenas are best seen as a terrain on which events, actions and diverse experiences unfold – the stage rather than the heroic actor.

'European identity' as a phrase is likely to be with us for some time, as various actors have reason to use it. Even empty phrases can be real in their consequences if enough people take them seriously, but it is not clear that we are at that point, or even heading in that direction. As something more substantial, the notion is yet more remote. European identity is an illusion, and some would say a foolish one. But it has been invented to respond to a genuine problem, one that will persist for as long as efforts to govern Europe as one.

Chapter 7

The Uncertain Future of the Euro

Editors' introduction

When the euro was introduced in 2002, many claimed that this was the most momentous event in the history of the European Union since the Rome treaties in 1957. And they were right: no other move towards integration has had the same potential of tying together the fates of the, currently, 17 member states in the eurozone. If any illustration were necessary for this, the eurozone crisis of 2010/11 has provided ample and unwelcome evidence. Since late 2010, the drama of a potential default of some highly indebted eurozone member states has kept EU leaders and global financial markets on their toes. The actual or looming contagion of the problem to the whole EU makes this crisis probably the most serious in the history of the Union.

Most experts recommend a move towards a real economic union, or else the eurozone will break up. In fact, some early proponents of a common European currency had hoped that its introduction would be a major step towards a truly federal state (Tsoukalis, 1977). No wonder then with the stakes so high, that emotions and controversy linked with the euro were always intense. Already the first plans for Economic and Monetary Union, culminating in the doomed Werner plan of 1970, were marred by conflicts between those who advocated a fiscal union and close economic coordination as essential parts of a common currency, and others who thought that a fixed exchange rate and transfer mechanisms in the case of imbalances would do. When, at the Maastricht summit in 1991, it was decided that the euro would be in fact introduced, there was a tacit hope among the deeply sceptical countries owning the most stable currencies, especially Germany, that the convergence which was necessary to sustain a common currency would happen over time (Dyson and Featherstone, 1999). A Stability and Growth pact was put in place in 1997 to force euro members to stick forever to the strict rules which had been required for accession. The European Central Bank was given unprecedented independence to pursue a monetary policy for the whole euro area. Nonetheless, the fact that the euro was a currency not backed by a truly federal structure caused lingering doubts about its future (Dyson, 2008; Torres et al., 2006).

As the Greek crisis has shown, the hopes for convergence were misguided, at least over the short run. Critics who had pointed to the flaws in the construction of the single currency saw themselves confirmed (Feldstein, 2012). Others interpreted the austerity measures imposed on Greece as just the most flagrant expression of the anti-growth bias of the euro (Schmidt, 2011). Increasingly, voices in Europe, especially from the far Left and Right, are calling for a reintroduction of national currencies. At an emergency summit in December 2011, the UK decided to opt out of the reform plans agreed to by the other 26 EU members. This conjured up the scenario of an eventual exit of the UK from the EU which is a prospect relished by many British conservatives. Most EU politicians, however, remain adamant in their support for the currency and do not tire to point out the advantages of the euro. Like the EU, and probably even more so, the euro remains a deeply contested project, the future of which is uncertain.

Amy Verdun argues that the euro has a future. The current crisis should be seen as an opportunity to remedy the undeniable flaws in the construction of the common currency. Tal Sadeh thinks that the euro in its present form will not survive. Due to the inherent tensions, he predicts that only a core of the former eurozone will remain.

The euro as a core project of European integration features prominently in other chapters of this volume. Its overall impact on the European project is discussed in Chapter 1, while Chapter 6 deals with its role in fostering a European identity. Chapter 7 discusses whether monetary union also led to a more efficient regulation of financial markets.

7.1 The euro has a future!

Amy Verdun

Since January 2010, the European Union (EU) has been on a rollercoaster ride. After a newly elected Greek government revised the figure for the country's deficit substantially upwards in late 2009 and subsequently conjured up the prospect of default for a member of the eurozone, European policy makers struggled in vain to contain the problems. At the time of writing (late 2011) these have taken on proportions so large that the future of the euro area as a whole appears to be at stake. An increasing number of commentators have begun to forecast the end of the euro. The surprising depth of the pessimism regarding the future of the euro shows that the revolutionary pooling of sovereignty implied by the common currency is still a phenomenon which people find hard to understand. This essay demonstrates why the euro might be more resilient than these doomsday thinkers predict. Rather than spelling the end of monetary union, I argue that the crisis offers an opportunity to deal with widely known flaws of euro governance, which, for political reasons, were not tackled during the creation and early years of the common currency (Heipertz and Verdun, 2010; Verdun, 2000). In order to make this assessment, I review the reasons for the creation of the euro, some of the problems of its institutional design, the challenges to making changes to its institutional architecture and, finally, I discuss why the crisis might offer an opportunity for the European integration process

The reasons that the euro is worth fighting for are well-known and many: the intimate link between the euro and European integration; the uncertainty about the cost of unwinding the common currency, the continued benefits of the euro in terms of strengthening the single market, such as the provision of transparent prices across Europe and increasing trade and economic activity across borders.

The benefits of Europe's single currency

The founding fathers of the European Union had already envisaged that a unified Europe eventually would need a single currency. In 1949, Jacques Rueff, advisor to French President Charles De Gaulle, famously said: 'L'Europe se fera par la monnaie ou ne se fera pas [Europe will be made by the currency, or it won't be made]' (cited by Van Raepenbusch, 2004: 61). Indeed academics and politicians alike have argued that the full benefits of market integration can only be realized by having a single currency. In the late 1960s, the leaders of the then European Community (EC) realized that a single currency among EC member states would lead to lower transaction costs for cross-border trade in the Common Market, eliminate the rampant exchange rate volatility in the EC, achieve more independence from the US dollar and US economic policy making, and create a symbol of greater unity amongst the members. Politicians and academics presented an increasing number of plans. At the Hague Summit of 1969, the EC members mandated an expert group under the chairmanship of Luxembourg's Prime Minister Pierre Werner to create a blueprint. The Werner plan was accepted in 1970. However, due to the oil shock and different national responses to the crises of the early 1970s, the plans to create a European Monetary Union (EMU) failed.

Instead, a European Monetary System (EMS) was established in 1979 and with it an Exchange Rate Mechanism (ERM) that ensured that European currencies stayed within agreed bandwidths. Stable currency rates were seen as fundamental for a common market. The system operated more or less well throughout the 1980s. By the end of the decade, renewed enthusiasm for European integration emerged and the seed to relaunch EMU was planted by mentioning it in the Single European Act. Under the leadership of Commission President Jacques Delors, another plan was drawn up in April 1989 to create Europe's EMU in three stages, culminating in the introduction of the euro no later than 1999. The Delors Committee started off reviewing the earlier 1970 Werner Report and discussed how much balance was needed between centralizing monetary integration versus other domains of economic integration, in particular fiscal policy. After all, if one compares the EU to a mature federation, a federal government has a number of instruments (taxing and spending) to deal with economic woes. The reason Europe's monetary union is called 'Economic and Monetary Union' was because the notion 'economic' still carries within it that 'something' needs to be done to balance monetary policy so as to have not only a good policy mix between fiscal and monetary policy but also to address the necessary convergence of macro-economic performance among member states. However, the enormous transfer of sovereignty required by a real economic union was politically impossible in the 1990s, and thus EMU's design remained asymmetric with economic integration lagging behind monetary integration (Verdun, 1996; 2000). It was assumed that this matter would be revisited in the future. The time has now come to revisit this part of EMU design and to write that unwritten chapter in European history which details the exact form of economic governance to accompany monetary integration.

By the early 1990s into early 2000s, the benefits of monetary integration fulfilled the objectives that had been spelled out in the late 1960s: reduced transactions costs, transparency of prices, easier operation of the single market by having a single currency in that market, and having a currency that would serve as a reserve and trading currency to rival the dollar. Moreover, another benefit had become even more prominent. The system of fixed exchange rates, that had been operational since the start of EMS in 1979, relied strongly on the Federal Republic of Germany. Its central bank (the *Bundesbank*) set interest rates which many other national central banks closely followed. Effectively, Germany had become the leader and other countries followed. They reached the same goal, namely stable exchange rates and low inflation rates; however, they had lost their autonomy in setting interest rates. For them, EMU was attractive because it would replace German dominance over monetary policy with a collective European alternative that would aim at similar objectives: price stability and economic growth.

With the creation of the European Central Bank (ECB), all member states in the euro area had some influence over the setting of European monetary policy. Before EMU, the German central bank would set policies mostly based on the needs of the German economy. In contrast, the ECB considers the entire euro area when determining the level of interest rates. Each of the governors of the national central banks of the eurozone countries has one vote on the ECB Governing Council as do the six members of the Executive Board. So except for Germany, everyone won influence over monetary policy by joining the euro. But of course Germany received something in return. During the ERM period, the deutschmark (DM) often appreciated against other European currencies and had to be revalued. This situation was challenging for German exporters as they competed against goods made in other European countries whose currencies would frequently devalue. High-level political negotiations surrounding revaluations were often challenging and made financial markets jittery. Many analysts also argue that giving up the DM was the price Germany had to pay for its reunification in 1990, so that the post-Cold War period would see a 'European Germany' rather than a 'German Europe' (Janning, 1996). Thus, the euro had and still has a powerful political logic in addition to its economic logic.

Despite some uneasiness about this new European project, Europeans readily accepted the new currency. Initially, consumers noticed increases in prices of day-to-day goods and perceived inflation to be higher than recorded by official statistics. However, in its first ten years, the euro delivered an enviable record of price stability in the eurozone with the inflation rate at less 2 per cent on average. In that sense it scored better than the DM since the Second World War, according to a recent study of the German Federal Statistical Office (Statistisches Bundesamt, 2011). In addition, European tourists enjoyed the ease of using a single currency in the euro area, trade increased substantially among eurozone members, as well as between the eurozone countries and those outside. According to a recent study by McKinsey, the euro boosted growth in all member states (*Die Welt*, 2012). Countries such as Austria, Germany and Finland saw their GDP increase by 6 per cent or more in 2010. While countries like Greece and France are estimated to have gained much less, the euro was still a factor enhancing growth. No wonder, that many of the new member states were keen to adopt the euro as soon as possible. The cost of borrowing money went down, particularly in those countries that suffered from high costs of attracting funds prior to euro adoption. They experienced a major increase in the availability of cheap credit in the first decade of EMU. While they did not utilize this opportunity to reform their economies, keeping the lid on budgetary deficits and reducing public debt in good times, one cannot really blame the euro for the ensuing opportunism of governments and investors in these countries. National governments and EU leaders chose to ignore the writing on the wall when various member state governments were openly flouting the budgetary rules. Despite this, the new currency still rose quickly to prominence in international currency markets as public and private investors purchased the euro in order to diversify their reserves (Zimmermann, 2012). The whole world has profited from the existence of a second reserve currency, which in the future also might be able to exact some discipline on US monetary policy.

An effective response to a serious crisis

Since the start of the euro, there have been sceptics across the globe arguing that the euro would collapse. Harvard economist Martin Feldstein, for example, famously argued in a 1997 *Foreign Affairs* article that the euro could lead to increased conflict (perhaps even war) within Europe and between Europe and the US (Feldstein, 1997b). Indeed, as we have seen above, the euro was created without a fully fledged federalist framework and thus lacked the necessary institutional structures to deal with difficult times. It does not have a centralized government or a central budget to deal with imbalances among member state economies. The creators of the euro had put their confidence in a so-called 'no bail out clause' and rules that would ensure that budgetary deficits and public debt of member states would not exceed agreed ceilings. Putting their trust in those rules, they chose to eschew institutional structures for situations in which a massive economic crisis would lead to heavy indebtedness in member states. The architecture also does not include effective oversight of banking and financial systems at the EU level or a sufficiently empowered statistical office to fight against the cooking of statistics as in the Greek case.

The 2007–8 financial crisis followed by the economic crisis of 2009 and the sovereign debt crisis of 2010–11 has exposed these flaws. In the first stage of the crisis, after the Lehman collapse, the ECB intervened quickly and decisively with huge funds that helped avoid a complete financial meltdown. In this phase, the ECB was rising to the occasion and the central bank would continue to do so in later periods when credit was tight or bond markets worried. The crisis, however, soon showed the limits of cooperation. The British economist Charles Goodhart (2009) put it bluntly, 'in the EU, banks are international in life, but national in their death'. Elaborating a common EU strategy to deal with the financial crisis proved too slow and member state governments thus turned to domestic solutions. Moreover, the EU did not have any large funds at its disposal that could be tapped into at a time of crisis. Another vulnerability is that collective action in the EU is reliant on national parliamentary approval. EU decision makers eventually sought to deal with this shortcoming by creating the European Financial Stability Facility (EFSF) and there is intense debate about a deepening of integration through eurobonds or a real fiscal union. They saw themselves also forced to harmonize economic policies faster than they would have liked.

These far-reaching developments are the ultimate result of the crisis that erupted when the newly elected government of Greece under George Papandreou let it be known that its budgetary deficit was much larger than reported by the previous government, namely 12.8 per cent instead of 3.6 per cent of GDP (see also Featherstone, 2011). The result was a chain reaction of responses ranging from rating agencies downgrading Greek debt to an increase in the cost of lending for the Greek government. The European member state governments had a hard time deciding what to do in response to this problem. They were facing two possible scenarios. They could decide not do anything because the Treaty on the Functioning of the European Union, Article 125, does not allow the EU to bail out a member state that is running a large debt and has difficulties to refinance this debt. Or they could decide to help out anyway, something that is allowed by Article 122. Germany, led by Chancellor Angela Merkel, was initially reluctant to help. Effectively a bail-out is a transfer from one group of people (tax payers in the member states) to those holding Greek debt. A default would affect not only investors within Greece but also outside Greece and many of them were banks in other EU member states (notably in France). Yet, for Greece to be able to pay back the loans implies that it would need to restructure to become more competitive and generate more growth. It also meant that if this were done for Greece then in future it should also be done for other member states, should that prove necessary.

None of this was planned for in the original architecture of EMU as per the Maastricht Treaty and changes made to the rules of the so-called Stability and Growth Pact (SGP) (Heipertz and Verdun, 2010). The SGP and the Treaty required that member states keep their debt to 60 per cent of GDP or – in case a country started at a high debt – would be reducing its debt and move closer towards the target. The budgetary deficit of member states was to be no more than 3 per cent of GDP. Throughout the 2000s, however, member states had difficulties at various times complying with these rules. Importantly, when France and Germany were violating the rules in 2003 they managed to obtain an exemption. This was widely understood to be against the spirit of the Pact and it undermined the belief in these rules as well as the credibility of sanctions if the rules were violated.

Eventually, in May 2010, the euro debt crisis came to a climax when EU leaders needed to decide whether they would let Greece default or if they would provide it with enough funds so that it could renew its loans. They opted for the latter and created a new European Union fund: the

European Financial Stability Facility (EFSF). In the first instance it received 750 billion euro. The EU and IMF made 110 billion euro available to assist Greece.

Unfortunately, however, the problems did not go away. They also affected the other countries in the periphery of Europe. By November 2010, Ireland was given a financial support package of loans for the amount of 85 billion euro with contributions from the eurozone member states through the EFSF, bilateral loans from Denmark, Sweden and the UK (countries not in the eurozone), assistance from the IMF and even an Irish contribution (from the national pension fund). In May 2011, Portugal also received a 'financial and economic support package' of 78 billion euro. The crisis reached a new stage when, in late 2011, the cost of borrowing for Italy, the eurozone's third-largest economy, and Spain started to rise above sustainable levels. Taken together, these countries would be considered too big to bail out. In July and August, the ECB had been buying up sovereign debt of countries in difficulty in order to provide those countries with the funds they needed. But in order to stabilize the euro further, institutional changes were required. The crises in Greece and Italy in November quickly entered the political domain, ultimately costing the political life of Prime Minister Berlusconi in the wake of the resignation of Greek Prime Minister Papandreou. Both men have been replaced by technocrats with ample experience in European institutions. Their choice of technocratic leaders with strong European credentials is an indication that the elites in both countries are reaffirming their support for a European future of their respective countries.

The way forward

As has been made clear, the original designers of EMU were aware of the asymmetries in the institutional design. What is often not mentioned is that this design was meant to leave the door open to the exact expression of what steps towards deeper political and economic integration would be needed in the future. The reason it was not initially designed as a fully fledged federal state or a larger mandate for EU institutions to borrow, tax and spend, or to coordinate budgetary policy through a supranational body, was the lack of clarity regarding whether there would have been sufficient support for these steps to be taken.

Many Europeans consider the euro now as an achievement, a right or entitlement they would loathe to give up. Indeed, for many the euro is the symbol of successful integration, one that gives consumers and citizens a concrete token of the entire European integration process that has brought to the European continent peace and prosperity.

Indeed, despite the enormous challenges, leaders of EU member states to date are determined to save the euro. The euro symbolizes many different aspects of successful European integration: it reinforces the advantages of the single market; it is something that every citizen can experience first-hand; and there is a widespread feeling that, although the problems in the eurozone were caused in part by poor accounting, poor governance and dishonesty by the Greek governments for their deficit reporting, it is short-sighted to blame only Greece for the problems. Some of the structural imbalances were insufficiently recognized in advance of the financial crisis, and it is challenging to determine who should pay for the cost of the situation and how best to devise a scheme that would spread the burden in a fair way.

What might be some solutions to the current problems? Some have already been considered and will likely be further consolidated in the near future. The EU will become more closely involved in monitoring the budgetary deficit and fiscal debt of member states; the ECB and the European Financial Stability Facility (EFSF) will remain important institutions in ensuring that credit is made available to member states that are suffering from the lack of confidence in financial markets. Various analysts think that so-called eurobonds would be the solution (Jones 2011; von Weizsäcker and Delpla, 2011). These bonds would be drawn on the collective instead of issued by individual member states. Having eurobonds would reduce the likelihood that financial markets would attack one particular country. Finally, an orderly Greek default would require more funds to be mounted centrally and the EU needs to find funders to assist with replenishing the EFSF. It would need to be prepared for the effects of this default in the region and draw up a plan for containing the contagion. It would also need to develop further the rules on budgetary policies, management of government finances and some core macro-economic indicators. Perhaps this episode will offer the Europeans another opportunity to review the democratic credentials of the EU, and ask itself the question whether the time might also be ripe for deeper integration in political representation, so as to include citizens and EU level politicians more explicitly. Early steps have been taken. At a European Council meeting of December 2011, all member states, but one, agreed to move forward towards a new enhanced system of surveillance which would lead towards closer integration of fiscal policy. The UK was the only member state that was uncomfortable with changing EU treaties to support such a solution to the euro crisis. Euro member states are also following the example of Germany by introducing so-called 'debt brakes' in their constitutions, which should put limits on future over-spending (*The Economist*, 2011). The alternative, demise and disintegration, is not something that is supported by many citizens or indeed by politicians. It is a time of opportunity for the European project.

Conclusion

As the euro debt crisis continuous to pose greater challenges, it is clear that the governance of the euro and of EMU has to change. To save the eurozone, deeper integration is needed, and should come as no great surprise to those who studied the origins of EMU. The original architects of EMU both in the 1960s and early 1970, as well as those who were instrumental in re-launching it in the 1980s and 1990s, knew they created a 'work in progress'. They foresaw that there would come a moment for change – a time that would demand further, deeper integration. As such, that is nothing new. It is also not exclusive to the EU or the eurozone: it is the basis of nation building, public policy and good governance across the globe. The part that worries people is that they feel the crisis and observe the political impasse in the run-up to the change. It sometimes requires that people observe an external threat before they can make a leap to deepened integration (Verdun, 2000). Of course the major problem that was not foreseen by the original architects is that too many people at this stage are distrustful of the EU, of political leaders in member states, and of leaders at the helm of the EU. They do not see deeper integration (more centralized rules of joint policy-making delegation to the EU institutions) as the solution. It makes the current crisis extra trying. Those in charge of EU institutional design and governance need to balance two tasks. First, they need to be visionary leaders who are crafting the best governance model for EMU, whilst at the same time finding ways to convince national parliamentary representatives and the general public that deeper integration is the way to go.

7.2 The end of the Euro Mark I: a sceptical view of EMU

Tal Sadeh

Between December 2009 and May 2010, and again in the autumn, Irish, Portuguese, Spanish and especially Greek sovereign debt faced huge pressure in the markets, as default risk, once unthinkable, began rising. The 1992 Maastricht Treaty, which established Economic and Monetary Union (EMU) in Europe, specifically ruled out mutual guarantees for member governments' debts ('bail-outs'). However, until 2009 many investors seemed to assume that economic interdependence among the member states would compel governments to do just that in case of a crisis. This assumption was put to the test, as European governments rushed to offer increasing amounts of loan guarantees, with the help of the International Monetary Fund (IMF). A Greek bail-out was followed by Irish, Portuguese and, yet again, Greek bail-outs. Social protest erupted in these countries at the austerity and reform measures imposed by the governments, as part of the loans' conditions. In the summer of 2011, even major member states came under pressure, in response to inconsistent Italian budget policy and concerns that the French government would not be able to fulfil its commitments to rescue the other member states. Political unrest grew in Germany at the prospect of seemingly endless rounds of bail-outs. These developments reminded everyone how difficult EMU is to sustain. Economically inconsequential, and indeed quite costly to some member states, and with little domestic political support to pay its increasingly transparent price, the fate of EMU is argued here to hang on its merits for Franco-German relations. This is why in the next few years the euro area, as we know it, is expected to dissolve in favour of a new currency area without some of the peripheral member states, but with an ever more committed core.

The economic costs of EMU

From a viewpoint of economic efficiency, EMU involves a trade-off between micro-economic gains and macro- economic costs. The gains are potentially derived from expanded trade in goods and services following the elimination of the trade barrier inherent in exchange rate fluctuations and currency conversion costs. However, the establishment of the eurozone increased trade in goods among its member states by no more than a cumulative 10–15 per cent until the mid-2000s, and little more trade creation can be expected in the future as a direct effect of the euro. Even this small effect is suspected as an over-estimation because it is difficult to separate the effect of the single market from the effect of the single currency. And the effect of the euro on trade in services, which form an increasing share of output in the eurozone, and are responsible for a great majority of jobs, remains obscure. Indeed, given the political difficulties in liberalizing trade in services in the EU little can be expected here. Neither can the euro be credited with price convergence in Europe, which is an indicator of trade-driven competition, because most of it is the result of the single market. As of yet, ten years after its launch, there is no evidence that the euro brought large economic benefits to Europe that could not have been realized without it.

The macro-economic costs associated with EMU derive from the loss of monetary policy autonomy and the resulting inability to adjust the exchange rate. Outside EMU, these policy tools are convenient when growth rates diverge significantly among the member states. For example, a eurozone member state undergoing a recession may want to lower the interest rate or see the euro depreciated, but these measures may not be simultaneously appropriate for another member state undergoing an economic boom. Thus, the costs of EMU are lower if growth rates are synchronized among the member states. Unfortunately the opposite is true for the 2000s (Enderlein and Verdun, 2009). Germany entered the eurozone with an over-valued exchange rate but regained competitiveness (and thus exports and growth) through labour market reforms. In contrast Italy (and France) entered with an under-valuation, and lost competitiveness with time. Of the 14 eurozone member states as of 2009, ten (all but Austria, Belgium, Italy and Slovenia) have grown less synchronized with German growth rates in the late 2000s than they were in the 1990s (or Germany became less synchronized with them).

If national growth rates are not synchronized, and fiscal and monetary policies are constrained in EMU, it is imperative to remove rigidities and allow market forces a greater influence on prices and wages. However, prices in the eurozone are known to change very slowly, because of product and labour-market regulations limiting competition. Unfortunately, reforms in the goods and labour markets in Europe have either slowed after the adoption of the euro, or were unaffected by it. Reforms in the goods market are largely attributable to the drive to complete the EU's single market. Substantial wage moderation and erosion of real wages is observed in countries preparing to enter the eurozone in the 1990s, but much less so after the adoption of the euro, with few notable exceptions such as Germany (Alesina *et al.*, 2010). Following the launch of the euro, all EU member states (with the exception of Austria and Spain) slowed their labour market reforms in areas that enhance national economies' capacity to adjust to recessions. Within the eurozone, the differences are huge: Greece has the least liberalized labour market, while Ireland is the most liberalized.

Economic openness can also compensate for the lack of monetary autonomy inherent in eurozone membership. International flows of capital and labour can stimulate a depressed economy. In addition, capital flows restrict a country's ability to set its own interest rate and thus reduce the opportunity cost of adopting the euro, especially in highly open (mostly small) economies (Jones, 2008). Indeed, openness, as measured by the ratio of total exports and imports of goods and services to output, has increased continuously in most member states, as have capital flows. However, on average, such openness is consistently lower in eurozone member states than in non-euro EU member states; within the eurozone it is relatively high in Germany but especially low in Greece, Portugal and Spain. Labour flows are known to be relatively small among EU member states and cannot compensate for the above.

Persistent differences in the rates of price inflation among the member states add to the costs of maintaining the eurozone, because industries in high-inflation countries lose competitiveness. During much of the past decade, Greece, Ireland, the Netherlands and Spain experienced significantly higher annual inflation rates than the eurozone average. Germany, by contrast, has had the lowest inflation. While, on average, inflation has been consistently falling and converging in the eurozone (Greece being an outlier) these differences have nevertheless accumulated. As a result, the common interest rate, set by the ECB, has had different effects on the member states' economies, and exacerbated variation in their growth rates (Enderlein and Verdun, 2009).

Difficult domestic political conditions and rising adjustment costs

From an economic view, therefore, EMU is at best inconsequential (in that observed processes would have occurred even without it), or worse, a wasteful project. However, the same can be said of many countries with a single currency and poorly integrated regions. Whether economic inefficiencies matter for EMU's sustainability depends on how they feed into the political realm. Every currency union has its winners (who then support membership) and losers (who promote opting out or defection). National policy preferences are shaped by the results of this struggle.

A thorough review of the many interest groups affecting the sustainability of EMU is beyond the scope of this short essay. However, it is relatively simple to predict the positions of a few economic groups in this debate, assuming that a high degree of capital mobility is a global feature that is independent of maintaining the euro. On the anti-euro camp are standard tradable goods' industries, especially if they are locked in an uncompetitive exchange rate. This description currently fits much of the industry in the Mediterranean member states. In addition, companies in import-competing and non-tradable sectors (mostly services to local communities) are probably unhappy with the eurozone's constraints on their government's ability to stimulate local demand (including for their products). The growing importance of the service sector and the difficulties (discussed above) of freeing trade in services in the EU (which keep them less tradable than they could be) are bad omens for the euro.

Many important economic groups may be ambivalent or indifferent about the euro. Large multi-national corporations are built to handle complicated country risks and manipulate prices, and in fact, their multinational activities hedge them against currency swings. Companies with innovative products compete mostly over the quality of their products, much less over prices; hence they may be indifferent about the euro. Banks and other financial institutions hold assets that are sensitive to currency risk, but they also profit from trading in such risk. Broadly, banks cheer for policies that help their customers repay their loans, so they tend to echo the other groups' interests. So who is solidly in the pro-euro camp? Exporters should be supportive, to the extent that they are concerned about competitive devaluations in other member states (devaluations designed to improve a country's trade balance, much like a tariff), but only if the exchange rate is locked at a competitive level. This description currently fits the German industry, which may explain calls in Europe for Germany to aid some of the other eurozone member states. This is a rather narrow basis of domestic support for EMU.

Which interest group has the upper hand in this political contest depends in turn on domestic political institutions. These determine the access different groups have to policy making, and the resulting aggregation of preferences into policy. Many institutions can be important here, from electoral laws, to legislatures' regulations, labour market regulations, industrial concentration, and others. For reasons of scope only two important institutional features are considered here, the first of which is cabinet duration (that is, how long governments stay in power).

Cabinet duration is important because long-term currency union membership is supported by durable cabinets, which are less sensitive to short-term calculations. Furthermore, when properly instrumented, cabinet duration can summarize the effect of a vast array of institutions (Sadeh, 2006b: 95–107). Cabinet duration depends on the length of the democratic experience in each country, whether it is a presidential or parliamentary democracy, the electoral law (whether it is majoritarian or proportional, the size of the legislature and the entry threshold to it), the laws governing the legislature's work (the legislature's official tenure, whether and how the legislature can be dissolved, the involvement of the head of state (a monarch or a president) in coalition making, and whether no-confidence motions must be constructive), and ethnic, religious and linguistic fragmentation in society. In the 1990s and 2000s, cabinet duration was on average higher and rising in member states of the eurozone compared with the non-euro member states. This should make EMU more sustainable.

Another important institution is the electoral cycle – unsynchronized electoral cycles among the member states may lead to unsynchronized growth rates, because EU member states manipulate their economies in election years (Sadeh, 2006a). Indeed, over the 1990s and 2000s, Germany's elections have roughly coincided with those of other European countries, but there are important exceptions, such as France, Greece and Spain.

The different economic and political factors that affect EMU's costs, as discussed above, are weighted against one another in an index developed elsewhere (Sadeh, 2006b), which indicates the potential magnitude of adjustments required to maintain membership in the eurozone. The same estimated equation is used here to produce forecasts with revised data for 1992–8, and 1998–2004, as well as new forecasts for 2003–9. Figure 7.1 reports the adjustment indicator for some of the eurozone's member states in relation to Germany, which is an indispensible member state.

This adjustment indicator is on average much higher in 2003–9 than it was in earlier periods. In 2003–9, Greece suffered from a combination of relatively low openness, and unsynchronized growth rates (in industrial output) and electoral cycles with Germany. France suffered likewise from low openness and unsynchronized electoral cycles. Ireland and Portugal's problems were mainly low growth rate synchronization and relatively high inflation. The Netherlands surprisingly also saw a deterioration of its growth rate synchronization, as well as falling cabinet duration. Spain's main (though not only) source of trouble is the low synchronization of its electoral cycle with Germany's. In contrast, Finland and Italy have maintained relatively low levels of the adjustment indicator, mostly because of improved growth rate synchronization. As

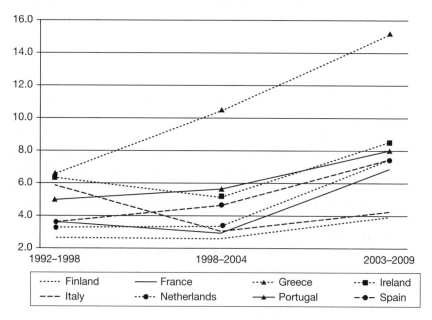

Figure 7.1   *Adjustment indicator with Germany*

explained above this process is not expected to continue in Italy in the long term, but it is consistent with its ability, at least until very recently, to escape the wrath of the bond markets.

Weak institutions and ideas, but strong Franco-German incentives

Might international institutions raise defection costs and maintain membership in EMU even if it is no longer efficient or beneficial to powerful interest groups? This could happen if exit costs are asymmetrically more expensive than entrance costs, because of the time that has lapsed between entrance and potential exit. During this time, integration has perhaps deepened among the member states in the monetary and other issue areas, and political bargains were struck among the member states, spanning a wider range of issue-area linkages. Thus, more would be politically disrupted from an exit than would have been disrupted had the member state not entered the union to begin with. Asymmetric exit costs can also result from highly centralized EU institutions, which would need replication at the national level to enable an exit. Indeed, eurozone member states are thoroughly integrated with the EU's institutional infrastructure, its laws, and its policy surveillance and review mechanisms (Heipertz and Verdun, 2010). EMU is one among many other frameworks of integration in the EU (such as a customs union or security cooperation), into which exit costs can spill. By leaving the eurozone a member states may suffer diminished reputation and influence in the EU, and relegation to a second league.

However, these arguments may be over-stated. For example, it is not clear that the standing in the EU of the UK, Sweden and Denmark would have been significantly enhanced had they joined the eurozone. Nor does it seem that their ability to bargain with the other member state and strike cross-issue deals was hampered. As for the centrality of EU institutions, the European System of Central Banks has a federal structure, which makes defection easier than a more centralized system would (Howarth and Loedel, 2005). National central banks were not abolished when the euro was launched, and they retain their own foreign currency reserves. An abrupt exit without due preparation would surely be disruptive but, in essence, if a member state is determined to leave the eurozone, all it has to do is stop taking phone calls from Frankfurt. Likewise, the growing importance in the past decade of the Council of Ministers (the EU's intergovernmental body) relative to the Commission's (its supranational bureaucracy) bodes ill for the sustainability of the eurozone. Indeed, the scepticism of governments of eurozone member states with regard to the authority of EU institutions has become more consensual, to judge by the manifestos of parties in governments (Sadeh, 2009; see also Chapter 3, this volume).

EMU can also be sustained by a shared set of beliefs and a strong sense of political community among the member states. Indeed, in their party manifestos governments of the eurozone's member states increasingly share core neo-liberal beliefs that underscore EMU (Sadeh, 2009). For example, they are in principle in favour of free enterprise, private property rights, reduced budgets (however difficult this is in practice for them) and a strong currency. However, some of their shared beliefs are inconsistent with the rules of EMU: support is growing for social cushioning mechanisms (social security schemes or social services such as health service or social housing). And member states are diverging in their support for micro-economic reforms. Specifically, they are diverging in their attitudes to the deregulation of markets, economic planning by the state, and their commitment to reduce taxes and to encourage competition by acting against monopolies in favour of small business and consumers.

If cognitive infrastructure is insufficiently conducive to a sustainable eurozone, perhaps the international distribution of power is. Member states of a currency union often need to rally around a dominant state willing and able to use its influence to ensure monetary cooperation (Cohen, 2000). For example, Estonia was arguably willing to maintain its currency link to Germany for many years as a way of escaping Russian domination. Estonia's situation may be common to other Baltic or small eastern European countries, but is not relevant for many other eurozone member states. Instead, Germany and France have traditionally been at the centre of EU politics, with small western European nations following their lead. And, as in the past, so perhaps it is today. Ever since the Cold War ended, Germany's influence in Europe is growing and France's is declining. Both countries still need the EU's multilateral organizations and a common currency, most prominently, to coordinate their adjustments to this process and reduce its costs. A common currency provides Germany's growth and power with legitimacy and acceptance, and prolongs the halo of France's influence in Europe. A Franco-German currency symbolizes this cooperation, and its demise would have great destabilizing consequences in European, and indeed in world politics. It is here where the best argument in favour of sustaining the euro can be found.

Conclusion

The economic arguments in favour of a single European currency were over-stated from the outset. The existence of different national currencies does not form an important trade barrier in economies with developed financial markets, or world trade would never have developed as it has. With hindsight, it is clear that little was gained in terms of trade, synchronization of growth rates and price convergence in Europe that would have not materialized without the launch of the euro. Worse, eurozone membership requires more reform than some member states' politics can swallow. Before the recent global crisis, they did not commit consistently to the imperatives of EMU. The eurozone has reduced interest rates on public debt and created more financial space for public spending (Enderlein and Verdun, 2009). Fiscal discipline was weak, and the costs of membership in the eurozone were piled into public debt. The global credit boom of the 2000s made this easier.

The euro crisis of 2010 exposed these tensions as never before. In response to the crisis, many governments reiterated their commitments to reform and austerity. However, now that the price for staying in the euro is more transparent, it is not clear that a strong supportive coalition exists within each and every member state. Social groups that are asked to make great sacrifices for the sake of fiscal stability may wonder whether leaving the euro is indeed worse for them than staying in. All the more so if they perceive that other groups gain more from membership in the eurozone, but are asked to sacrifice less. Time will tell whether the recent reform efforts are credible and adequate, and whether austerity will not plunge some member states into spirals of falling output and rising deficits. No matter how preferences are aggregated in the different member states, policy making cannot be forever isolated from the interests of EMU's losers. EU institutions cannot prevent a determined member state from leaving the euro, and even a country determined to stay in the eurozone may be pushed out of it by sceptical bond markets. Some of the member states whose membership is more expensive to maintain, will have to leave the eurozone at some point. Of course, departing from the club would be extremely costly for them (Eichengreen, 2010), but staying in may be costlier still, at least for those who suffer from ever harsher austerity packages. Any departure from the eurozone would probably occur under conditions of crisis, as in liberalized markets such a move cannot be managed in a tranquil manner. A departure by one member state might very well set off a domino effect, and it is not clear which country will be the last piece to fall.

That being said, for as long as France and Germany are interested, a common currency between them will survive. Whichever member states remain in the club would have to regain the credibility of their commitment (especially in the wake of a major crisis) by giving up more of their sovereignty (such as the final dismantling of national central banks). This can be tantamount to launching a new currency. Call it the Euro Mark II.

Chapter 8

Can the EU Tame Big Finance?

Editors' introduction

Is the EU able to quickly react to political emergencies? Can member states achieve the required degree of cooperation when they are faced with surprising developments which demand a coordinated response? The global financial turmoil after the collapse of Lehman Brothers in September 2008 was a major test case for the capacity of the EU to meet new challenges. Faced with chaotic markets, a potential meltdown of financial systems in many member states, and the ensuing global momentum towards the re-regulation of 'Big Finance', the EU was called upon to provide a quick and coherent answer to the crisis.

Financial governance seems to be a prime example for a policy field in which experts and bureaucrats decide complicated matters which are not suited for public debate. This technocratic policy making is one of the criticisms which are most frequently levelled against the EU. In that sense, financial regulation is also a test case for the legitimacy of European policy making. This topic therefore encompasses many of the most salient questions in this volume: the efficiency of EU policy making, the debate about the balance between national and supranational competencies, the reconciliation of widely diverging national positions, or the problem of the democratic quality of EU decisions.

Finance was not one of the issues which was high on the agenda of the European Communities during their first decades. The financial systems of the member states displayed very diverse national characteristics. Limited financial integration across borders meant that there was little pressure to coordinate policies in this area. Functional necessities to integrate emerged only slowly when markets in financial services were progressively liberalized during the 1970s and 1980s. The decisive event, putting the problem of financial market regulation firmly on the EU agenda, was without doubt the decision to establish a common currency, which was taken at the Maastricht conference in 1992. It was inconceivable to have a monetary union and at the same time widely diverging national rules on the governance of financial markets. The Commission took the lead in formulating a response to this problem. In 1999, with the so-called Financial Services Action Plan, it published comprehensive recommendations for an integrated financial market

(Dür, 2011). After it became clear that the coordination of the numerous different policy bodies in this area made decision making helplessly slow when faced with the breakneck speed of developments in financial markets, a Committee of Wise Men, chaired by the Belgian economist Alexandre Lamfalussy, established a new framework for expedited decision making by expert committees (Quaglia 2010). The financial crisis provided the impetus to put a comprehensive governance framework into place. Again based on an expert report (the so-called de Larosiére report), a new European System of Financial Supervisors (ESFS) was formed, consisting of a European Banking Authority (EBA), a European Insurance and Occupational Pensions Authority (EIOPA), and a European Securities Authority (ESA). Established on 1 January 2011, this new architecture was supplemented by a European Systemic Risk Board, chaired by the ECB. The EU now has a shining new set of institutions administering a policy field which not long ago was firmly in the remit of national jurisdiction. Will it work?

Daniel Mügge and Jörn-Carsten Gottwald use the case of financial market regulation as a lense to address various dimensions of EU policy making. Gottwald claims that the EU has so far successfully responded to the need for a new regulatory framework. Given the complicated subject matter, it is utopian to expect broad public participation as well as sweeping reforms within a short time. Daniel Mügge disputes this positive assessment and identifies a democratic deficit in this area. According to him, the process also has been cumbersome and ineffective, due to the habitual EU way of muddling through crises. This controversy forms part of the debate in Chapter 7 and illustrates the points made by the authors of Chapter 2 on the efficiency of the EU.

8.1 Regulating financial services in the EU: a case of successful institutional learning

Jörn-Carsten Gottwald

One of the rarely told success stories of European integration is the establishment of a new regulatory regime for financial services between 1998 and 2005. The Financial Services Action Plan (FSAP) of 1999 profoundly changed the regulation of banking, securities trading and insurances within the European Union. A new streamlined method of decision making, the Lamfalussy procedure, allowed for the surprisingly rapid completion of 41 of the 42 policy measures outlined in the FSAP within five years (Commission of the European Communities, 1998; 1999).

The EU had no time to consolidate these huge advances. In 2007, the sub-prime crisis began to hit the United States, triggering the bankruptcy of Lehman Brothers one year later. In turn, the home-grown property bubbles in the United Kingdom, Spain and Ireland burst. National governments all over the globe stepped in to avoid the complete implosion of global finance. Bail-out transfers from the public coffers and anti-cyclical investment programmes to soften the rapid decline of growth rates left national treasuries depleted. The banking crisis spilled over into a sovereign debt crisis, with several members of the European Union classified as being technically insolvent.

In view of these developments, the European architecture for the regulation of financial services has been criticized from various perspective (Posner and Véron, 2010). These negative assessments usually take an over-optimistic view about what financial market regulation can actually achieve. In an ideal world, prudent foresight and effective political leadership by democratically legitimized governments and parliaments would prevent the excesses that triggered the current crisis. The political and economic reality, however, looks strikingly different. For a full understanding of the weaknesses and strengths of the EU's financial regulation, its performance should be neither measured against a utopian benchmark, nor market-based criteria alone.

A broader approach that acknowledges the enormous pressure on regulatory adaptation linked to the specific nature of globalized financial markets, and one that takes into account the limits defined by the European political order, leads to the conclusion that the EU's regulatory regime for financial services is working surprisingly well (Gottwald, 2010). The EU's regulatory regime in this field has been characterized by constant learning from prior experiences, intensive exchange between policy makers, regulators and market participants, as well as the establishment of fast-track procedures to allow for quick action.

Aiming at a moving target: regulating financial services

Financial market regulation is a difficult challenge for every political system: market developments are truly global, 24/7. They are based on the real-time provision of information and the movement of vast amounts of capital around the globe within seconds. Large investment banks, hedge funds or insurance companies have access to capital exceeding most public budgets. They also have an enormous information advantage over political actors. Even the, presumably, most powerful nation in the globalized world, the United States, acts under constraints set by private authorities and companies in global finance. The breakdown of the highly regulated system of Bretton Woods in the early 1970s saw a paradigm shift from finances as a catalyst for trade in 'real' goods and services, to financial services as a profitable market in itself which is often decoupled from the underlying products. Human creativity, ambition and increasingly sophisticated software and technology have triggered a highly lucrative scramble for the creation of ever-new products promising huge returns. In essence, global finance has turned into a global betting game with highly leveraged stakes.

The role of governments in this game is complex: they are referees who supervise the players, the rule-setting bodies; they investigate, judge, and punish foul play while at the same time sending their own players – government controlled banks, debts management agencies, and ministries – on the pitch. To come to terms with these multiple, often contradictory roles, governments needed to diversify their appearance: they sought to pool certain competencies in the hands of more or less independent organizations, such as central banks and committees of experts. But the basic fact remains: governments are in no sense independent authorities *vis-à-vis* private enterprises, customers and investors, but they are fully engaged on all levels and in nearly all areas of financial services. The simple dichotomy of markets versus governments is invalid and politically misleading: in modern societies, governments in nearly all political systems are very active in the markets.

As referees of the game, governments need to be able to compete with the enterprises for information and talent. Revolving doors between financial enterprises and market watchdogs have become a common phenomenon. Leading experts are moving between regulatory bodies and private enterprises fuelling a spiral of innovation: enterprises seek to exploit loopholes in regulation to introduce new products – for example sup-prime mortgage or securitized assets – with which public authorities have to come to terms. The time lag between the introduction of a new product and its regulation can hardly be avoided. Therefore, regulation has to be understood more as a process than a static set of institutions. Any assessment of a regulatory regime for financial services should question how capable it has proved in dealing with changes, the persistent need of being able to provide crisis management and to draw the necessary conclusions in addition to the standard factors, such as transparency, accountability, efficiency and impact on global governance.

Can European member states deal with these challenges? Given the degree of economic and social integration, strictly national answers are not possible any more in the EU. Given that there is no single EU government, the member states have gone for the second-best solution by installing flexible and dynamic structures and committees merging US influences with European traditions.

Learning and adaptation in EU financial services regulation

Financial services regulation in Europe requires the integration of a plethora of different national systems. Dealing with divergent interests and traditions induced a strong dose of creativity and flexibility into the politics of regulatory reform.

Before the crisis of 2007/08 hit Europe, financial services were of little interest to the public. Members of the European Parliament, government representatives and civil society organizations found this highly complex and technical area to difficult to sell to their audiences. In the late 1990s, the gap between the establishment of the single market for goods and services plus the introduction of a single currency and the absence of a EU level of market regulation for financial services became a serious threat to European integration. Without the interest of a broader public – including many academics in the field of European studies – a small group of Brussels-based experts developed a programme to overcome the existing deficits. The resulting FSAP attempted to square several circles: to balance the lack of public interest with the need for democratic legitimacy; to pacify the objective of a single market in financial services with strong objections from member states to allow a transfer of competencies form member states to the EU; to merge significant ideational and practical differences between the member states into a coherent regulatory arrangement: and, finally, to strike a balance between creating ample space for market innovation and consumer protection (including the protection of public authorities and their capacity to fund public expenditure). The Financial Actions Plans paved the way for the recommendations of the Group of Wise Men under Baron Alexandre de Lamfalussy.

The Lamfalussy report called for the definition of a EU regulatory philosophy to produce coherent objectives and attitudes for the development and regulation of financial services, the introduction of a new decision-making procedure to improve the quality and the speed of regulation as well as a new set of regulatory bodies to assemble the necessary expertise and to allow for smooth cooperation between market experts and decision makers. By 2001, the Lamfalussy procedure was put in place and with it a new group of regulatory agencies and advisory bodies.

The Lamfalussy procedure, which was originally introduced for securities regulation and only later extended to the regulation of banking and insurance activities, distinguishes between the underlying broad principles which are still defined in the traditional co-decision method by the European Parliament and the Council of Ministers. Once the basic principles for dealing with a clearly defined matter have been established, however, the decision transfers specific rights to regulate matters to three committees for securities, banking, and insurance (Moloney, 2008). Each regulatory committee consists of representatives from member states' ministries. They work closely with advisory committees consisting of representatives from the member states' regulatory bodies. While in theory these bodies have advisory functions, in practice they wield substantial influence as they bring together those experts who are in charge of implementing regulation at the national level. In most member states, the ministries depend heavily on the input from the regulatory bodies due to their superior expertise. This structure aims at a balance between public oversight, input from democratically elected governments under the general supervision of the EP and the need to have a high level of understanding of market developments and market practices. It takes into account that financial services are too dynamic to leave their oversight to static ministries or traditional state administrations. In addition, it allows for a central role of member states' organizations, which has been a key condition of national governments.

Bringing together representatives from the national regulators alone was considered a major step forward in European regulation, especially so because finally everyone knew whom to contact. In the absence of an explicit politically defined regulatory philosophy, pushing for a better understanding and long-term convergence in regulation was the only chance to slowly overcome the lack of consensus in Europe. Of course, from the perspective of democratic theory, this process should have been led by public discourse and the members of the European and member state parliaments. Given the initial lack of interest, however, keeping the member states in a central role has proven the best track available to overcome the political and sectoral diversity. Overall, the new framework integrates national supervisors but does not substitute them with an EU political order.

In setting up the new regulatory regime, the EU proclaimed transparency, fairness and the development of stable and efficient financial markets as key criteria. Transparency was pursued by documenting all measures proposed and decided on the internet. Online forms invited the interested public to participate in the measures followed by documentation summarizing these submissions. Finding one's way through the draft regulation, statements, commentaries, and calls for proposals, however, requires substantial resources and while the procedures are technically transparent and open for participation from the general public, the old imbalance between well-organized and well-linked industry representation and less-organized and less well-resourced representation of consumer interests remains fundamentally unchanged. Transparency in itself might be a prerequisite for fairness and accountability, but where market participants commented upon the difficulties of obtaining relevant information before the new procedures, the introduction of the Lamfalussy process has generated an information overflow.

Nevertheless, the new regime at least provides the necessary access and tries to integrate societal input into the regulation. According to members of the regulatory networks in Brussels, it is less the actual procedures which limit the involvement of a broader public but rather the wide disinterest in regulation prior to the crisis. Various members of the European parliament who played an active role in the FSAP faced serious challenges to re-nomination and re-election. In their own views, their work on financial regulation had proved very difficult to sell to their constituencies. Therefore, the deficits of public oversight of financial regulation cannot be reduced to insufficient integration of the European Parliament in the development of new regulation. A stronger and more persistent public interest in issues of financial regulation would be a prerequisite for a broader and potentially fairer interest representation. However, matters as technical and complex as financial regulation do not qualify easily as subjects of major public discourse.

The EU regulatory regime and the fall-out from the global crisis

This lack of public interest in financial regulation disappeared instantly with the outbreak of the global financial crisis 2008. Soon, most member states of the EU faced serious difficulties. Quickly, the usual complaints about a lack of leadership by the EU in reacting to the crisis emerged. Most national governments at some stage took measures without proper consultation of European partners and EU institutions. Within two years after the collapse of Lehman Brothers, however, the European Union combined incremental improvement of the existing structure with substantial institutional innovation. Proposals developed by a new group of experts, the so called de Larosière report, fed into the 'Omnibus-Directive' of 2009 creating the European Systemic Risk Board (ESRB) which took up its work in January 2011 to improve the forecast and assessment of financial risks within Europe. A European Banking Authority (EBA), a European Insurance and Occupational Pensions Authority (EIOPA) and a European Securities and Markets Authority (ESMA) were set up. The new European Financial Stability Facility (EFSF) was established in 2010 to support national governments in financial distress. The FSAP had managed to overcome the deeply ingrained national reservations against transferring competencies in the regulation of financial services from the member states to the EU. The current crisis management process, beginning in 2008, even introduced measures of improved budgetary control and strengthened the transfer of competencies from member states to the EU. The interconnectedness of macro-economic policies and financial regulation is thus acknowledged and institutionalized.

While the final outcomes are yet to be seen, the EU regulatory regime has shown a remarkable capacity for adaptation to a profoundly changed international and market environment. Institutional and policy learning is currently driving a broad and deep revision of the existing regime, although these so far represent more of an add-on to the existing structures than a completely new alternative model. Nonetheless, the EU regime for financial services shows a significant ability of adapting to a dynamic market.

In addition to improving financial oversight within the EU, the reforms since 1998 have raised the EU's profile in setting global standards. It has been convincingly argued that the EU is a taker rather than setter of global standards in financial regulation. The crises of the US model in the wake of the collapse of Enron and Worldcom in 2001(Posner, 2010), and again since 2008, however, have opened room for European initiatives. This can be seen in the revision of the Basel rules or in the field of accounting standards, where the EU took the lead and increased the pressure on the US to at least partly adapt. The reforms have made the EU a respected partner in global regulation and increased the European influence on attempts to improve global financial governance within the G20 by extending the scope and reach of supervision.

Conclusion: the benefits and limits of regulation financial services in the EU

If stability and crisis prevention are the gold standard of assessing a regulatory regime for financial services, then the EU has failed. Europe is experiencing one of the worst financial crises in its history, with profound consequences for public budgets and the long-term economic prospects of member states. However, it is simply asking too much of EU financial regulatory policy to prevent such a crisis. Financial markets are too dynamic because they are driven by human creativity and greed, which challenges all attempts at political control.

The European Union still lacks a consensus on the objectives and broader implications of financial services. The huge differences between the financial sector in, for example, the UK or Ireland and continental Europe remain in place. An increasing number of European politicians call for a stronger respect of national interests while the crisis management requires new and deeper forms of integration. Either way, the EU's regulatory regime is destined to continue to change.

This highlights again the ability to adapt to a changing environment and to improve the venues for participation and oversight. In this crucial regard, the EU regime for the regulation of financial services is remarkably successful. Without it, most member states would have been unable to meet the challenges of the current crisis. Globally, the EU has raised its profile and influence regarding future standards and policies. Extensive dialogue with leading powers as well as emerging markets strengthened the EU's representation in regulatory networks. In the G20, the major global forum for coordinating the regulatory and policy responses to the financial crisis, the EU plays an important role as an alternative model to the US and significant rule-setter. Domestically, while the regulatory regime has not been successful in preventing the current crisis, decision makers have established numerous venues for input and representation of societal interests in the process of reform. Transparency and access have improved enormously, as has coordination and cooperation within Europe. The main deficit has been the lack of public interest in the evolution, workings and outcomes of financial market regulation. The underlying weakness of this institutional and procedural arrangement has not been addressed yet. The current crisis might well have the unintended side-effect of addressing these shortcomings.

8.2 The pitfalls of EU governance in financial markets

Daniel Mügge

The times when financial regulation was only of interest to bankers in dark suits are long gone. The rules that govern banks, stock markets, insurances and the like have taken much of the blame for the so-called credit crisis – the financial maelstrom that has engulfed the EU economy since 2007 and has since morphed into a full-blown sovereign debt crisis. Bank losses over the past years have risen steeply. In late 2009, the International Monetary Fund estimated that UK banks alone were heading for losses totalling US $604 billion by the end of 2010 – more than 25 per cent of British gross domestic product (GDP) for 2009. Eurozone banks were set for a further US $814 billion losses, amounting to 7 per cent of eurozone GDP. European citizens have had to foot the bill, with budget cuts hitting everything from welfare provisions to infrastructure investment across the continent.

Unsurprisingly, the credit crisis has challenged EU citizens and policy makers alike to take a hard look at the way financial market rules had been drawn up before the crisis. In particular, has the integration of financial rulemaking in the EU been a boon or a bane for European citizens? Taking stock of the twenty years of uploading powers to Brussels, the overall assessment cannot be anything but sobering. In a nutshell, while EU financial integration failed to live up to its promises, the complex web of multilevel financial institutions that were set up since the late 1990s has shown real flaws: it has dented the European voice internationally, it has spawned more lenient regulation than would have been desirable, it has further removed financial governance from the citizens it should have served, and it has repeatedly been rendered ineffective – both before the crisis and in its direct response to it – by complexity and fragmentation. Grave as they are, these defects come as no real surprise once we disentangle the origins of pre-crisis financial governance in Europe.

Perilous incrementalism and private interests in EU integration

In spite of all their differences, theorists of European integration by and large agree that past integration steps can beget additional reform down the line. In the benign account of this spillover mechanism, any given level of economic integration, for example, a customs union, makes further integration more appealing. Stripped to its essentials, regional integration becomes self-reinforcing. The somewhat less benign version of this mechanism adds an extra twist: integration is not moved forward by the ever greater benefits that each consecutive step towards closer union reveals, but by the shortcomings that become apparent at each level of economic integration. Faced with policy failure, policy makers have to choose between disintegration – which is largely considered unpalatable – or yet further integration. EU integration is a patchwork of incremental policy fixes without any overall master plan that puts everything in its place.

Commonly, this stumbling forward of European integration is not considered a major problem in itself. In the run-up to the credit crisis, however, it was fatal. The eternal construction site, which EU economic governance has been over the decades, turned out to be ill-prepared for the policy challenges that the credit crisis of the late 2000s forced its way. Worse still, the substantive policy generated by fragmented institutions aggravated the financial meltdown and its economic aftermath.

This incrementalism has been compounded by the key role that private interests have played in shaping EU policy and institutions in the financial sector (Mügge, 2010). Over the past two decades, banks, investment banks and stock exchanges have been core players in the policy community that has reformed financial governance in Europe. Industry influence over regulation is nothing new, and it is certainly not limited to the EU (Johnson and Kwak, 2010). Private interests as a driver of, or obstacle to, regulatory and institutional reform have meant, however, that eventual policy has frequently been a compromise between multiple imperatives pulling in different directions (for example, Gadinis, 2008; Singer, 2004), of which the wider public interest in financial stability has been only one. In short, the heavy industry role in financial regulation reinforces its patchwork character – the dangers of which the credit crisis has starkly illustrated.

The elusive benefits of financial integration

To be fair, drawbacks of financial integration and supranational governance in Europe could be balanced by their economic benefits to citizens. The multilevel governance of financial markets in Europe – including their regulation and supervision – is tightly linked with the project of building an integrated market for financial services and capital, and the desire to do the latter has normally been the key justification for a partial up-loading of competencies to the supranational level. Also empirically, integration of governance has been a corollary of market integration, meaning that in any assessment of their merits, the two cannot be completely disentangled.

The official justification for building a single financial market – removing capital controls, allowing financial services to cross borders freely and partially centralizing governance in Brussels – was that it would boost efficiency in capital allocation and lower the cost of funds to governments and enterprises. This latter effect was deemed to be most pronounced in the peripheral regions of the EU, where financial markets had remained under-developed by Northern European standards.

In the years before the crisis, the Commission set out to gather empirical evidence to see whether financial integration had lived up to its promises (European Commission, 2007). The findings were mixed. Many indicators seemingly pointed in the right direction, including the convergence of interest rates paid by EU governments for their debt. Others underlined that much financial activity continued to be concentrated in Europe's traditional financial centres, while a catch-up of the Mediterranean countries in particular proved elusive. The record looked positive, if less impressive than had been hoped.

The crisis that erupted in the late 2000s has shattered this optimistic view. Greece emerged as the obvious example of how, what looked like, beneficial effects of EU financial integration turned out to be a treacherous mirage. To cut a long story short, the extension of 'sophisticated' finance to ill-prepared countries meant that the latter would be swamped in credit, generating temporary economic calm that could masquerade as economic progress. With financial markets lulled into complacency by economic and monetary union (EMU), which eradicated exchange rate risk, the abundance of funds fuelled not sustainable investment, but excessive consumption relative to productive capacity and bubbles in unproductive sectors such as real estate. To complete the picture, 'modern' financial techniques could be used to hide the true state of financial affairs from outside observers, including other European governments. A Goldman Sachs-arranged swap agreement of the Greek government, which turned sovereign debt into a financial service and thereby allowed Athens to fool its EMU partners, was a stark example (Hope *et al.*, 2010).

Even in light of this, it remains plausible – not more and not less, given the lack of hard empirical evidence – that EU financial integration has also had some positive effects. But with the belief in the unequivocally and automatically positive effects of unfettered markets dented by the recent crises, such arguments surely are not enough to justify the Europeanization of a policy domain that after all stands central to national economies.

Which other yardsticks should then be applied to assess whether, on balance, pre-crisis arrangements in EU financial integration have served European citizens well? Three stand out which the remainder of this contribution will assess. First, have multilevel institutions enhanced the stability of financial systems – arguably the second core feature of financial systems in addition to their effect on economic performance? Second, have they rendered policy making more democratic, allowing citizens to shape policy in light of their own preferences? And third, have they ensured a greater voice for these preferences in global financial governance?

Multilevel governance and financial stability

In addition to a cheaper cost of capital through cross-border integrated markets and hence higher levels of liquidity, the second professed goal of EU financial integration was to make the European economy more like the American one with its central role for capital markets. In the mid-1990s, the US economy appeared to have found the key to combining economic vigour and growth with low inflation. The bursting of the dot-com bubble already undermined the myth of the new IT-led economy. The real challenge to the ostensible strength of the American growth model came with the sub-prime crisis, however, which exposed just how much of the US economic miracle since the early 1990s was built on financial quicksand. If it were not for the global pre-eminence of the US dollar, the USA might easily face fiscal and financial challenges not unlike those of the Southern European economies. The downgrade of the USA's credit rating by Standard & Poor's in August 2011 brought out these difficulties for the world to see.

The European financial regulatory project has been bent on imitating US 'success' in the mid-1990s – and hence exposed the European economy to similar dangers when the sub-prime house-of-cards finally came tumbling down. A corollary to increased cross-border integration was increased competition – advocated forcefully by the champions league of European financial firms in the erroneous belief that it would suit their long-term interests. To be sure, this competition was an artefact of the rules prevailing in Europe more than of the fact that they were generated through multilevel institutions. That said, one key argument in favour of such governance – argued to outweigh potential disadvantages – was that it was necessary to allow intra-European financial integration and the competitiveness of European firms in the global market place. In this way, multilevel governance and the emergence of super-charged investment banking in Europe were tightly linked.

The credit crisis exposed the limits and, indeed, inherent fallacies of finance as a turbo-booster for economic growth. More importantly for the present argument, however, it revealed the detrimental effects of using reformed European governance as a tool in a transatlantic competition that in the end generated only losers. Countries such as Canada and, to some degree, Australia refused to be lured into this competitive game – and the limited fall-out of financial crisis there has proven them right. The project of EU integration in financial governance certainly did not produce the financial stability that would have been in the interest of all EU citizens.

The democratic deficit in financial regulation

Of course, able financial governance produces not only collective goods, such as economic growth and financial stability. It also has a plethora of socio-economic effects whose costs and benefits are distributed unevenly throughout society. Financial system design structures the way in which citizens accumulate their pensions, it influences the availability of mortgages and credit in general, and it affects employment opportunities and conditions through the terms on which it supplies credit to corporations.

If citizen preferences about these characteristics of financial governance diverge, and if there is no obvious optimum solution, it becomes imperative that financial governance is in some form democratic, meaning that it allows citizens to formulate and articulate policy preferences and to make them count in the policy process.

The complexity of financial governance and regulation makes citizen input into rulemaking inherently difficult – whether in the EU or elsewhere. That said, multilevel governance has further damaged democratic citizen participation – 'input legitimacy' in Scharpf's (1999) terms. Lest the EU regulatory machine become atrophied to the point of complete immobility, key decisions have been outsourced to a web of expert committees. In the early 2000s, much of the rule design was handed to the so-called Lamfalussy committees, EU-level clubs of national regulators (Mügge, 2010; Posner, 2009; Quaglia, 2008). Post-crisis reforms adopted in 2010 will further strengthen these committees and, now re-branded as fully fledged 'regulatory authorities', equip them with their own staff. The net effect of such reforms have been that national parliaments have been reduced to all but rubber stamping policy negotiated between the supranational committees, EU finance ministries, the European Commission and the European Parliament (EP).

The latter would seem the most likely substitute for citizen representation in regulation. But European citizens themselves largely refuse to be won over by the EP's claim to citizen representation. More gravely, the crisis has starkly illustrated the deficiencies of a one size fits all-approach to regulation (Mügge *et al.*, 2010). The regulatory preferences of stakeholders will differ with the specific 'variety of capitalism' within which they find themselves, given the way financial systems interact with pension arrangements, labour markets, corporate governance, and the like. The EP is unable to accommodate these differences, let alone heed them in its own policy output. *Ceteris paribus*, the multilevel governance arrangement in EU finance has further removed financial rule making from European citizens without any unambiguous improvement in the quality of regulation it produces compared to member states themselves.

A European voice in global financial governance?

Financial transactions face no border controls when leaving the EU. Finance is integrated globally, and even though Europe has furthered rather than obstructed this globalization of finance, the latter is still a constraint that cannot be ignored. The crisis has demonstrated just how important global rule coordination is, and scholars of EU finance have argued that the uploading of governance in the EU itself has also boosted the standing of supranational bodies in the rest of the world, particularly *vis-à-vis* their US counterparts (Bach and Newman, 2007; Posner, 2009). The European Commission and even the Committee of European Securities Regulators (CESR), the Lamfalussy committee for capital markets that was founded less than a decade ago, have been in formal dialogue with non-European authorities and participated in some key forums, including for example the G20.

In principle, pooling European influence to shape global rule making more effectively could be a powerful argument in favour of the EU institutional set-up. The boosted role of supranational representation on the international scene is only one half of the equation, however. The competencies that EU bodies now enjoy are those that member states had held earlier – and they have now lost. The incremental and patch-work character of European integration has fragmented responsibilities between national and supranational authorities. Member states are commonly locked into legally binding EU-level agreements, robbing them of the freedom to actively negotiate revised rules internationally. At the same time, new rules can only be introduced in Europe by qualified majorities in the European Council with the approval of the EP. The room for manoeuvre of the Commission or CESR is thus also strictly limited.

This internal complexity has meant that no-one can represent European citizens at the global negotiating table – neither individual governments nor supranational bodies. As member states struggle to find compromises that are workable within the EU itself, coordination with the rest of the G20 largely falls by the wayside. EU multilevel governance in finance has not boosted the chances for effective global governance with a strong European imprint.

Conclusion

Has the multilevel set-up in EU financial governance been a boon or a bane for European citizens? The complex division of tasks between supranational bodies and member states has clear downsides while the concrete benefits remain elusive. To be sure, a number of these shortcomings could be remedied by more daring concentration of competencies in supranational hands – think for example of the external representation of European interests or a stronger and more effective role for the EP.

The history of European integration is a cause for scepticism, however. The plethora of interests within the EU, and the institutional complexity that the union has developed to deal with them, mean that grand designs have rarely been implemented – and even those that have been, such as EMU, have a mixed record at best. As new challenges to financial governance emerge, the EU will therefore probably not respond with a massive regulatory overhaul but with its customary mode of reform and adaptation: muddling through.

Chapter 9

The EU's Cohesion Policy: Reducing Disparities?

Editors' introduction

The origins of the EU's cohesion policy, the EU's only broadly redistributive policy, go back to the Rome Treaties (1957). Ever since, its central aim has been to reduce disparities across European regions, reflecting a belief that market mechanisms alone would not achieve this objective. Over time, however, member states have asked the Community institutions to address an increasing number of goals with the EU's cohesion policy, from strengthening the EU's competitiveness to modernizing education systems and combating unemployment. In parallel, the EU's structural funds that finance the EU's cohesion policy have been steadily increased so that they now take up more than one third of the EU's budget.

This development begs the question of how effective the EU has been in realizing its aims, mainly with respect to reducing disparities, by way of its cohesion policy (see, for example, Cappelen et al., 2003; Geppert and Stephan, 2008; House of Lords, 2008). Critics of the EU's cohesion policy point out that it has been largely ineffective. Little convergence has been achieved at the regional level despite spending several hundred billion euros, with the regions eligible to receive support from the EU – such as Italy's Mezzogiorno and French Corsica – largely remaining the same over time. Moreover, those states among the pre-2004 members of the EU that received the largest cohesion payments relative to their gross domestic products (Greece and Portugal, and traditionally also Ireland) are at the forefront of the current sovereign debt crisis. Neither has the EU managed to increase its competitiveness relative to other world regions. Critics partly point to fraud and mismanagement of funds when explaining this failure. But there may also be deeper structural reasons: when deciding on the broad guidelines and objectives of cohesion policy, member states often are not only motivated by economic concerns but also by other considerations, such as the principle that every member state should get something out of cohesion policy. In the wake of the EU's first enlargement, for example, cohesion policy got a major boost for the simple fact that states were looking to find a budget line that would partly compensate the United Kingdom for its net contributions to the Common Agricultural Policy.

By contrast, backers of the EU's cohesion policy stress the positive consequences of cohesion policy. They allege that cohesion policy was necessary for the political cohesion of the EU that benefited both rich and poor regions. Indeed, member states explicitly linked the implementation of both the single market programme and monetary union to a reform and strengthening of the EU's cohesion policy. They also suggest that while not all structural funds were spent well, over time member states and the Community institutions have learned and improved the governance of structural funds. Finally, they maintain that the challenges posed by various rounds of enlargement that brought in poorer member countries (Ireland in 1973, Greece in 1981, Portugal and Spain in 1986, and the central and eastern European countries in the 2000s) were so large that any policy instrument would have had difficulties to cope.

The following two contributions take up this debate about the effectiveness of the EU's cohesion policy. Dirk Ahner backs the EU's regional policy, arguing that it brings EU policies closer to the citizens and fostering European integration. Marco Brunazzo and Vincent Della Sala, by contrast, stress the shortcomings of the EU's cohesion policy: confusion about objectives, lack of focus, and lack of an effective monitoring mechanism. This controversy mainly relates to Chapter 2 on the efficiency of the EU.

9.1 Cohesion policy: fostering European integration through development

Dirk Ahner

Since its inception, the weight of cohesion policy in the EU budget has steadily grown. Today, it accounts for more than one third of the EU budget, being the second biggest spending item after the Common Agricultural Policy. This reflects the major role cohesion policy plays for the European integration process. Indeed, by promoting a balanced and sustainable development of Europe's regions, it contributes to the wide geographical and societal dissemination of the benefits associated with the integration of EU markets and thus helps build consensus around this process.

Moreover, cohesion policy contributes to the process of integration itself. A significant part of cohesion policy resources are spent on transport and telecommunication infrastructure, which foster exchanges of goods, services and technologies. Investments of cohesion policy in the field of human capital also contribute to integrate further EU labour markets. The mobility of workers and their capacity to grasp professional opportunities outside their region of origin is indeed highly correlated with their level of educational attainment. Finally, cohesion policy is a key instrument for fostering cooperation between regions and countries as well as between various levels of government in Europe, making it possible for national, regional and local governments to engage in overarching strategies and networks across policies and country borders.

For all these reasons, cohesion policy greatly contributes to the widening and deepening of the European integration process. However, this contribution is often overlooked or not well understood. In fact, a lot of the criticism regarding cohesion policy would appear to be based on misconceptions. This text therefore aims at clarifying the foundations, the objectives and the operation of cohesion policy to highlight its value added to European integration.

The origin of cohesion policy

'No Community could maintain itself nor have a meaning for the people which belong to it so long as some have very different standards of living and have cause to doubt the common will of all to help each Member to better the condition of its people' (European Commission, 1973: 4). This citation of the so-called Thomson Report of 1973 summarizes the original political vision which inspired cohesion policy. Its central idea is that in order to maintain a strong (political) cohesion around the European project, policies aimed at integrating markets should be complemented by policies ensuring that all EU member states, regions and citizens could benefit from such integration. In fact, it was feared that letting countries or regions with marked differences in their economic development compete on open EU markets would lead to a situation where 'the realisation of global economic equilibrium may be dangerously threatened by differences of structure' (Werner, 1970).

Instruments aimed at improving the structure of EU economies have been created since the onset of the European Community. The European Social Fund (ESF) and the European Investment Bank (EIB) were established in 1958 while the European Regional Development Fund (ERDF) was created in 1975 to ensure a Community contribution to the regional development in the different member states of the EU in the context of the first enlargement of the then European Community. However, with the accession of Greece in 1981 and then Portugal and Spain in 1986, regional disparitiesin the Community of 12 member states widened significantly. Before the accession of Greece, the proportion of European citizens with an annual income 30 per cent below the

Community average was around 12 per cent;this became 20 per cent after accession in1986. At the same time, the EU integration process was deepened with the project of completing the Single European Market. The opening of the market in the enlarged Community was expected to have strong distributive effects among member states and their regions. Against this background, the Single European Act in 1987 introduced the concept of cohesion into the European Economic Community (EEC) Treaty. The 'structural' policies of the Community were reviewed and reorganized under a common heading of 'cohesion policy' while levels of financial support through the Community were increased substantially. Article 130A of the EEC Treaty was amended to provide that 'In order to promote its overall harmonious development, the Community shall develop and pursue its actions leading to the strengthening of its economic and social cohesion. In particular the Community shall aim at reducing disparities between the various regions and the backwardness of the least-favoured regions'.

Cohesion policy is therefore a development policy which complements the actions taken by the Community in order to realize the liberalization of the internal market. It aims at fostering sustainable growth and jobs, improving the wellbeing of citizens in all EU regions, and promoting the integration of regional economies. In doing so, it ensures that EU citizens, wherever they live, can benefit from, and contribute to, the common political project of achieving a deeply integrated European space.

A development policy tailored to the local context

In recent years, cohesion policy has adopted the guiding principles of a new paradigm in regional policies, evolving from a policy aimed at compensating regions for their handicaps to a policy designed to improve regional growth and competitiveness based on regions' endogenous potential and assets (strengths). With this in mind, cohesion policy is meant to support development strategies that cover a wide range of direct and indirect factors affecting regional social, economic and environmental performance (see European Commission 2010b for a wide overview of cohesion policy and of the main regional trends in the EU).

Like every development policy, cohesion policy cuts across sectors, promotes multidisciplinary approaches, and involves many levels of decision and jurisdiction. As a result, it is difficult to reduce its purpose to one single, clear-cut objective. Nevertheless, it operates within a logical framework linking investments in pursuit of an over-arching objective ('regional development'), through a number of operational and specific objectives.

The legal basis of cohesion policy derives from Article 3 and Title XVIII of the Treaty of Lisbon. The treaty sets out the over-arching objective of cohesion policy which, as explained above, is to promote development of the EU and its regions. This objective is supported by three strategic objectives. The first one is the strengthening of EU regions' competitiveness by fostering growth-enhancing conditions. In least-developed member states and regions, the policy concentrates on factors leading to real convergence, while in others the focus may be more oriented towards supporting economic change through innovation and the promotion of the knowledge society. This is mainly achieved through interventions aimed at improving the business and innovation environment, improving infrastructure such as transport and telecommunications, and investing in human resources.

The second objective is the improvement of people's wellbeing, notably through the promotion of employment and job opportunities by enhancing workforce skills, facilitating access to employment for minorities, enhancing the social integration of disadvantaged people, and providing access to services of general interest. The third pillar is the quality of environment and is supported by measures aimed at cleaning up polluted areas, boosting resource efficiency (and in particular energy efficiency) and the use of alternative (renewable) resources, promoting clean public transport, and drawing up plans to prevent and limit natural and technological risks.

Cohesion policy adopts a territorial approach to reach EU citizens. This responds to the mandate given to cohesion policy by the Treaty to promote regional development. But such an approach is also based on the fact that development has a strong local dimension and that development strategies need to be tailored to the local context and need local ownership to be effective. Most mechanisms of development are indeed highly context dependent. They rely on the complex interplay of different factors, spanning from the engines of economic growth to the working of societal institutions, which are likely to change from one place to the other or to work principally at a given spatial scale. One example is innovation which has been shown to critically depend on the interactions between various actors and/or institutions. Such interactions are generally hampered by distance and hence more likely to take place at a local level (Polenske, 2007).

Development strategies must therefore be differentiated to account for the specificities of the context to which they are applied. This implies that the choice of the geographical area on which a development policy is applied is a key determinant of its success. In the EU, economic and social performance strongly varies within each member state and it is therefore relevant to choose regions as the geographical level to implement development policies as they are likely to constitute much more homogenous contexts than member states. The EU's cohesion policy has been successful in doing so.

Clarifying some misconceptions

Cohesion policy significantly contributes to the development of the EU and its regions while at the same time providing support to the EU integration process (see for instance the recent report summarizing the evaluations of cohesion policy programmes 2000 6, European Commission, 2010a). However, cohesion policy is subject to controversies, some of which are based on a misunderstanding of its objectives and the manner in which the policy operates. It is therefore useful to clarify the value added of a EU-level cohesion policy, its contribution to the efficiency of the European economy as a whole and its ultimate objective in terms of reducing regional disparities.

The EU value added of cohesion policy

Why should the EU be involved at all in promoting regional development and greater cohesion? Three main reasons may be invoked to justify the setting up of regional policy actions at the EU level. First, cohesion policy complements national and regional resources and capacities, in particular in the poorest member states and regions of the EU. It is the expression of the principle of solidarity that constitutes one of the foundations of the European project. In a number of cases, investments necessary to improve economic, social and environmental conditions or to comply with EU legislation would have been impossible without adding cohesion funding to national or local resources.

More generally, cohesion policy promotes the development of a multilevel governance system where the capacities of each level complement and reinforce each other. Sub-national governments are often in the best position to decide where the priorities lie for optimal regional development programmes. However, higher levels – including the EU level – are needed for supporting capacity building, financial support, and orienting regional development policies towards the maximization of positive spillovers to the member states and the Union as a whole. Cohesion policy also plays a key role in ensuring consistency among the interventions of the various levels by reducing the asymmetry of information, and by identifying and disseminating good practices.

Second, cohesion policy is a major instrument for mainstreaming the EU policy agenda to national and regional levels, thereby bringing it closer to EU citizens. Growth and development in EU regions are partly determined by other EU policies. Cohesion policy complements other

EU policies so as to ensure that all regions are in a position to benefit from these policies and to better participate in the delivery of their expected outcome. For instance, cohesion policy has contributed to the restructuring of a number of EU regions, thus easing their adaptation to the progressive liberalization of the EU's external trade policy.

It helps regions to meet EU policy goals in transport, innovation, information society, environment and energy and to translate them into, or to combine them with, development on the ground. In addition, cohesion programmes often encourage national and local governments to develop and sharpen their strategies in implementing EU policies. Some of the most striking examples can been seen when observing the policy's support for environmental priorities, the EU enlargement process, and activities to underpin the Lisbon Agenda – the EU's blueprint for competitiveness and sustainable growth. This role will be reinforced in the future, as cohesion policy will be a key delivery mechanism to achieve the new Europe 2020 strategy priorities of smart, sustainable and inclusive growth.

Third, cohesion policy fosters integration between EU member states and promotes exchange directly by improving communications and transport infrastructure as well as cooperation between EU regions that facilitates not only inter-regional flows of goods, services, capital and labour, but also the flow of ideas and technologies. The EU territory is a complex system of interconnected places whose individual performance combines to greatly impact economic, social and environmental outcomes of the Union as a whole. Cohesion policy has the important task of deepening the integration and networking between EU regions. These are indeed key factors of EU competitiveness, which allow reaching critical mass and activating agglomeration economies, exploiting synergies and complementarities between European cities and regions, and overcoming possible divisions stemming from administrative borders.

The impact of cohesion policy on EU growth

The argument is often made that cohesion policy would be detrimental to EU growth by transferring resources from rich regions with high potential for growth to poor regions where there would only be gloomy prospects. Cohesion policy would therefore work against efficiency, and hence global economic growth. However, there is no firm evidence that such a trade-off exists and there are even a number of reasons to believe that cohesion policy could very well contribute to a more efficient allocation of factors across the EU. As the literature shows (Romp and De Haan, 2007), adding public infrastructure in a place where it is critically lacking produces much more global growth than augmenting it in place where it is already abundant. This is precisely what cohesion policy is doing when it focuses its investments in transport and telecommunication infrastructure in the poorest member states and regions of the EU. For investment in R&D, places where the stock of knowledge is already high may be those where the impact is the highest and accordingly so, cohesion policy in more developed regions may favour this priority.

Another argument is that since agglomeration fosters efficiency, cohesion policy limits the possibility of the Union to fully exploit agglomeration economies, since it forces activities to stay in places where they would not in the absence of policy. However, cohesion policy does not limit but, as emphasized above, fosters the integration of EU markets and hence facilitates the movements of people and firms across the Union. The policy cannot be blamed for limiting the agglomeration of economic activities. Rather, it seeks to create the conditions to fully enjoy the benefits of agglomeration and avoid its possible negative side-effects by promoting a balanced development of EU territories. In the real world it is therefore likely that cohesion policy contributes to global growth. This is because it mobilizes under-utilized resources in various types of regions; it helps reducing agglomeration diseconomies, notably by improving infrastructure in urban areas; and, it promotes the exploitation of inter-regional synergies, notably by enhancing the capacity of poorer regions to interplay with more developed ones.

Reducing regional disparities in the EU

According to the Treaty of Lisbon, the objective of cohesion policy is to reduce disparities between the various EU regions. On this basis, it is sometimes argued that the policy aims at equalizing performance and situations across regions. Obviously, this is not correct. It is true that a priority of cohesion policy is to help poorer regions to reduce their development gap with respect to the EU average. However, this does not mean that the policy expects all EU regions to converge to the same living standards and economic performance. Rather, it recognizes that, even in the case where potentials are fully exploited, large differences would inevitably remain between EU regions, reflecting the specificities of the regional context. In other words, the policy has an objective in terms of conditional convergence but certainly not in terms of unconditional convergence.

This has important implications when it comes to gauge the evolution of disparities among EU regions. For example, evidence suggests that convergence is effectively taking place among EU regions (Geppert and Stephan, 2008), but disparities are currently growing inside some member states (in particular the new member states). This is, however, not in contradiction with the convergence objective of cohesion policy since such disparities mainly reflect the extraordinary performance of some (typically capital city) regions. These very positive results do not prevent growth from taking place in other regions, even if it is at a more moderate pace. On the contrary, these regions most likely benefit from the high growth of outstanding performers and the real objective of cohesion policy is to make them capable of exploiting the opportunities this high growth creates.

Conclusion

This contribution highlights the role played by cohesion policy in the European integration process. It stresses that when it comes to discussing the achievements of cohesion policy, one cannot overlook that the contribution of the policy is often of both economic and political nature. Cohesion policy is a key complement to the spatially blind policies that underpin the integration and liberalization of European markets, such as the European Single Market, the Economic and Monetary Union, the EU trade policy or the enlargement process. By providing EU regions with the necessary support to take advantages of wider and deeper integration, cohesion policy strengthens the political project of the European Union while at the same time contributing to the full exploitation of all of its potential benefits. In this sense, cohesion policy is an element of consensus building around the project of European integration.

However, it also contributes more directly to economic and social integration. Infrastructure investments in transport, energy and telecommunication, as well as investments in human capital and technology transfers, promote EU markets' integration and economic development. Investments in connective infrastructure reduce the distance between firms and people. It facilitates access to the most prosperous places while at the same time allowing EU regions to interact and benefit from the opportunities created in these fast-growing areas. This not only implies an ability to connect leading and lagging areas but also to invest in education, training and lifelong learning, while at the same time contributing to improve the business environment all over Europe.

Last, but not least, one of the principal foundations of the European project is solidarity between its people. Cohesion policy is the expression of this principle, providing resources to those most in need and ensuring that the European integration will effectively contribute to improve their well being.

9.2 A good idea that lost its way: cohesion policy in the EU

Marco Brunazzo and Vincent Della Sala

It might be easy to see the various elements of the EU's cohesion policy – which comprises various programmes and funds that aim to reduce inequalities and promote economic growth, including regional development and structural funds – as a resounding success. They constitute an important redistributive policy in the EU's budget and even if the sums are not great with respect to overall GDP of member states, they fund important initiatives. More importantly, there is widespread consensus that the EU needs a 'cohesion' policy. As many have pointed out, there are strong economic, political and social reasons for some form of transfer to less wealthy regions (Barca, 2009; Hooghe, 1996). Having a central institution allocate transfers is almost essential in a single market, otherwise the costs of ensuring a level playing field for firms would be unsustainable. More importantly, leaving outcomes entirely in the hands of market forces in a single market risks the widening of income gaps within and between states, thus undermining support not only for economic liberalization but also for closer European integration. This is one of the rare cases when there might not be any evident clash between political and economic agendas and objectives.

Yet, despite the resources that have been dedicated to it along with the political support for the notion of cohesion, the policy has been far from a success. Indeed, as we will argue below, there is a need to address fundamental structural and political problems with cohesion policy. In particular, it suffers from: a lack of clarity and even confusion about objectives (growth versus solidarity); a lack of a strategy that identifies clear priority areas rather than trying to spread as many funds as widely as possible; and a lack of an effective mechanism for monitoring. While the rosy picture is one of a Union committed to 'cohesion', the fact is that a majority of the funds in the current allocation remain unspent, not to mention various forms of misappropriation. More importantly, what emerges is a policy that has incrementally grown in size and complexity but without a vision or direction. We do not mean to challenge the economic rationale for a cohesion policy at the EU level nor the laudable political objectives assigned to it. Rather, we will argue that cohesion policy risks being undermined in the long run if it does not address major structural problems: that is, that there are gaps between policy objectives and implementation; and that states are unable or unwilling to narrow the choice of objectives if it affects their perceived interests. A more focused, redistributive policy would mean that some member states would have to give up access to cohesion policy funds.

Lack of clarity

Despite its humble beginnings as a regional development policy, cohesion has become a complex and at times confusing (if not confused) policy. As the EU has widened and deepened over the last fifty years, so have the problems that cohesion policy was supposed to address and the objectives it should reach. Reducing economic differences between the various parts of Europe has always been a central objective of the EU. But so has the creation of economic conditions that will make the European economy more competitive on a global scale. This has often been interpreted as giving greater space to market forces. This is where we get to the crux of the problem, one that has not escaped member states: that is, trying to reconcile what may be, at times, the conflicting objectives of promoting economic growth through liberalization and reducing inequality or enhancing 'solidarity' and 'cohesion'. This lack of clarity has not prevented – indeed, it may have even facilitated – the various forms of regional policy to expand over the decades, so that it now funds close to 600,000 projects in both the under-developed peripheries of the European economy as well as some of its more advanced industrial economies. On the one hand, it is indeed an impressive feat that Europeans are willing to transfer resources across borders. On the other hand, it is not entirely clear that this can compensate for some other imbalances that may emerge with the erosion of national borders.

A lack of clarity about what is to be the nature and objective of cohesion has meant that it has been relatively easy to expand the ways in which the funds have been used. More often than not, it has meant that both objectives – growth and reducing inequality – have been promoted. For instance, nearly one-third of structural funds go to member states which have a GDP above the EU average. These figures have prompted some member states, such as Denmark, to suggest that structural funds should be concentrated so as to benefit only the least prosperous regions in the least prosperous member states, producing a substantial cut in the share of the EU budget allocated to structural and cohesion funds. The Swedish government in January 2011 emphasized the need for deep cuts in the budget devoted to cohesion policy as a prerequisite to accommodate spending in other policy areas. At the same time, the UK government has declared its support for the idea of phasing out the provision of cohesion funds for some of the richer member states. While there may remain, for different reasons, important regional imbalances in cases such as Germany and Italy, these have paled in comparison to some of the broader inequalities that have emerged as the EU has expanded to 27 members. It suggests that it is easier to feel 'solidarity' when funds do not flow in only one direction. It also raises the question of whether this is the most appropriate way to use scarce resources to meet objectives such as enhanced competitiveness through improved infrastructure and innovation.

Another issue related to the lack of clarity of cohesion policy refers to the policy objectives. It is certainly true that at least since the 2007–13 allocation of structural funds, cohesion policy has broadened its final aims to include areas, such as, technology and the environment. At the same time, in the debate about the post-2014 period, we find a general agreement among the member states on the need to include policy areas such energy use and supply, demographic challenges, climate change, and, more in general, the objectives contained in the Europe 2020 strategy. However, it is plausible that the pursuit of too many objectives can weaken the overall objective of cohesion policy, that is, the reduction of economic and social disparities.

There can be no doubt that the objective of promoting economic growth and improving competitiveness in peripheral regions has been partially met in many regions of the EU. In absolute terms, the evidence demonstrates that according to a range of indicators – from percentage of average GDP to investment – economic and social conditions have improved in absolute terms. The cases of Spain and Ireland are always, at least until the recent economic crisis, trotted out as evidence of how both the economic and political missions of cohesion policy have been achieved. However, as even the Barca report (Barca, 2009) mandated by the Commission to assess the effectiveness of cohesion policy claimed, it is not always easy to identify whether it was general macro-economic conditions and policies that were responsible for past successes (suggesting that rising tides lift all ships) or whether such praise could be laid at the doorstep of structural funds. In other words, it is not just that the objectives may be confused but that we do not always know whether the policies designed to meet them have been responsible for success.

Problems of implementation

There are a number of structural flaws in the design of the cohesion policy. While it may make sense to have a centralized policy and machinery to ensure a level playing field, the nature of the EU has meant that the implementation has been highly decentralized, with a prominent role not only for member states but local and regional governments as well. This has raised a number of important problems that need to be addressed as cohesion policy goes forward.

First, probably for good reasons, most funds allocated at the EU level require matching funds or at least that funds are first committed by some other level of government. This means that quite often local and regional levels of government first need to develop the technical capacity to devise plans of action in order to access funds at the national level which will then allow them to seek out European funding. It also means that they already need to have some financial resources that will be a gateway to EU funds. If, on the one hand, shared management can be considered an instrument promoting actors' learning, then on the other hand it can constitute a problem for the less developed territories. Regions needing help may not have the technical and financial resources to tap into funds waiting in Brussels. One of the reasons why so many of the structural funds have remained in Brussels during the current economic crisis is that as governments at all levels have cut spending, they do not have the means to access structural funds. Faced with the choice of whether to provide essential services to the citizens in the short-term *or* to pursue a wiser long-term investment through obtaining structural funds, governments have opted for the former. For this reason, a further simplification of cohesion policy implementation mechanisms has indeed been one of the main aims of every intended future reform. Second, the original schemes for cohesion policy were designed primarily for dealing with the consequences of industrial change and de-industrialization. Those phases of economic development had largely played themselves out in the pre-2004 EU member states. Thus, the kinds of challenges they face are of a different nature than those of the newer member states. A centralized policy makes sense for the single market but a one-size-fits-all, centrally directed initiative may be too inflexible for the different needs of the different regions of the European economy. Efforts have been made to recognize local diversity but there remains a problem of balancing common objectives and criteria with differentiated experiences, capacities and aims.

Problems of monitoring

A great deal of aggregate data has been produced outlining the successes of cohesion policy. The most recent Fifth Report on Cohesion provides extensive data that covers the most recent enlargement countries, illustrating that gaps are diminishing between old and new members (European Commission, 2010b). However, some of the problems mentioned above point to another challenge for cohesion policy: how to assess the impact of interventions carried out in its name. This is not unique to the EU or to any form of redistributive policy but there are some particular features that are rooted in the very nature of cohesion policy in the EU.

First, and at a general level, if the nature and objectives of cohesion policy are not clear, then it becomes difficult to monitor performance of specific programmes and interventions. What exactly are we supposed to measure in terms of success? While we have had a decrease in many regional imbalances, economic growth throughout the EU, and especially the eurozone, has been tepid at best in the decade from 2000. If this is a trade-off that is integral to the policy, then there is not a problem. Yet, cohesion policy was to pursue both objectives and we have no clear way of knowing how interventions may be affecting each or both, either positively or negatively. There is no systematic way to ensure that the results of cohesion policy interventions are consistent with their objectives. The fragmented nature of the current policy ensures that.

Second, it is to be expected that any policy area that funds over 600,000 projects across 27 member states and involves a countless number of other authorities, not to mention an array of public–private partnerships, is going to have problems keeping track of how funds are used. It also should come as no surprise if this involves a misappropriation of funds. Yet, what is troubling in the case of cohesion policy is that there is no systematic, centralized mechanism to keep track of the use of funds. While this may seem as merely a technical problem of finding ways to better monitor the use of funds, it is something much deeper that reflects the politics of cohesion policy. The attempt to balance the needs to have a central policy aimed at ensuring the proper functioning of the internal market with those of local authorities means that great latitude is given to how the latter will interpret how the funds should be used. EU institutions lack the resources and capacity for a close monitoring of funds, therefore having to rely on national and regional authorities to do much of the filtering of projects and control of their outcome. It thus becomes difficult to keep track of the rivulets of funds dedicated to a policy that has broadened in its scope and lost its focus. It is not surprising, then, to read reports of abuses such as the €1million spent for a concert in Naples or the €600,000 for a Slovakian football club.

For these reasons, at least two challenges appear particularly relevant for future cohesion policy: the need to promote interventions with clear objectives and intervention logic, taking into consideration cross-cutting themes and actions; and the need for transparent and results-oriented spending, able to avoid (or at least limit) a misuse of the EU funds.

Finding a way back

Finding a way to retrieve the essence and the functioning of what was a good policy idea requires some reflection on how it is that we lost our way. Clearly, it is a policy idea in search of a clear direction, requiring some difficult decisions that need to be made. Too often, the incremental nature of decision making and the seemingly eternal search for compromise has led to a wayward drift in cohesion policy. Righting the course will require difficult decisions about what should be the priority with respect to objectives.

All roads lead to a political commitment for a more focused cohesion policy with a set of clear objectives and responsibilities. An important step in this direction, as Barca (2009) suggests, would be to create a specific Council of Ministers for cohesion policy. An affirmation of a commitment to a more concise cohesion policy is also necessary to ensure that tendencies to re-assert national prerogatives do not take over a policy that is vital for the functioning of the internal market, to improving competitiveness and for sustaining support for the European project.

Chapter 10

The Big Waste? The Common Agricultural Policy

Editors' introduction

If there were a prize for the most reviled European Union policy, the Common Agricultural Policy (CAP) would most likely be the winner. And that despite the fact that for decades the CAP has been at the heart of European integration and was the policy area into which most of the money for the European Community went. Initially consuming almost the whole budget, the share of agriculture in total EU spending has declined only slowly and now stands at about 40 per cent. The heydays of the CAP were the decades in which European integration was still an unquestioned good. Nonetheless, CAP was unpopular already then, although it achieved its most obvious purpose spectacularly – European self-sufficiency with regard to food. This was no mean feat after the deprivations of the post-Second World War period. Another objective was to placate and satisfy a group of voters, which in many countries used to be core constituencies of conservative parties and were often prone to follow rightwing demagogues. Producers in other areas of the world produce food at much lower cost – therefore European farmers had to be protected from the impact of world markets. They needed a fair standard of living, especially compared to the rising post-war wages of industrial workers (Rieger, 2005).

The European Union tried to achieve these objectives through a complicated system of tariffs and quotas, as well as an extremely cumbersome system of price guarantees for agricultural products. The CAP had become an entrenched policy sub-field with extreme resistance to change. This sparked endless conflicts with major agricultural exporters, particularly the United States, and resulted in giant over-production in the 1970s. Images of wine lakes, butter mountains and tomato hills – produce that had to be destroyed or distributed cheaply on world markets – dominated media attention on the CAP. Numerous reform efforts followed and they continue until this day (Garzon, 2007). Recent enlargement rounds which admitted economies with comparatively large agricultural sectors intensified the need for substantive and sustained change (see Chapter 13). External pressure during successive rounds of

160

global trade talks, most recently the so-called Doha round, also played an important part in the many reform attempts by the European Union. Policy instruments shifted to direct income support for farmers. This support was linked to objectives other than production, such as rural development and the preservation of landscapes. In the past two decades, issues of food safety and environmental policy have increasingly become key issues in European agriculture policy (Jones and Clark, 2001). For both these problems, the CAP has been seen as the problem as well as the cure. The emphasis on environmental sustainability has also put the Common Fisheries Policy (CFP) in the spotlight, which stands accused of leading to over-fishing and the depletion of marine life. Both the CAP and the CFP are often seen as policies which allow well-organized groups to exploit their privileged access to decision makers and information and, thus, to make reforms in the interest of the common good almost impossible (see also Chapter 11). Despite many changes over the past decade, these policies remain among the most contested among the many activities of the European Union. Eugenia Conceição-Heldt argues that the CAP and CFP still remain economically wasteful and environmentally disastrous policies, which urgently need further reform. Ann-Christina Knudsen counters that the CAP has to be understood as a public policy with broader objectives than those specifically linked to agricultural production. To her, the CAP is an essential part of the European way of life.

10.1 EU Agricultural and Fisheries Policies: an economic and environmental disaster!

Eugénia da Conceição-Heldt

The EU's agricultural and fisheries policies are an economic and environmental disaster. The huge amount of subsidies lavished on European farmers, the trade distortions created inside the EU and on world markets, and their negative impact on the environment make these policies particularly telling cases of misallocation which absorb more than 40 per cent of the EU's budget. The CAP protects EU farmers from international competition through import tariffs, direct payments and export subsidies. This increases prices for European consumers and creates problems for farmers in foreign countries. Moreover, by coupling subsidies with production until the beginning of the 1990s, the CAP regime had a distributional effect that benefited big producers to the detriment of small farmers. Finally, the subsidies encouraged intensive methods of production that have had a negative impact on the environment. Since the end of the 1990s, under external and internal pressure, EU member states have agreed on several CAP reforms. International pressure during global trade negotiations made a shift of domestic support subsidies from income support to rural development policy necessary in order to make the CAP compatible with WTO rules. However, the EU still highly subsidizes its agricultural sector and continues to stick to a very defensive position on agricultural trade issues in negotiations aimed at trade liberalization.

At the same time, the challenge of eastern enlargement, which brought in a number of countries with large low productive agricultural sectors, made a reform of the CAP necessary to avoid a huge increase in budget costs. Nevertheless, the EU missed the opportunity to achieve a fundamental reform that would have shifted agricultural subsidies towards more productive purposes and would have, in the long term, improved the EU's competitiveness. The CAP system was simply transferred to the new member states with the objective of keeping the CAP as a safe haven for farmers. The same happened with the Common Fisheries Policy (CFP), which is a complex system of regulations and subsidies to shield the European fishing industry from foreign competition. The CFP with its total allowable catches system has failed to achieve its principal aim, the conservation of fish stocks. Like the CAP, it has come under attack from the outside as well as the inside.

Under attack from the outside: the impact of the CAP on world trade

The CAP is an economic failure because it inhibits agricultural trade liberalization, thus hurting foreign agricultural producers and domestic exporters in other sectors. Dumping on the world market makes it almost impossible for developing countries to compete with highly subsidized European agricultural products. CAP reforms as a result of pressure in international trade talks have not resolved these problems. One of the main difficulties in changing the CAP arises from the fact that member states are unable to agree on a reform of the general objectives and principles of the CAP as they were defined in the Treaty of Rome in 1957. The CAP basically aims at increasing agricultural productivity, ensuring a fair standard of living for farmers, stabilizing markets, providing sufficient supplies of food and ensuring that these reach consumers at reasonable prices (Art. 39 TEU).

In the late 1950s and 1960s, member states were particularly concerned with self-sufficiency, food security concerns and the satisfaction of farmers as a group of voters prone to follow right-wing demagogues. In order to reach these objectives, the then six EC member states established the three main CAP principles: the unity principle, the Community preference and the principle of financial solidarity. The unity principle of the CAP meant that the agricultural markets of all member states were to merge into one single market with a common price level and unrestricted trade between member states. The Community preference principle refers to the CAP regime of import tariffs and export subsidies designed to give preference to EU products over imported ones. This principle *de facto* protects domestic producers from foreign competition through a system of variable import levies (customs duties). It basically means that no trade agreement should damage domestic producers. Moreover, EC member states set a target and intervention price, as well as a common market organization (CMO) for each agricultural commodity. CMOs fixed a minimum price by which national agencies would buy products and take them off the market with the aim of reducing supplies and encouraging higher market prices (intervention prices). Each year, the Agricultural Council sets a target price at a level that is expected to provide a satisfactory return to farmers. The CMOs were to intervene by purchasing as much of the produced agricultural commodities as necessary to keep the price above the set level (the 'target level'). The principle of financial solidarity says that the cost of doing so would be covered by the Community budget.

In order to protect European farmers from the competition of international production, a system of high and fluctuating prices was introduced on all agricultural products from non-members. Products could generally only enter the European market if their price was equal to or above the price on the EC market. This price is commonly referred to as the 'entry price'. When a given target price level on the international market was lower than the EC's, the EC introduced a system of export subsidies enabling European farmers to export agricultural products that had not been sold on the EC's market. These export subsidies reimbursed producers the difference between world prices and the EC price level. Export subsidies and import tariffs are still very high, in general more than 50 per cent higher than the world price. For example, rice has the highest tariff of 361 per cent, followed by sugar (297 per cent), wheat (156 per cent) and beef and veal (125 per cent) (Conceição-Heldt, 2011: 91).

The three CAP principles are closely interrelated. First, the establishment of a European market for agricultural products guaranteed the free flow of products within the common market. The Community preference principle provided a means of protecting the single market from external products produced at lower prices. Finally, through the principle of financial solidarity, the support mechanisms were centralized at the supranational level. All this created a protectionist system contrary to the principles of non-discriminatory trade. CAP export subsidies have been widely criticized, especially by agricultural trade exporters, such as the US or Australia, but also by emerging countries, such as Brazil and many least developing countries (LDCs). These criticisms are related to the internal support prices that created excess production with the surplus being dumped on world markets at a lower price than products of non-subsidized exporters, many of them LDCs.

In this way, the CAP regulatory system protects farmers from the now 27 EU member states from international competition through import tariffs, direct payments and export subsidies. Due to the large amount of subsidies paid every year to European farmers, the CAP is one of the main obstacles to agricultural trade liberalization. As a result of pressure from LDCs and NGOs supporting them, the EU responded with the so-called 'Everything but Arms' initiative. Since 2001, this initiative gives LDCs preferential treatment by granting them 97 per cent duty-free access without any quantitative restrictions to imports of all products, except arms and ammunitions. At the same time, at the WTO ministerial conference in December 2005, the EU agreed to abolish all export subsidies by 2013. However, since the Doha round is deadlocked and WTO members agreed on the 'single undertaking principle' (nothing is agreed until everything is agreed), this concession will not take effect if there is no progress on the other issues that are on the negotiating agenda (for example, domestic support and market access).

Domestic support subsidies have been the other major bone of contention in international trade rounds. Under the 1994 Uruguay Round agreement on agriculture, domestic support measures are differentiated according to their degree of trade distortion. Domestic subsidies have been divided into three categories, called 'boxes': green box, amber box, and blue box subsidies. Green box subsidies are direct payments not linked to production. They include measures that are assumed to have no effect on production, such as set-aside programmes or environmental protection. Amber box subsidies affect trade directly and include market price support (linked to production) or direct payments. Finally, blue box subsidies include direct payments that compensate producers for income loss when production is reduced (Conceição-Heldt, 2011: 44).

In the current Doha round of trade liberalization, negotiations on agricultural issues focus on better market access, the elimination of export subsidies and the reduction of domestic support in these different 'boxes'. The EU has a defensive position on all three pillars. EU member states only agreed on reducing market access tariffs, under the condition of taking into account the geographical indications for EU products. Moreover, the EU argued that it would only accept reductions in export subsidies if less transparent forms of export support (such as export credits, state trading enterprises and food aid) were also included in the negotiations. At the same time, the EU wanted to keep the system of domestic support covered by the blue and green boxes (European Commission, 1999). Finally, the EU asked for the inclusion of the controversial principal of multifunctionality in WTO negotiations. This refers to the non-trade objectives of agriculture, such as environmental protection, food security and rural development. This demand was initially opposed by the US, Australia, Brazil and many other countries, who considered this principle to be a ruse that would allow the EU to circumvent WTO rules on domestic support (Conceição-Heldt, 2011: 126).

With the 2003 CAP reform (the so-called Fischler reform), member states shifted market price support to direct aid payments on the basis of the area farmed and the livestock kept. In this way, the EU shifted blue box support to payments into the green box category, creating at least some bargaining leverage at the WTO level (Swinbank and Daugbjerg, 2006). The main objective of the Fischler reform was not to reduce support to farmers, but to shift payments from the first pillar (market production) to the second (rural development policy). Thus the new CAP rules for the single payment scheme were formulated to comply with the green box rules, which require that payments must be determined by clearly defined criteria. Altogether, this reform neither came anywhere close to meeting the demands of other WTO members for a rapid elimination of export subsidies, nor did it significantly reduce import barriers. This is why the CAP remains one of the most contentious issues between the EU and its international trading partners, creating costs for other sectors of the European economy that would benefit from international trade liberalization.

Agricultural interest groups, especially the peak agricultural confederations at the European level, the Committee of Professional Agricultural Organizations (COPA) and the General Confederation of Agricultural Cooperatives (COGECA), remain the greatest opponents of further agricultural trade liberalization and CAP reforms. In the Doha round, the COPA has criticized the European Commission sharply for using the CAP as a bargaining chip. The main argument put forward by agricultural interest groups is that reduction in domestic support would undermine the European multifunctional model of agriculture, and force farmers to abandon agricultural activity. French farmers, who are the main beneficiaries of CAP subsidies, would be the main losers from agricultural trade liberalization. This explains why they continue to successfully lobby French governments against further CAP reforms and global trade liberalization. A tight coalition of member states and producers makes the CAP extremely resistant to reform demands from the outside.

Under attack from the inside: budgetary, environmental, and consumer costs

CAP reforms in the 1990s and 2000s were not only driven by external pressures from multilateral trade negotiations. They also reflected sharp attacks from within the EU, due to the policy's high cost for taxpayers and consumers and the general agreement among member states that the CAP could only 'survive' enlargement to the east after undergoing a fundamental reform. On the budget side, the CAP is a subsidy-devouring monster that absorbs a large part of the EU's budget. In 1984, the share of the CAP in the EC budget represented 70 per cent. Today, even though agricultural subsidies have decreased greatly, they still make up about 43 per cent of the EU's budget (Oersted Nielsen *et al.*, 2009: 371). At the end of the 1990s, increased budgetary pressures occurred largely in connection with the enlargement to the central and east European countries (CEEC). First, because agriculture's share of total GDP was larger in these countries than in the EU, a direct transfer of the CAP subsidies to the CEEC would enormously increase the CAP costs and thus the EU's budget. A second major concern was that injecting large subsidies in the form of direct payments into the new entrant countries would undermine restructuring efforts of the unproductive farm sector. In the end, however, EU member states decided that the ten candidate countries would receive the same direct payments as the EU-15 countries, but gradually phased-in over a period of ten years from 2004 to 2013. Thus, the enlargement of the EU was not used to achieve a fundamental reform of the CAP, but simply to transfer the system to the new member states. The EU missed a unique opportunity to shift agricultural subsidies towards more productive purposes and to improve the EU's competitiveness in world markets.

A second internal criticism concerns the negative environmental effects of increased production (for example, water pollution, soil and air quality) of the CAP. Since the CAP subsidies were from the very beginning coupled to production, this sent a signal to big farmers to intensify production, with grave consequences. High levels of production and the use of chemical fertilizers cause contamination of ground and surface waters, especially where intensive livestock and grain production takes place. Agriculture contributes to around 8 per cent of total greenhouse emissions and is the principal source of methane (from cattle production) and nitrogen oxide (from grazing livestock). CAP subsidies boosted the farmers' prices above market prices and encouraged farmers to produce too much, to use too much fertilizer and pesticides, and to keep unprofitable tracts of land in production. Decoupling subsidies from production is a way of lowering returns and changing the incentives to boost production levels through the use of agrochemicals (Oersted Nielsen *et al.*, 2009: 375). Even though emissions from European agriculture are modest compared to other sectors, agriculture remains the main source of methane and nitrous oxide emissions. Of course, this problem may not be solved by increased agricultural imports, as it is not clear that production in the United States, Australia or Brazil and transport from these countries would cause less environmental damage. Instead, to decrease greenhouse emissions in the agricultural sector, the EU would have to support small, local farmers.

Several reforms have tried to address these problems. The 1992 Mac-Sharry and Agenda 2000 reforms gradually shifted subsidies from production to direct payments and reduced intervention prices for the grain sector by 30 per cent and by 15 per cent for the beef sector (Daugbjerg and Swinbank, 2007). At the same time, direct income payments to all farmers were introduced to compensate for cuts in support payments. In order to be eligible for compensatory payments, farmers had to lay fallow 15 per cent of their arable land. The 1999 Agenda 2000 reform extended the 1992 reform by reducing price support and creating the second pillar within the CAP (rural development policy) to take into account the principle of multifunctionality in farming activities. Finally, the 2003 Fischler reform decoupled direct payments from production and replaced them with income support in terms of a single payment scheme (SPS). In addition, the SPS was made dependent upon farmers compliance with certain standards for animal welfare, food quality and the environment (Nedergaard, 2006). The introduction of this principle of cross-compliance was a way to enforce compliance with environmental regulations, to make farming more sustainable and more compatible with the expectations of consumers and taxpayers (Oersted Nielsen *et al.*, 2009: 370). While these reforms addressed some of the CAP's problems, they did not substantially reduce EU spending on agriculture nor did they shift the CAP towards a more competitive approach. For example, the main aim of the 2003 Fischler reform was not to reduce agricultural support, but rather to shift subsidies from the production to the rural development policy pillar. The CAP instruments were reformulated to comply with the less trade-distorting WTO green box rules that require domestic subsidies to be determined by clearly defined criteria.

The Common Fisheries Policy

Despite the fact that the CFP was set up in 1983 to conserve and manage fish stocks by limiting fishing activities, the problem of resource scarcity has hitherto not been solved. The total allowable catches (TACs) system does not contribute significantly to maintaining fish stocks and conserving resources (Conceição-Heldt, 2004). Studies diverge greatly in explaining the causes of this failure. Christian Lequesne (2000) explains the poor performance of the CFP with a flawed set of policy instruments for reducing fishing efforts, such as the TAC assessments. Other authors blame the failure of resource management on the unanimity requirement in the Council of Ministers (Franchino and Rahming, 2003; Payne, 2000).

The negotiations on the TACs and the allocation of national quotas that take place every year in December show that each member state is first and foremost concerned with maximizing its own benefits. National government representatives are preoccupied with short-term opportunities for their national fleets with little apparent regard for wider conservation issues or for environmental protection. There is little sense of sharing responsibility for a common resource. The protection of fish stocks was never the most important priority in the negotiations at the EU level. The CFP instruments of TACs and national quotas are more suitable for conserving fishermen's incomes and employment than fish stocks.

Conclusion

The CAP represents one of the main obstacles to worldwide free trade and is a constant source of dispute between the EU and its international trading partners. With its system of export subsidies and domestic support, the CAP impedes imports from developing countries and hurts their domestic agricultural sectors. Despite several reform attempts in the last two decades, the CAP is still a safe haven for farmers. CAP reforms have not really reduced support for farmers, but simply shifted subsidies from the production to the rural development policy pillar. Moreover, the critical juncture of the EU eastern enlargement did not move the CAP towards a more competitive path, but simply kept the CAP's regulatory system that insulates European farmers from world markets competition. Similar to the CAP, the CFP is a complex system of regulations and subsidies designed to protect the European fisheries sector against foreign competition and is unable to protect fish resources. Together, the two policies are an economic and environmental disaster.

10.2 Europe's common values and agricultural policy: a defence of the CAP

Ann-Christina L. Knudsen

In a 2010-Eurobarometer survey, 90 per cent of respondents answered that agriculture and rural areas are important to Europe's future, and an overwhelming majority were also in favour of continuing support for farmers' incomes through the EU's budget in return for the delivery of safe, healthy, high quality and organic food products, respectively (Eurobarometer, 2010c). The survey also showed that a large majority of respondents thought that the sector would be a strong force in the future of Europe through the use of new biotechnologies and production of renewable energies. The high approval ratings reveal that there is solid public support towards one of the EU's primary areas of activity and spending – its common agricultural policy (CAP) –even in an atmosphere of severe financial and economic constraint. This is not necessarily because citizens have become EU-enthusiasts overnight in the classical for-or-against-positioning, but rather because they realize that the CAP plays a key role in catering for the lifestyle and type of society that European citizens enjoy and expect. The CAP builds upon common European values and deep-rooted political priorities, as this contribution will demonstrate, and it embodies an impressive combination of the modern and progressive with the preservation of unique landscapes and diverse local traditions across the vast territory. No other EU policy contains such riches, yet this essay shows that the CAP needs not be analysed as an insular or *sui generis* phenomenon.

Critics of the CAP, however, look elsewhere. They routinely point out that it is a paradox that around 45 per cent of the entire EU budget goes to a sector that merely employs 4–5 per cent of the work force, ranging from 29 per cent in Romania to just over 1 per cent in Britain. Such figures nevertheless give an inadequate picture. The small size of the EU budget compared to state budgets means that the CAP claims no more than around 0.5 per cent of the total gross domestic product (GDP), distributed widely across the 90 per cent of the EU's territory that is classified as 'rural', and that is home to more than half of the entire population. A more substantial criticism of the CAP has however revealed that the major recipients are large businesses operating in the food and farm sector, and they obtain millions of euros in CAP subsidies (as listed on the website, www.farmsubsidy.org). The beneficiaries include royal families, multinational food and investment companies such as Nestlé, Unilever and Kraft Foods, and even current and former EU ministers for agriculture who, incidentally, are often farmers themselves.

The (mis)allocation of public funds on this scale should, in a well-functioning democracy, be monitored and questioned. It is not the intention of this text to justify or hide such flaws in the policy's architectural details. The contribution instead aims to move focus to the bigger picture of identifying and exemplifying what the socio-cultural mechanisms behind the political priorities embedded in the CAP are, as this will help us evaluate what role to expect for the CAP in the future EU.

Three vital political priorities

Born during the 1960s, the CAP is one of the EU's foundational policies. Unlike other original activities such as competition and industrial policies that primarily aim at regulating markets through legislative measures, the CAP is essentially a public policy (Knudsen, 2009). Importantly, public policies are not neutral mechanisms, but give testimony of what type of values and ideals we can find in a given society (Lascoumbes and Le Galés, 2007).

At the heart of the CAP is a redistributional mechanism that can allocate funds to both private and public actors through a wide range of subsidies and support programmes. The CAP is therefore one of the EU's few spending policies, and its primary political priorities can be summarized as maintaining a constant and safe food supply, providing an income safety net for farmers, and preserving certain common European values. To appreciate why the CAP is designed in this way, the following sections will identify and critically assess central structural determinants that have shaped these political priorities.

Food

Europeans today are accustomed to an unwavering supply of safe and varied foods, so much so that it might be easy to forget that the food chain is complex and fragile and does not function automatically. The upkeep of a modern food infrastructure across a large territory like the EU demands intensive regulation and the CAP is one of the world's most reliable at this job. At a general level, the priority stems from a belief that agriculture holds a strategic position in society. Everyone must eat regularly and an adequate food supply is necessary to keep a society socially and politically stable. Yet food production is an unpredictable enterprise, subject to conditions that the farmer cannot control individually, such as, weather or diseases. More particularly, when the CAP was first created, it was against the historical context of two devastating world wars that turned fertile farming areas into battlefields and made most Europeans at the time experience shortages, under-nourishment or even starvation. After the Second World War, policy makers were acutely aware of the destabilizing effects of a faulty food chain and their construction efforts sought to restore as well as to modernize farming. By the time the Rome Treaty was signed in 1957, the food supply had long been restored, but the memories of shortages were not far away and the particular idea of agricultural exceptionalism – namely that this sector needs special political attention for a society to function – gained particular prominence. An efficient food chain depends on a long range of private actors, but it is above all CAP regulation that assures that certain rules and standards are upheld at the common market for food products in the EU.

Consumers become particularly alert to the functioning of the basic food infrastructure when something goes wrong. In the summer of 2011, an E.coli-contamination of cucumbers was discovered in the EU and was directly tied to several deaths and hundreds of cases of food poisoning. Even more fatal was the so-called mad-cow disease that caused a major scandal and food crisis during the 1990s. These two examples show how the EU's food security responses have developed and improved over time. When the mad-cow crisis broke out, the EU experienced a toxic combination of unsafe feeding practices for bovines and lax oversight from public authorities. This led to a public outcry across the EU, but the CAP had no instruments to deal with these problems. In fact, more than 2 million infected cattle and sheep had entered the food chain before the problem was disclosed publicly and scientists have directly connected this breach to more than a hundred human deaths (Budka, 2011). In the name of precaution, several millions of cattle were slaughtered. Consumer trust in the authorities' abilities to provide safe foods plummeted. As national authorities were unable to cooperate and exchange information in an efficient way, the EU stepped in and began to play a key role in the restoration of consumer confidence in foods (Ansell and Vogel, 2006). One strategy was the Commission's integrated strategy – called From Farm to Fork – that sought to establish a clearer link between food producers and consumers. Another strategy was to improve coordination of specialized scientific information, alerts and advice in relation to communicable diseases, as well as setting up an independent scientific risk assessment and advisory agency called the European Food Safety Agency. Food risks can never be completely eradicated, but we saw that these networks and agencies all responded immediately to the spread of the cucumber incident in 2011 to ensure that the risks were identified and communicated quickly and that the spread of contamination was contained.

Regarding external trade relations, the EU similarly plays a crucial role in managing food standards in imports and, based on the precautionary principle, it has, for instance, taken part in some rather tough confrontations with the United States over issues such as hormone in-jected beef and the so-called Frankenstein foods, that is, food produced with genetically modified organisms.

Welfare

The year 2013 has been set as a target date for reform of the CAP, and a top priority for the European Commission as well as many member states is the provision of a 'basic income safety net' for farmers. Income redistribution is typically the authority of national welfare state policies and the CAP is practically the only EU policy area that is concerned with income transfers to individuals. This priority has been a constant feature throughout the CAP's life and is what the EU's Court of Auditors has called 'the real leitmotif running through the whole CAP' (Court of Auditors, 2004: item I). Already the Rome Treaty stipulated that the policy's aim should be 'to ensure a fair standard of living for the agri-cultural community, in particular by increasing the individual earnings of persons engaged in agriculture' (Treaty, 1957: article 39b). It was a reaction to a situation where income levels and standards of living were generally rising in post-war Western Europe, but much less so for those employed in agriculture. At a time when technological innovations were behind continuous growth in the industrial sector, many farmers found it difficult to follow suit. The introduction of, say, a tractor on a farm is not likely to bring similar growth and wealth increases as a conveyer belt in an automobile factory. Moreover, the labour intensive nature of farming, the immobility of land, complex ownership structures, and low levels of education among farmers were basic conditions that hindered a fast rise of incomes in farming. Some farmers certainly earned well, especially those who took advantage of the new and increasingly cheap technologies such as combine harvesters and milking machines. But oth-er farmers lacked the means to participate in the modernization process and either continued to live on low incomes or left the profession en-tirely. Attempts to offset the farm problem, as it was called in the 1950s, developed into what is now known as the agro-industrial complex, and income problems in the sector continue despite CAP support. One rea-son is that modern farming is extremely investment intensive and many of those who have invested are now caught up in massive debt. Another reason is that the strong regional differences provide unequal condi-tions for fortunes in farming, something that is also highlighted in every enlargement scenario.

Public interventions into agriculture were, however, not invented in the European Community. The idea of agricultural exceptionalism in national policies became particularly pronounced after the outbreak of the agricultural crisis in the early 1920s. The extent of the national agricultural welfare state policies differed, but by the end of the 1950s they all broadly consisted of a mix of policies that included income redistribution, extensive domestic market support and external trade barriers. The political goal of income parity in farming was not easy to fulfill, and when the Rome Treaty entered into force, national agricultural welfare states were struggling to live up to their solidaristic aims. To try and rectify this, the income gap problem became the absolute priority in the negotiations shaping the CAP in the 1960s and this objective has remained stable ever since. The original market and price support had, however, certain problematic features and led to a bias in financial benefit for the larger farmers that we can still observe today, as mentioned earlier in the chapter, as well as massive over-production that has been referred to by media as butter mountains and wine lakes. In an attempt to rectify these problems, the key policy instruments were altered from the early 1990s onwards in a series of reforms that moved away from price support – and thereby indirect income support – to direct income transfers. This gave the CAP a more clearly defined redistributory profile and also made it more efficient.

The CAP is supplemented by national and local policies that range widely from tax benefits to planning permissions for farmers. While public intervention has reached an unprecedented degree of refinement in the EU, most other industrial states have similar measures, though not necessarily with the same type of priorities as in the EU. The average level of public support to producers (called Producer Support Estimate, PSE) in the OECD countries was 22 per cent of aggregate gross farm receipts in 2007–9 (OECD, 2010: 5). The PSE in the EU was an estimated more-or-less average, namely 23 per cent. This is much above the United States (9 per cent), but well below countries such as Norway (61 per cent), Switzerland (58 per cent), South Korea (52 per cent), Japan (47 per cent) and even Turkey (34 per cent).

Values

A key set of priorities in the CAP has been to preserve and promote values that relate to farming and food. First, while the CAP does not set direct limits to the size of farming units, it is clear that it builds up a particular ideal for what the good properties of a farm are. Europeans tend to be alienated by images of helicopter-flying cowboys that manage herds of millions of cattle in the United States and Australia, portraying industrial farming on an immensely large scale. Instead, CAP legislation has for the first four decades systematically referred to a conception of the 'family farm'. The family farm was not just any farm, as the presence of the 'family' implied the political support for a moral economy involved with running the business. The farmer, his family and their relation to the soil and locality, have been important symbols in the narration of belonging and nationhood cross much of Europe (for example, Weber, 1976). The adoption of this terminology into both national and CAP legislation implied a political accept of the obligation to preserve this feature of the European socio-cultural landscape.

Since the turn of the millennium, the terminology related to the farm unit has begun to change but still builds on an ideal. Europe's new farmer is 'multifunctional'. The principle of multifunctionality rewards the farmer for undertaking certain tasks beyond traditional agricultural production. These tasks include, for instance: nature conservation, upholding biological diversity, securing animal welfare, environmentally friendly production techniques, and facilitating agro-tourism. This moves away from the original priorities of attaching values directly to the (family) farm unit, to a broader range of priorities and values that are related to rural areas and the life that it also enables. In policy terms, the consequence of this reform is that farm support and incomes are increasingly de-coupled from the agricultural production *per se* and instead there has been a political definition of other 'services' that farmers are best placed to provide and that are in demand with the general public.

The farm is the backbone in rural communities and when farms disappear, it becomes a struggle to uphold adequate facilities for everyday lives to function in such areas. Yet rural communities contain something of fundamental value to Europe, as captured well by former Commissioner for Agriculture and Rural Development, Mariann Fischer-Boel: 'Rural regions are indeed the soul of Europe. ... They represent the environmental, socio-economic and cultural richness of our continent even more than European urban areas. Farmers and farm households will be important providers of public goods' (Fischer-Boel, 2007). Concerted efforts to preserve this socio-cultural heritage began in the framework of the CAP in the early 1970s when it was realized that along with the de-population of the countryside, many local communities were dying, and with them also dialects and traditions. Efforts to counter such tendencies were integrated into the structural and cohesion policies that were subsequently developed. In debates over CAP reform, there is now a strengthened emphasis on what role the ideal European countryside should play in the future EU. It is clear that when on holiday, Europeans do not want to be faced with a string of industrial-scale farms as in the mid-west of the United States and increasing emphasis is placed on maintaining village life, a varied and distinct countryside and well-kept farms. This ideal is in fact also a key feature of the emerging EU-tourism strategy, which is an expanding sector that already generates more than

5 per cent of the EU's GDP and keeps many small and medium-sized businesses running in rural areas.

Second, another clear values emphasis in the CAP relates to the choice of promoting food products that rely on proud craftsmanship and strong traditions bound to certain localities. In the wake of the single market project, an EU-wide labelling system was introduced in 1992, and since then more than a thousand products have received that label, for instance the prized Italian *parmigiano* cheese. It has the most restrictive label, the Protected Designation of Origin (PDO) which the EU Court of Justice has found to be an integrated part of EU food law that trumps the principle of free enterprise in the common market (Official Journal of the EU, 2008). Hence, only producers in the Emilia province that live up to certain production standards have the right to name their products as '*parmigiano*'.

The practice of such EU labelling has come as a reaction against mass-produced food products. Some have criticized this as a Proustian search for lost time and authenticity that privileges middle-class consumers to whom such products are primarily a marker of distinction. Yet studies have demonstrated that 'gastronationalism', as these labelling practices have also been called, not only reflects a resistance against trends of global homogeneity in food as created by companies such as Kraft Foods and Unilever in collaboration with large retailers, but also that it can shape production and marketing positively (DeSoucey, 2010). This also informs the strategy behind the delegation headed by EU commissioners for agriculture going to emerging markets such as China to promote 'quality products' with the geographical indications labels. Interestingly, when, in March 2011, Commissioner Dacian Cioloş went to China the programme for the visit included, among others, the area where the *Longjin* tea is grown and few months later this product became one of the first produced outside the EU to receive a PDO-label. Food values, it appears, can also be translated into reciprocal strategies in trade and heritage.

Conclusion

The looking-glass through which the CAP makes sense is not the typical economistic or rationalist one that is often used to analyse the EU. The CAP is a public policy, and scholars of public policy have pointed to the need to identify and analyse the types of priorities, values and ideals that have been chosen for policy. The text has shown that the CAP rests on a deep-founded platform of the need to secure a safe food supply, farmers' incomes and the values stemming from Europe's rural areas and food traditions. In the past two decades, the CAP has shown a remarkable ability to accommodate new demands in its priorities, and embodies a unique link between economic entrepreneurship and the common values that make Europe distinctive to both Europeans and others. Europeans are expressing a continued support towards this, as the initial Eurobarometer survey showed, and the CAP should be strongly placed in shaping the EU's future. Perhaps the main task ahead is of a different nature, namely for critics – wherever they reside – to admit that when they go home from work at night, uncork a bottle of good wine and treat themselves to a nice bowl of pasta ritually sprinkled with freshly grated *parmigiano*, the CAP has ultimately been a central gateway to their comfortable lifestyles.

Chapter 11

Foreign Economic Policies: How Much Power for the Lobbyists?

Editors' introduction

A large number of interest groups and companies aim at influencing EU decision making (Coen and Richardson, 2009; Greenwood, 2011). More than 1,000 Euro-groups now have an office in Brussels, including business associations, such as BusinessEurope, labour unions, such as the European Trade Union Confederation, *professional associations, such as the* European Medical Association, *and public interest non-governmental organizations (NGOs) such as the* World Wide Fund for Nature. *Many more groups send lobbyists to Brussels to influence specific policies. The European Parliament thus lists more than 4,000 individuals as 'accredited lobbyists'.*

But how much influence do these groups exercise on EU decision making? The response to this question is of major importance for our normative assessment of European integration. Interest group dominance creates the danger of socially inefficient policies that only serve the interests of a few. Such policies in turn may undermine public support for European integration. By contrast, if the EU's political institutions are autonomous actors, they may be able to pursue socially efficient policies. Autonomy is not without dangers, however: an integration process that is detached from societal actors' preferences also creates the possibility of a popular backlash that may undermine the very foundations of the Union.

The following two contributions tackle this debate with respect to the EU's foreign economic policies, that is, trade, foreign financial, and development policy. The EU is a major actor in the world economy: it is the largest trading power and largest donor of development assistance. Most of the competencies in this field have been moved from the member state to the EU level (Dür, 2012). Against this background, the analysis of interest group influence in this policy field is of particular interest. The same question has been discussed in the context of United States' foreign economic policies for many years (Bauer et al., 1972).

In the first text, Andreas Dür adopts the position that interest groups are powerful actors in shaping the EU's foreign economic policies. He sees interest groups using their resources to influence decision making in the EU, a political system that offers many access and veto points to well-organized domestic interests. Cornelia Woll counters, arguing that interest groups often are not independent actors but subject to 'reverse lobbying'. The European Commission, rather than being controlled by interest groups, may use them to pursue its own interests vis-à-vis member countries or third states. Which of these two perspectives better captures reality has major implications for our expectations about the EU's foreign economic policies: does the EU mainly defend business preferences or does it manage to pursue broader interests and normative goals? This chapter's debate relates to issues taken up in Chapter 3 (how much power do the supranational actors have in the EU?) and Chapter 12 (is the EU a normative power in international relations?).

11.1 Why interest groups dominate the EU's foreign economic policies

Andreas Dür

In a report on the negotiations for a free-trade agreement between the EU and India that have been ongoing since 2007, two non-governmental organizations, the Corporate Europe Observatory and India FDI Watch, denounce the EU's 'corporate-driven trade agenda' and 'incestuous relationship with vested interest groups' (Corporate Europe Observatory and India FDI Watch, 2010: 37). Is this portrait of the EU's foreign economic policies, and here especially the EU's trade policy, as dominated by business interests correct? This text's argument is that interest groups representing concentrated interests indeed have a large influence on the EU's foreign economic policies. By lobbying decision makers, they often manage to shape policies to their advantage. I back this argument empirically by showing that interest groups have excellent access to EU decision making, highlighting the coincidence between preferences and policies adopted, and drawing attention to groups' self-assessment of their influence.

In defending the argument of interest group dominance, I make a case against studies that suggest that the delegation of trade policy competencies from the national to the European level has undermined the influence of societal interests (Meunier, 2005; Zimmermann, 2007). The main idea behind this argument is that the delegation of trade policy competences from the national to the EU level insulated decision makers from interest group pressures, and in particular from lobbying by interests that demand greater protection of domestic markets. Delegation may have this effect for several reasons: it increases the number of actors that have a stake in trade policy decisions and thus aggravates free-rider problems; it increases the heterogeneity of interests that take opposing stances on trade policy decisions and thus gives decision makers more leeway to create coalitions in support of their policies; and it exacerbates information asymmetries that favour public to the detriment of private actors.

My argument about interest group dominance does not rely on the assumption of highly effective and resource-rich business associations. Clearly, many EU level peak associations (these are groups such as the European Association of Mining Industries or the European Engineering Industries Association) lack the resources and internal decision-making procedures that are necessary to pro-actively influence the agenda of EU policy making (Gerlach, 2006). Often, they only have a few full-time staff members, and even fewer employees that focus on foreign economic policies. Moreover, the need to gain and maintain members distracts them from their objective of influencing public policies. Given these constraints, my argument is that most lobbying on the EU's foreign economic policies is reactive, namely in response to either foreign policies that hurt European economic interests or policy proposals formulated within Europe that are likely to impose concentrated costs on economic actors. Only a few groups will be able pro-actively to influence EU foreign economic policies; nevertheless, the reactive lobbying is sufficient to ensure that few EU policies run counter to concentrated economic interests.

Access to EU decision making

Groups aiming to influence EU trade policy have excellent access to decision makers. They can direct their lobbying effort at several different political actors, including national governments, the European Commission, and the European Parliament. Given the important role that they play in determining EU trade policy, most lobbying can be expected to be channelled through national governments. In the EU's institutional framework, national governments have the final say over most aspects of trade policy making, with consensus (in cases in which qualified majority voting applies) or unanimity (at the end of major trade negotiations that cover topics that require unanimity) decisions prevailing in the Council of Ministers. The available evidence indicates that interest groups have excellent access to national governments. Many ministries that are responsible for formulating trade policy have established formal or informal dialogues with societal interests with a stake in trade policy. In the United Kingdom, this dialogue is known as the Trade Policy Consultative Forum and in Denmark the 'Beach Club process'. Also through indirect channels, interest groups may influence the positions adopted by national governments. These indirect channels include attempts to shape public opinion (which in turn should influence government positions), lobbying of legislators and parties, and the provision of information and expertise to public officials.

Societal actors can also strive to influence the European Commission. The Commission plays a key role in decision making, as it both has the right of initiative and represents the EU in negotiations with non-member countries. Contrary to claims made in some studies, I suggest that even though the European Commission does not face elections, it has ample incentives to listen to societal interests. A key interest of the Commission is to avoid situations in which its proposals fail to get passed in the Council of Ministers (Woll, 2009). Knowing that societal interests can influence the position of member state governments, this interest ensures that the Commission will try to integrate the position of European industry and service providers at an early stage, thus allowing it to present member states with proposals that are "'pre-approved" by European industry' (Cowles, 2001: 171). For that reason, the European Commission has been proactive in searching for input from interest groups of all shades (Gerlach, 2006: 178). The resulting ease of access to the Commission is illustrated by the fact that nearly 900 groups from all over Europe (and a few from beyond) were registered with the Civil Society Dialogue (a series of meetings between Commission officials and stakeholders on specific topics) organized by the Directorate General for Trade in 2009.

Finally, groups can lobby the European Parliament, which gained substantial powers over EU trade policy with the entry into force of the Lisbon Treaty in December 2009. This institution is very accessible to groups representing societal interests. While most research has shown that non-economic interests have relatively better access to the parliament than to national governments or the European Commission, this does not mean that economic interests cannot wield influence over this institution. The upgrading of the parliament's role resulting from the Treaty of Lisbon thus will not result in policy outcomes that run counter to the interests of concentrated interests. At most, it has introduced a further veto player – that is, an actor that has the formal power to block political decisions – that makes movement away from the status quo even more difficult.

The EU's institutional set-up thus offers many veto points for societal interests, favouring groups that defend the status quo over those that want to change the EU's foreign economic policies. After the creation of the European Economic Community in the late 1950s, the resulting bias benefited protectionist interests. That protectionist interests were the beneficiaries of the EU's institutional framework runs counter to the argument that sees delegation as an attempt by decision makers to keep protectionist pressures at bay (Meunier, 2005). Only for a variety of exogenous reasons, including technological change and the incentives offered to European societal interests in international trade negotiations, did the EU's status quo move towards freer trade over time (Dür, 2010). In the meantime, the EU's trade policy status quo, with the notable exception of agriculture, is relatively close to the free trade end of the continuum, which in turn is locked in by societal interests benefiting from an open trading system.

Preference attainment

Given the excellent access that organized economic interests have to decision makers, it is no wonder that they have seen their preferences reflected in policy outcomes. The EU's negotiating position in the Doha Development Agenda (which was started in 2001 and is ongoing at the moment of writing), a major round of trade talks in the framework of the World Trade Organization, illustrates this point. The EU has been at the forefront in pushing for the launch of this round from the mid-1990s onwards. It has demanded a further reduction of tariffs on industrial goods, a liberalization of services trade, international rules covering trade facilitation, public procurement, competition policy, and investment (these were known as the Singapore issues at that time), and a limited liberalization of agricultural trade.

On all of these aspects, the EU's position has received substantial backing and only very limited opposition from business interests (Dür, 2008). All broad business associations, both EU-level and national-level ones, supported the launch of the negotiations. They also demanded a further liberalization of trade in industrial goods. The liberalization of trade in services (such as financial services, telecommunications and transport) was backed by a particularly broad alliance of societal interests, including both service providers and producers of industrial goods (many of which sell hardware together with complementary services). The only services sector in which European providers have taken a protectionist stance is cultural services. Given the argument made here, it is no wonder that the EU's position was to ask for an exception to this service sector (maintaining the EU's *exception culturelle*).

The demands voiced by societal interests also explain the Commission's insistence on talks about trade facilitation, that is, the reduction of costs that hamper the movement of goods across borders. The Commission's position on this issue has been supported by actors such as the Foreign Trade Association, the European Round Table of Industrialists, the chemical industry, and the European Information and Communication Technology Industry Association. In the negotiations concerning the liberalization of agricultural trade, the EU's position – although a stretch between interests that want the EU to open this sector in exchange for foreign concessions and interests that support a protected European agricultural market – has been supported by a surprisingly broad coalition of societal interests. In short, across the full agenda of the Doha Development Agenda, the EU's position reflected the preferences of economic pressure groups.

Equally, European societal interests have consistently seen their interests reflected in bilateral trade negotiations between the EU and non-member countries. In fact, major agreements negotiated by the EU can mainly be seen as a response to lobbying by European exporters. For example, after the United States, Canada and Mexico signed the North American Free Trade Agreement, European exporters mobilized to ensure continued access to the Mexican market (Dür, 2007). In particular, the automobile, chemical, pharmaceutical, telecommunications, and textile and footwear sectors were active in lobbying both member states and the European Commission. Not least responding to this lobbying effort, the EU concluded a far-reaching free trade agreement with Mexico in 2000. Similarly, there has been a strong mobilization of export interests in favour of the negotiations between the EU and South Korea, which resulted in a free trade agreement in 2009. Other trade agreements, such as the Economic Partnership Agreements between the EU and a large number of developing countries in Africa, the Pacific, and the Caribbean, while not being pushed by European economic interests, did not run counter to their interests either.

Importantly, my argument is not that all societal interests are equally able to shape the EU's trade agenda. Non-governmental organizations that defend positions that do not directly, and in a concentrated manner, affect the economic interests of their supporters (such as groups working in the fields of environmental protection, poverty eradication, and human rights) in most cases are not able to counter the influence wielded by concentrated economic interests (Dür and De Bièvre, 2007). This is so even though they, just as the economic interests, avail themselves of good access to decision makers. Rather, the reasons for their limited influence are to be found in the lack of resources that groups need to sustain a long campaign and the fact that the positions that they defend are far from those that the European Commission considers to be in the (international and intra-European) win set.

Self-assessment of influence

By itself, a coincidence between preferences and outcomes is not proof of influence. Such a coincidence could also be a result of either luck or 'reverse lobbying' that leads groups to adopt the positions pushed by public officials (Woll, 2009). The above discussion of interest group access and the level of interest group activity already partly responds to the concern that preference attainment may only be a result of luck. Also supportive of the causal argument that sees societal interests influencing EU trade policy is the observation that many groups assess themselves as having considerable influence. This self-assessment of influence can be witnessed in groups' statements praising the EU's negotiation position and portraying the European Commission as a service institution to European business. A survey of a random sample of groups registered in the Civil Society Dialogue database of the European Commission also backs this point (Dür and De Bièvre, 2007). Asked to assess the extent to which their activities affect European trade policy (with the possible responses being to a large extent, to some extent, not really, and not at all), 95 per cent of respondents representing business and agricultural interests replied 'to a large extent' or 'to some extent'.

Conclusion

I have argued that societal interests dominate EU foreign economic policy making, and especially trade policy, under most circumstances. In fact, this finding is not particularly astonishing. Trade policy (and foreign economic policy in general) has had low public salience in the EU for a long time. Its aggregate economic effects are not particularly large either, at least when compared to fiscal policy or the setting of interest rates. According to most estimates, a successful conclusion of the current round of negotiations in the World Trade Organization, for example, would only have minor consequences for the gross domestic products of most EU member states. At the same time, trade policy can have very large (and in many cases easily predictable) distributional consequences for individual producers and providers of goods and services, with internationally competitive firms winning and import competitors losing as a result of a liberalization of trade. These are ideal pre-conditions for pressure groups to influence policy. The available evidence suggests that they make ample use of this opportunity.

11.2 EU foreign economic policy: the autonomy of EU institutions

Cornelia Woll

Demonstrators at global trade talks and economic summits regularly point out that business lobbies dominate the making of foreign economic policy. The EU is not exempt from this critique. In fact, interest groups regularly participate in EU policy-making processes and they are very well established in the national capitals and Brussels, where about 15,000 lobbyists are currently active. This level of activity is not astonishing since the stakes for powerful economic actors are high in areas such as trade and investment. Policy makers also openly declare that the objective of such policies is to create the most beneficial context for their industries. At the same time, NGOs argue that it is precisely the undue influence of business lobbyists that explains the biases of foreign economic policies in favour of big companies and they denounce what they call 'corporate globalization'.

And yet, it appears that business influence depends on the willingness of European officials to listen to their demands. Successful lobbying is built on cooperation with European decision makers not traditional pressure politics. Moreover, many of the associations criticized by activists were actually founded with the support of the European Commission, for example the Transatlantic Business Dialogue or the European Services Forum. Does business lobbying then really play such a central role in the making of the EU's foreign economic policy?

This contribution examines the dynamics of EU trade policy making and counters the assumption that interest groups call the shots when it comes to defining European policy objectives. It argues that the degree of lobbyists' influence depends on the interests and choices of the policy makers, which retain enough autonomy to ignore societal demands. I argue that this is in part due to the institutional set-up of the EU. EU trade policy is marked by a phenomenon of reverse lobbying, where the European Commission encourages business interests to become politically active in order to gain legitimacy on policy issues *vis-à-vis* the member states. To study only the distribution and strength of lobbying demands would thus provide a misleading picture of EU trade policy and EU foreign economic policies more broadly.

The dynamics of EU trade policy making

Fundamentally, analyses of economic lobbying divide into two camps: a first strand argues that foreign economic policy is tailored to serve the interest of firms; the second points to the institutional framework of policy making and argues that decision makers are sufficiently autonomous from societal pressures and can make policy choices based on a mix of motives. The first line of argument relies on a political economy framework, where governments directly respond to business demands. Scholars in the second group stress the mechanisms of delegating policy authority from the electorate and its representatives to public actors. They argue that public actors, and the Commission in particular, maintain an important degree of autonomy. It is helpful to look at the three main actors of EU trade policy – the Commission, the member states, and interest groups – in order to understand the dividing lines between these two camps.

The European Commission

Following the establishment of a common external tariff, trade policy has turned into one of the most integrated policy areas in the EU. The setting of the agenda and the conduct of negotiations is the responsibility of the Commission, in cooperation with the member states. Results are adopted by the foreign ministers of member states in the General Affairs Council either by qualified majority voting under exclusive competence or by unanimity under mixed competence. In practice, however, consensus decisions are the norm. Moreover, the European Commission faces its external negotiation partners and has to be accountable to a myriad of stakeholders – the member states, of course, but also the European Parliament, the European Court of Justice, and, last but not least, economic and social interest groups. Using this complexity, it can assume leadership and increase its room for manoeuvre by referring to tensions between the different demands (van den Hoven, 2004). Delegation from the member states to the supranational institutions thus created a kind of 'autonomy by design' (Elsig, 2007).

Advocates of this argument have proposed several hypotheses about the ends to which the Commission will use its autonomy. For some, the insulation from protectionist pressures was a means to cement the policy objective of trade liberalization (Meunier, 2005: 7–8), because Commission bureaucrats do not depend on re-election. Young (2004), in turn, points out that the EU is not necessarily liberal, but that the Commission pursues solutions that fit the goals of the member states collectively. These goals can either be the liberalization of trade policy or the imposition of regulatory constraints that apply to the entire EU and shield it from the outside. Realist approaches have pointed out that the Commission can also pursue geo-political strategies, such as balancing against the US or containing China (Zimmermann, 2007). Which of these objectives will most likely determine EU trade policy choices appears to depend on the context of international pressures and external challenges. Nonetheless, all authors within this literature strand concur that the role of the supranational institutions in EU trade policy goes beyond pure intergovernmental decision making.

The member states

To oversee the actions of the Commission, member states have put in place multiple control mechanisms (De Bièvre and Dür, 2005). Long before the formal adoption of a mandate, the Commission submits the proposal to member states to prepare for discussions with the Committee of Permanent Representatives (COREPER), which is composed of national trade officials, and eventually the Council. Since opposition from the member states can entirely block a proposal, achieving consensus during these negotiations is crucial for the Commission to act effectively. The extensive formal and informal procedures that help to coordinate the interests of the member states with the actions of the European Commission are at the heart of current analyses of EU trade policy making (De Bièvre and Dür, 2005).

With reference to these control mechanisms, several authors argue that it is the interests of the member states that determine trade policy. While some claim that member states are motivated by geo-political considerations, others highlight economic interests. Dür (2010) makes the case most forcefully by tracing EU policy objectives back to the interest of exporters, who successfully lobbied their national governments and thereby shaped external policy. Similarly, Ehrlich (2009) demonstrates the importance of member state control by showing that despite common tariff schedules, member states are actually subject to quite different conditions depending on the bundle of goods that they import. The resulting difference in the actual trade-weighted tariffs of each member states is intentional, he argues, and results from the pressures of the affected industries in each country. For Ehrlich and Dür, the economic interests of domestic firms are thus key to understanding member states' behaviour on trade policy. Protection for import-competing firms is achieved through differential tariffs and protection for exporters through targeted trade agreements with key markets.

Interest group influence

This brings us to the third potential driver of EU trade policy: interests groups, which can be both economic actors and NGOs interested in trade-related issues such as labour standards, the environment or economic development. The previous discussion has highlighted that interest groups can become active at the national level and pressure member state governments to defend their interests on external trade *vis-à-vis* other member states. Relying on an extensive literature on the political economy of trade, the causal argument employed by these authors postulates that government officials seek to increase campaign financing and/or their chances of getting re-elected and are therefore attentive to interest groups with strong preferences on trade policy. Public interest NGOs (that is, groups pursuing policies that do not have concentrated benefits or costs for their members or supporters) are likely to find it difficult to become politically active on trade policy, so the main focus in this domestic lobbying literature has been on firms and business associations.

Alternatively, interest groups can become active at the European level and try to enter the EU trade policy-making process at various stages. Indeed, the Commission consults extensively with firms, business and professional associations, and NGOs in order to define specific stakes in its proposal. Furthermore, the Commission is also the main lobbying target for groups that demand protection against 'unfair' foreign competition through anti-dumping procedures or countervailing duties. Interest groups are thus present at both the domestic and the European level.

However, very few observers contend that the mere presence of private interests is sufficient to explain the evolution of trade policy, with the exception of advocacy groups warning against the increase of lobbying in Brussels. In the scientific literature, the role of interest groups depends on the ways in which they contribute to shaping the economic preferences of member states or the policy objectives of the Commission, which reflects the two camps on the governance of EU trade policy cited in the beginning. Intergovernmentalists tend to evaluate the importance of interest groups with a rational choice perspective where domestic politics shapes member state preferences. Supranationalists concentrate on the coalitions between European institutions and lobbyists active in Brussels and most often adopt a perspective close to the 'autonomy by design' argument.

Commission autonomy from societal demands

It is difficult to determine whether intergovernmentalists or supranationalists provide a more accurate picture of EU trade policy, because the absence of conflict can be interpreted as either complete autonomy of the European Commission or perfect control by the member states. Moreover, the fact that businesses voice demands which are actually reflected in policy choices says little about the mechanisms at work. Taken together, these two problems highlight the weakness of political-economy approaches, which tend to over-estimate the weight of interest groups in EU trade negotiations.

By contrast, I argue that the main difficulty with interest-group fo-cused accounts is the assumed uni-directionality of influence going from interest groups to policy makers. To see this missing link in the dynam-ics of EU trade policy making, it is important to consider, (1) how the Commission relies on interest groups and actively solicits their help through reverse lobbying, and (2) how interest groups adapt to these opportunities by choosing their policy venue according to the demands they would like to voice. This adaptation results from the discretion the Commission has in responding to lobbying.

Reverse lobbying

Over the course of trade talks, in particular during the Uruguay Round (1986–94), the Commission had to face US negotiators with very strong business support behind them, and openly complained about the ab-sence of European firms. Integrating business interests into the formu-lation of trade objectives therefore became an important goal for the European Commission in the 1990s, with the aim of strengthening its negotiating position. The creation of interest groups and fora such as the Transatlantic Business Dialogue, which brings together CEOs from both sides of the Atlantic, or the Civil Society Dialogue, which focuses on non-profit organizations, illustrates that the Commission actively so-licits participation from private actors and is willing to listen to their suggestions.

On the one hand, private actors can supply expertise and information about their competitive position, which help to bolster the EU's nego-tiating stance *vis-à-vis* the outside. On the other hand, business sup-port helps the Commission to gain information about potential lines of conflict between the member states and to increase the urgency of its proposals. Both externally and internally, business support and inter-est group activity more generally is thus an important resource for the Commission. This explains why business–government relations are tight during trade negotiations, but it also indicates that we should not neces-sarily equate this closeness with one-sided influence (Woll, 2008).

Commission autonomy

Since Commission officials do not depend on re-election by constituency interests, firms cannot exert direct pressure on European officials to re-inforce their demands. Therefore, business access is not automatic; it de-pends on the degree to which private actors can offer the resources the Commission is interested in. Business lobbying on trade is thus marked by a particular exchange logic, where firms provide expertise and sup-port in order to gain access to the policy process (Bouwen, 2002). Not the intensity of lobbying activities, but the way in which it corresponds to Commission objectives is key to success.

The selective access at the European level creates a two-channel logic for business lobbyists, which specifies different routes according to the content that firms seek to defend. Export-oriented industries lobby the Commission to press for further liberalization and market access, while import competing industries concentrate on instruments of commercial defence such as anti-dumping and countervailing duties and work with their national governments. Put differently, classical protectionism is easier to achieve in interaction with national governments, while cooperation on the elaboration of pan-European solutions – such as liberalization or new regulation – promises an excellent working relationship with the European Commission.

Several authors have shown how business lobbying has changed over time to take into account the institutional environment of EU trade policy. In particular, firms that lobby at the supranational level have moved from protectionism to non-tariff barriers to preferences for multilateralism in order to lock in national regulatory models (Woll, 2008). Concerning bilateral or regional trade agreements, exporters who can benefit from market access have formed coalitions with the Commission and their national governments to support negotiations. This adaptation of trade lobbying shows that firms have learned to move certain demands to other levels, once they realized that the Commission would remain unresponsive. The adaptation of lobbying strategies thus testifies to the autonomy the Commission enjoys from societal demands that do not fit its own agenda.

Conclusion

In sum, business lobbying is an important element of EU trade policy making. However, business activities are dependent on the opportunities offered by the European Commission. The reverse lobbying in turn creates a two-channel logic, which implies that interest groups face a trade-off when lobbying the European Commission: if they adapt their demands to the Commission's objective, they will find an open ear; if they press more narrowly for their own interests, they risk being ignored. Explaining EU foreign policies as the result of extensive business lobbying thus overlooks both the capacity of European institutions to ignore certain demands and the reverse influence, whereby EU institutions actually shape what businesses will publicly engage on. Analysing European trade dynamics must entail an understanding of the institutional set-up, because the ways in which lobbyists can successfully influence policy depends on the balance struck between the European Commission and the member states.

Chapter 12

Does the EU Act as a Normative Power?

Editors' introduction

For centuries, states were the main actors on the global stage. International organizations and supranational institutions, such as the EU, were seen as little else but instruments in the hands of powerful governments and their constituents. Thus, it is not surprising that few commentators cared to think about the EU as a global actor during the early decades of European integration. Events in the early 1990s changed all this. The end of the Cold War removed the umbrella of bipolar great-power rivalry under which the Europeans were hiding. The Maastricht treaty institutionalized a common foreign and security policy as part of the EU, and the bloody break-up of Yugoslavia brought home the need for common approaches to many pressing international issues, which were beyond the problem-solving capacity of single member states. In more and more areas, ranging from foreign trade to development aid, environmental diplomacy, human rights policy, financial regulation, energy issues, and so on, the European Union became an international actor on its own right (Bretherton and Vogler, 2006). The earlier debate on whether the EU should be seen as an independent actor on the world stage petered out. Now the focus was on the issue of precisely what kind of an actor the EU was. Does it act increasingly like a traditional state with similar means and ends or does it constitute something entirely new?

Already, after the first attempts of the Europeans to coordinate their foreign policies in the quite inefficient EPC (European Political Cooperation) framework, some authors speculated that the then European Communities would not only become a new type of actor but that it would behave in a different way, namely as a so-called civilian power (Bull, 1982; Duchêne, 1972). Civilian powers were expected to put an emphasis on non-military means in their international behaviour, to prefer multilateral diplomacy to traditional power politics and to try to promote democratic values. The reaction of the United States to 9/11, in particular the Iraq War, which was opposed by many EU members, seemed to emphasize this distinction. While the US and other great powers ultimately relied on hard power, the EU seemed to be equipped with a different kind of power: soft power (Nye, 2002). A comparison of the National Security Strategy 2002, issued by the Bush administration, and the European Security Strategy of 2003 (ESS, 2003), underlined this. In 2002, Ian Manners published an article in the Journal of Common Market Studies *in which he claimed that the EU indeed acted differently, in a way which makes it possible to call the EU a 'normative power': not only its means, but, above all, its ends are shaped by normative concerns. Given that its very existence was based on multilateral understandings, an emphasis on shared values and the rejection of traditional great power diplomacy, the EU was supposed to base its external actions on the same principles The article has become one of the most widely quoted pieces in research on European integration, and ever since, the debate has continued on whether the EU behaves really differently in the international arena. The controversy about 'Normative Power Europe' feeds into wider debates on the 'nature' of the EU as an international actor and on the relevance of norms, perceptions and 'roles' in international relations.*

Ian Manners restates his argument in the ensuing pages, showing how a normative power approach can lead to a better understanding of how the EU acts in the global arena. Mark Pollack challenges this notion and thinks that the EU is not different from traditional state actors, as it employs material and ideational power resources to further its goals and often acts rather hypocritically. The debate illustrates not only different ways of seeing the EU as global power, but also different methods of analysing this question: while Pollack's analysis is an example of a rationalist account, Manners shows how a reflexive approach, which sees the interests of actors not as reflections of their capabilities and constraints but as derived from their idea-based interpretations of reality, can enrich our understanding of the EU. These two contributions thus represent not only one of the most pervasive controversies in EU studies and the discipline of international relations in general, but they are also of huge relevance to the external dimension of various EU policies, such as agriculture (Chapter 10), foreign economic policy (Chapter 11) and security (Chapter 14). The issue of normative power is also a core part of the identity debate (Chapter 6).

12.1 The European Union's normative power in global politics

Ian Manners

How can we best understand the European Union (EU) in global politics? The most popular approaches to this question seek to answer it in a number of ways – by comparing it with other actors such as states, regional organizations or international organizations – or by declaring it unique and beyond comparison. Both political and scholarly assessments argue that 'we are one of the most important, if not the most important, normative powers in the world' (Barroso in Peterson, 2008: 69) and that 'Europe has tremendous normative power' (Moravcsik, 2010: 18). The normative power approach set out here makes it possible to explain, understand, and judge the EU in global politics by rethinking the nature of power and actorness in a globalizing, multilateralizing and multipolarizing era. The EU uses normative power in global politics but the question is whether it is more prone than other actors to do so? In areas which are core to the 'European project', it seems clear that the EU is more disposed to use normative power.

This short contribution sets out the normative power approach by asking four further questions about, (1) the *meaning* of normative power; (2) normative *pouvoir* as an ability; (3) the method of *analysis*, and; (4) an *assessment* of the EU's normative power in global politics.

Three meanings of normative power: what does 'normative power' mean?

Over the past decade there have been wide-ranging debates over the meaning of the EU's 'normative power' in global politics. These evolving debates have been covered in numerous volumes (Adler *et al.*, 2006; Aggestam, 2008; Gerrits, 2009; Laïdi, 2008a, 2008b; Lucarelli and Manners, 2006; Manners, 2010; Sjursen, 2006; Tocci, 2008; Whitman, 2011; Whitman and Nicolaïdis, forthcoming).

The social sciences have many different understandings of 'normative power', but in EU studies normative power has three particular meanings, as illustrated in Figure 12.1. The first is its emphasis on normative theory, that is, how we judge and justify truth claims in social science. The second meaning of normative power is as a form of power (*pouvoir*) that is ideational rather than material or physical. The third meaning of normative power is as a characterization of an ideal type of international actor (*puissance*).

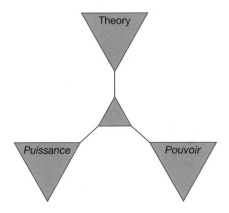

Figure 12.1   *The three meanings of normative power*

Theory

Normative theory is commonly believed to lie in opposition to empirical experience or positive description. The justification of the selection of empirical data, the value given to a particular interpretation of data, and the claims regarding why such research should be judged important, however, all involve normative truth claims. The emphasis on normative theory in the study of the EU's normative power makes clear that simply focusing on empirical truth claims is unsustainable – analysis needs to also account for how we judge and justify such claims, as well as engage in critique. Thus engaging with normative power suggests, first and foremost, that the analyst needs to think about their understanding of normative theory, regardless of whether it is more empiricist or more critical in orientation. An example of the deployment of such normative approaches is found in the argument that 'an EU capable of acting as a normative power and a major player on the global scene is a basic prerequisite if our goal for the EU is to secure peace, maintain stability, foster economic prosperity and preserve our lifestyle over the next 50 years' (Bonino, 2007).

Pouvoir

The emphasis of a normative form of power, or *pouvoir*, is on the ability to use normative justification rather than an ability to use material incentives or physical force (see discussion below). This ability to use a normative form of power, in the shape of normative justification, has to constantly come to terms with the intersection and interaction of other forms of power (material incentives or physical force). Whether focused on EU norm promotion, trade practices, or peacekeeping missions, this dilemma of combining normative power with material or physical forms of power arises. The emphasis on normative forms of power assumes that the prioritizing of normative power may help ensure that any subsequent or parallel use of material incentives and/or physical force is thought about and utilized in a more justifiable way. The EU's use of security-community practices in the Euro-Mediterranean represent an example of the application of 'normative power' (*pouvoir*) in international relations (Adler and Crawford, 2006: 4).

Puissance

A normative ideal type of actor, or *puissance*, places the focus on the extent to which the EU or any actor in global politics may be characterized by its use of non-coercive normative forms of power in the promotion of international norms . In order to assess this, analysis of the principles, actions and impact of norm promotion is necessary. Such analysis makes it possible to disaggregate the role of international norms and use of non-coercive actions in order to judge whether actors in global politics can be characterized as *more* or *less* normative types of actors. One example of normative *puissance* can be seen in the EU's civilian missions (EU Police Mission, EUPOL Proxima, EU Police Advisory Team, and EULEX Kosovo) in the former Yugoslavia since 2003, although this is qualified by inconsistencies over time in a difficult environment (Juncos, 2011: 97).

Pouvoir: ability – what form does normative *pouvoir* take?

As introduced in the previous section, normative *pouvoir* takes a form of power that is ideational rather than material or physical. It is necessary to differentiate the ability to use normative justification from that of the use of material incentives or physical force (see Figure 12.2).

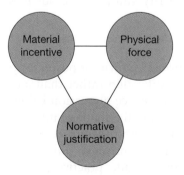

Figure 12.2   *Forms of power*

Material incentives

Material incentives represent the most common understanding of the EU's ability to exercise power in global politics. General examples of the use of material incentives by the EU might include trade preferences, trade sanctions, technical assistance, or development assistance. All of these policies involve the offer or denial of material benefits for the receiving parties. The most obvious exercise of material incentives can be found in the use of 'transference' when the EU trades goods, or provides aid or technical assistance with third parties through largely substantive or financial means. Such transference may be the result of the 'carrot and stick' approach of financial rewards and economic sanctions. Examples of transference and material incentives have been seen in the impact of pre-accession assistance to countries joining the EU, as well as development assistance to Cotonou states. An example of the combination of material incentives and normative persuasion is found in the EU's promotion of labour standards through trade (Orbie, 2011: 179).

Physical force

In contrast to material incentives, physical force involves the physical presence and/or overt use of coercive force by the EU in global politics. General examples of the use of physical force by the EU might include the deployment of EU rule of law, border, police, or military operations. All of these operations are capable of using physical force such as imprisonment, policing activities, or military action. The 'overt presence' of the EU in third states and international organizations may also contribute to the emphasis placed on physical force. Such physical presence, including the role of the European External Action Service or EU member states' participation in UN peacekeeping missions, may lead to greater concern for, and use of, physical force in global politics. An example of the interplay of normative justification and physical force is found in the EU's emphasis on human security in its engagement with the Democratic Republic of Congo (Martin, 2011: 207).

Normative justification

The third form of power is that of normative justification which, if it is to be convincing or attractive, must involve persuasion, argumentation, and the conferral of prestige or shame by the EU in global politics. General examples of the use of normative power by the EU might include the promotion of UN conventions, the creation of fora for dialogue and persuasion (such as association councils), or the socialization of candidate countries into international norms. Normative justification may be facilitated by 'procedural diffusion' involving the institutionalization of a relationship between the EU and a third party, such as an inter-regional cooperation agreement, membership of an international organization or enlargement of the EU itself. Examples of these three procedural factors might be the inter-regional dialogue with the African Union, membership of the EU in the World Trade Organization, or the current enlargement negotiations taking place with the accession countries of southeastern Europe and Turkey. There are examples where normative power discourse may allow EU actors to have positive influence in conflict situations (such as Cyprus and the Middle East), but these are not without problems such as inconsistency in the Israel/Palestine case (Diez and Pace, 2011: 211 and 223).

Analysis: what is the best method of *analysis* to understand normative power?

Having set out the *meanings* of normative power, including normative *pouvoir* and normative *puissance*, the question immediately arises of the best method of *analysis* to study the EU (or any actor) in global politics. The normative power analytical approach combines a tripartite analytical framework, which can be used causally or constitutively to understand the EU's normative power. The tripartite analytical framework involves examining the principles the EU promotes, the actions it takes in their promotion, and the impact of such promotion. The framework provides a causal method of explaining how principles can lead to actions; how actions may have an impact: and how any such impact might change the principles. Following a different approach, the framework provides a constitutive method for understanding how principles, actions and impact construct the EU as an actor in global politics (see Figure 12.3].

Principles

The first part of a normative power analysis is to examine the principles at work in the understanding of normative *pouvoir*. Principles in the EU

Figure 12.3 *Tripartite analytical framework*

and its relations with the rest of the world draw upon the principles of the UN Charter, as well as the Helsinki Final Act, the Paris Charter, the Universal Declaration of Human Rights and UN Covenants, and the Council of Europe/European Convention on Human Rights. In practical terms such principles can be differentiated into the prime principle of sustainable peace; core principles of freedom, democracy, human rights, and rule of law; as well as the general provisions on equality, social solidarity, sustainable development, and good governance. The analytical challenge is to explain the extent to which such principles *cause* the creation of EU policies to promote them. In parallel, there is the challenge of understanding the way in which such principles *constitute* the EU as an actor, and thus the way their promotion is an extension of the EU polity. Example of differing EU principles at work can be found in the combination of cosmopolitan law (such as the UN charter) and communitarian social preferences (such as member state preferences) found in particularly difficult cases such as the EU's mission in Kosovo (Bickerton, 2011: 32).

Actions

The second part of a normative power analysis is to examine the actions an actor takes in the promotion of its principles. As discussed in the previous section, the use of normative justification in the promotion of principles would involve persuasion, argumentation, and the conferral of prestige or shame. EU actions in the promotion of principles cover a full spectrum of practices and policies, encouraging a more holistic, or comprehensive, approach to the many challenges of global politics. The EU has historically been better at addressing more structural challenges through development aid, trade, inter-regional cooperation, political dialogue and enlargement. The focus at this stage of analysis is explaining how these actions may *cause* an impact in target sectors and on other actors. At the same time, understanding how such actions *constitute* both the EU as an actor and other actors in the target sectors is analytically important. Examples of EU actions include support for regional integration in other regions such as South America, Africa and the Pacific (Grugel, 2004: 621; Meunier and Nicolaïdis, 2006: 914).

Impact

The third part of a normative power analysis is to examine the impact of actions taken in the promotion of principles. The impact of normative justification in the promotion of principles could involve socialization, partnership, and ownership. Socialization means being part of an open-ended process of engagement, debate and understanding. Partnership may involve the institutionalization of relationships created by the participating parties whether multilateral or plurilateral, international or transnational. Ownership might involve practices of joint or local ownership as a result of partner involvement and consultation. The emphasis at this third stage of analysis is explaining how any such impact may *cause* a rethink of the principles being promoted. In contrast, understanding how the responses of other actors and partners impacted by the EU may *reconstitute* the EU as a global actor is critical here. The example of EU development policy suggests a commitment and impact of actions in terms of Millennium Development Goals (Birchfield, 2011; Bonaglia *et al.*, 2006).

Assessment: how can we best assess the EU's normative power in global politics?

This short contribution has set out the normative power approach to understanding the EU in global politics. It has done so by suggesting there are three *meanings* of normative power; that normative *pouvoir* can be seen as a form of power distinct from material incentives or physical force; that normative *puissance* can be seen as an ideal-type actor in global politics; and that a tripartite *analysis* of principles, actions and impact can help causal explanations and constitutive understandings of normative power. This final section concludes by suggesting there are at least four ideal-type global actors with which to think about assessing and typifying the EU in global politics. By asking whether the EU or any global actor promotes more self-understood or more international principles, and whether it engages in more or less coercive actions, it may be possible to imagine four ideal-type global actors (Thomas Diez in Tocci and Manners, 2008: 304–6) as shown in Figure 12.4.

By using a comparative analytical approach for assessment it makes it possible to ask whether the EU is relatively prone to the promotion of more self-understood or more international principles; whether the EU is relatively more likely to engage in more coercive or less coercive actions; and whether the EU is having a relative impact of strengthening of solidarism or pluralism in international society. For example, aspects of the *realpolitik* ideal-type may be seen in the EU's self-understood and economically coercive trade policies (Orbie, 2011; Smith, 2011). In contrast, aspects of the *civilian power* ideal-type may be seen in the EU's self-understood and relatively non-coercive (in the sense that no state is forced to join) enlargement policy (Schimmelfenning, 2011: 728). By comparison, aspects of the *liberal internationalist* ideal-type may be seen in the emerging internationally understood and relatively coercive (involving localized engagement) EU peacebuilding framework, although this is more accurately described as 'post-liberal form of peacebuilding'

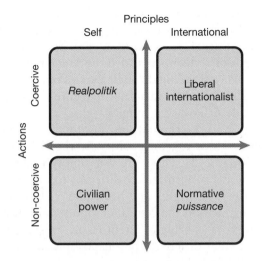

Figure 12.4 *Ideal-type global actors*

(Björkdahl, 2011; Richmond *et al.*, 2011). Finally, aspects of the *normative puissance* ideal-type may be seen in internationally understood and relatively non-coercive EU climate change policies (Lightfoot and Burchell, 2004, 2005; Scheipers and Sicurelli, 2007, 2008). What this assessment suggests is that we can find aspects of the EU in all four ideal-type actors. In areas, which are core to the global aspects of the 'European project', such as international public policy of climate change or the pursuit of multilateralism, the EU appears more like a *normative puissance* ideal-type. However, it also appears that in areas such as EU enlargement and peacebuilding, non-coercive actions or international principles are important aspects of other idea-types. Thus the EU uses normative power and analysts believe it to be important in both core and non-core areas of understanding the EU in global politics.

12.2 Living in a material world: a critique of 'normative power Europe'

Mark A. Pollack

There is, in contemporary literature on European Union foreign policy, a broad consensus that the EU today constitutes a 'normative power'. As first articulated by Ian Manners (2002) in an extraordinarily influential article, the idea of 'normative power Europe' (NPE) combines two fundamental claims.

The first of these claims is about the EU's 'normative difference', the notion that the EU, by virtue of its history, its nature as a hybrid polity, and its political and legal framework, is *constituted* by a commitment to certain constitutional norms that determine its international identity (Manners, 2002: 241). Reading through a series of historic declarations, policies and treaties, Manners identifies five core norms (peace, liberty, democracy, the rule of law, and human rights) and four minor norms (social solidarity, anti-discrimination, sustainable development, and good governance) which together constitute the EU's normative identity (Manners, 2002: 242). These are not simply universal or western norms; rather, 'the EU is normatively different to other polities with its commitment to universal rights and principles' (Manners, 2002: 241). Indeed, 'in my formulation the central component of normative power Europe is that it exists as being different to pre-existing political forms, and that this particular difference pre-disposes it to act in a normative way' (Manners, 2002: 242).

Manners' second claim is about the nature of the EU's 'normative power'. After reviewing traditional views of Europe as a 'civilian power' wielding material economic resources, and contemporary views of European Security and Defence Policy (ESDP) wielding military power, Manners suggests that these views need to be augmented by a consideration of Europe's normative power – a 'power of opinion', *'idée force'*, or the ability to shape conceptions of 'normal' in world affairs (Manners, 2002: 239). More specifically, he identifies six 'factors' or mechanisms of norm diffusion, which he refers to as contagion, informational diffusion, procedural diffusion, transference, overt diffusion, and a 'cultural filter' (Manners, 2002: 244–5). While not rejecting entirely the significance of material economic and political power, Manners argues that, 'the ability to define what passes for "normal" in world politics is, ultimately, the greatest power of all' (Manners, 2002: 253).

In the language of rational-choice theories such as intergovernmentalism, institutionalism and realism, NPE proposes a new and novel explanation of both the *preferences* and the *power* of the European Union in world affairs – the former generated by constitutive norms and the latter driven primarily by symbolic and ideational processes rather than by material resources.

There is something very powerful in this formulation. There can be little doubt that, with respect to human rights, the death penalty, multilateralism and the rule of law, European leaders see and present themselves as driven by sincere normative convictions in their interactions with the rest of the world. As Manners rightly pointed out, it would be difficult, if not impossible, to explain EU policies on an issue like the death penalty through any appeal to the material interests of the

member states, and the notion of the EU as a normative power has precipitated a series of books, articles and edited volumes in recent years
(see for example, Aggestam, 2008; Laïdi, 2008a; Lucarelli, 2007; and
Tocci,2008). Beyond the academy, NPE has penetrated the thinking of
EU practitioners, who increasingly present themselves as uniquely normative actors on the world stage. Whether this influence is due to the
accuracy of its claims, or the heroic light in which it paints the EU and
its leaders, however, remains an open question.

In fact, recent events in world politics, and contemporary scholarship by students of EU foreign policy, have begun to question the rather
heroic depiction of the Union as an inherently normative power, pure
in motivation and noncoercive in its behaviour. Across a range of issue-
areas frequently considered to be 'normative' in character, new scholarship suggests that material interests, and material power resources, are
at least as significant as normative ones. The image of the EU as a purely
normative actor, I argue, is an ideal type – one that illuminates certain,
perhaps more admirable, features of the EU as a global actor, but one
that should not be confused with a realistic portrayal of what the EU is
and does in world affairs.

Preferences

With respect to preferences, a growing body of scholarship challenges,
or at least lends nuance to, Manners' portrayal of the EU as an actor
uniquely driven by normative considerations. Manners, in his original
statement, simply accepts at face value the various declarations, policies
and treaties that spell out the EU's core normative principles. And his
illustrative case study of the EU's global campaign against the death
penalty emerges as an 'easy' case – one in which no EU member state
appeared to have a discernible material interest that might cut against or
undermine the Union's collective normative commitment.

By contrast, other recent scholarship suggests either that material
interests may underlie the EU's normative declarations (thus masking
the EU's hidden motives), or that EU normative and material concerns
may intermingle in determining EU preferences (the notion of 'mixed
motives'), or alternatively that material interests may cut across and
undermine the EU's public normative stance (hence generating charges
of hypocrisy; see for example, Aggestam, 2008: 7).

Claims that the EU's normative preferences are in fact a mask for
its hidden material interests are commonplace among the Union's conservative critics, who question the source and the sincerity of the EU's
commitment to multilateralism and the rule of international law. Robert
Kagan, for example, has famously suggested that the EU's embrace of

such principles actually reflects an effort to compensate for Europe's military weakness and tie down a hegemonic United States (Kagan, 2002). Others, for instance, Jack Goldsmith and Eric Posner, suggest that the EU's commitment to the rule of law and multilateralism is insincere, as witnessed by the Union's willingness to violate international law, where doing so will serve its material interests (Goldsmith and Posner, 2009). Such accounts serve a useful purpose in questioning the purity of the EU's motives, but they almost certainly go too far in reducing the EU's normative beliefs to hidden material preferences.

More convincing, in this context, are other studies that demonstrate mixed motives and even hypocrisy in the EU's 'normative' foreign policies. In their study of the EU's environmental diplomacy, for example, Daniel Kelemen and David Vogel (2009) suggest that, while the EU's global environmental leadership is consistent with EU norms such as multilateralism and sustainable development, a pure NPE approach pays inadequate attention to the role of economic interests. In their alternative, 'regulatory politics' approach, the EU has sought to export or upload its high environmental standards, not simply out of normative concern for the global environment, but at least in part in an effort to level the economic playing field *vis-à-vis* states with more lax economic standards. Indeed, the EU's environmental diplomacy is just one part of a broader Commission initiative to 'promot[e] European standards internationally through international organization and bilateral agreements', which, the Commission argues, 'works to the advantage of those already geared up to meet those standards' (European Commission, quoted in Pollack and Shaffer, 2009: 129).

We can also find mixed motives in other cases, where the EU's normative declarations can and sometimes do come into conflict with the material interests of EU member governments and their constituents. In the area of arms trading, for example, the EU's members expressed a genuine normative concern for preventing armed conflicts, which helped lead to the establishment of an EU code of conduct for arms trading with third countries, yet the large material interests of arms exporters in the various EU member states has resulted in provisions that are often politically rather than legally binding, and sufficiently vague as to impose few significant restrictions on such sales (Webber, 2010). Similarly in the human rights realm, the EU has been inconsistent in its insistence on observance of human rights, treading more softly in its criticisms of economically or strategically important states, such as Russia and China (Smith, 2001). Perhaps the most obvious case of EU hypocrisy, in which economic interests trump normative declarations, is the area of trade policy. Here, notwithstanding admirable normatively motivated efforts like the 'Everything but Arms' initiative, the Union's defence of the protectionist Common Agricultural Policy stands as a significant global impediment to economic development in the world's poorest nations, and perhaps the greatest single obstacle to further trade liberalization (Oxfam, 2003).

Power

Even if one concedes that the EU's foreign policy is motivated exclusively by normative ends, there remains the question whether the means or sources of EU power are normative, material, or – as seems likely – some combination of the two. To his credit, Manners did not argue that EU power arose *solely* through ideational processes – and indeed the experience of EU foreign policy in a range of areas has revealed the limits of normative power and the importance of material economic and, in rare cases, military power to promote the EU's values and interests in the world.

Take, for example, the case of EU enlargement, which is often seen as a triumph of the EU's normative power spreading democracy and free markets to the post-Soviet republics of central and eastern Europe. In fact, however, careful studies of EU enlargement have demonstrated that, while some of the effects of the EU might be partially attributable to learning from the EU's normative example, on balance 'the external incentives provided by the EU can largely account for the impact of the EU on candidate countries' (Schimmelfennig and Sedelmeier, 2005: 210–11; see also Vachudova, 2005; Zürn and Checkel, 2005). By contrast, in other post-Soviet states, such as Russia, Ukraine and Belarus, the EU's normative example, without the material promise of membership, has not been enough to prevent a backward slide into authoritarianism.

A second case, namely the EU and global human rights, similarly points to the importance of material pressure and economic conditionality in securing implementation of human rights norms in third countries. In the United Nations system, for example, the EU has been a consistent and impassioned advocate of human rights worldwide, but has few material incentives to offer other states, relying primarily on its normative example – and here we find the EU's consistently pro-human rights position losing ground to authoritarian defenders of national sovereignty like Russia and China who regularly defeat EU proposals on issue after issue in the UN Human Rights Council (Gowan and Brantner, 2008). By contrast, the EU has been found to have much greater influence on human rights practices when it explicitly links human rights performance to the material benefit of trade access to EU markets (Hafner-Burton, 2009).

Indeed, surveying the EU's human rights and environmental foreign policies in recent years, it is hard not to conclude that the EU foreign-policy practitioners have drunk the NPE Kool-Aid, believing that the force of the EU's normative example really could change the world, uncoupled from the EU's material sources of bargaining leverage. That view has served the EU poorly in the UN human rights realm, and condemned the Union to near-irrelevance at the Copenhagen climate-change negotiations in December 2009, where the final agreement on the 'Copenhagen Accords' was negotiated by the US, China, India, Brazil and South Africa without EU participation.

The limits of the EU's normative power, and the significance of its material power, are arguably most evident in European countries' controversial but ultimately successful military intervention in Libya, which succeeded in removing Colonel Muammar al-Quaddafi from power after four decades of authoritarian rule. Indeed, the Libyan case illustrates both the kernel of truth in, and the limits of, the NPE thesis. One could, with Manners, make a strong case that normative concerns about human rights and democracy were foremost in the minds of European leaders, yet those leaders were sharply divided about the use of military force, with Britain and France taking the lead in a NATO military operation while Germany opposed the use of force and abstained from the UN Security Council resolution authorizing the operation. In this case, the EU's normative position was not inherent in its nature but was rather deeply contested, and the means by which European countries effected change in Libya was not primarily normative but military. The success of the Libyan campaign does not, of course, suggest that the EU should seek to become a global military actor, but it does suggest that normative power alone has its limits, and that EU leaders should be prepared to supplement normative influence with the use of material (economic and occasionally military) power in defence of it its values and interests.

Conclusion

A careful reading of the EU's role in world affairs suggests a far more mixed and nuanced story than the heroic image of 'Normative Power Europe.' For those who believe in human rights, democracy, and the rule of law, there is little question that the contemporary EU and its member states have been, on balance, a force for good in the world. However, if we want to understand and use that force for good in the future, we would be better served to jettison the idealistic and heroic image of the EU as a purely normative actor, and instead understand the complex mix of material and normative preferences and power that make the EU an admirable, but also a flawed, inconsistent and sometimes failed advocate of its values on the global stage.

Chapter 13

Turkey and Beyond: Is EU Enlargement a Success Story or Has It Gone Too Far?

Editors' introduction

Enlargement has often been seen as the EU's greatest success story. From the first enlargement in 1973 to the most recent one in 2007, no fewer than twenty-one states have acceded to the EU. Many of the acceding countries were politically and economically weak when starting accession negotiations. Greece, for example, had been ruled by a military junta between 1967 and 1974, and still had to be considered a weak democracy when it joined the EU in 1981. Similarly, Portugal and Spain, the two countries that acceded in 1986, had been dictatorships until 1976 and 1975 respectively. All of these countries not only became stable democracies after entry to the EU, but also – at least until the recent sovereign debt crisis – witnessed economic development. No wonder that soon after the fall of the Iron Curtain and the transition to democracy in central and eastern Europe many of the formerly Communist countries deposited their wish to become members of the EU. As a consequence, the EU now has 27 member countries, with five more countries enjoying the status of official candidate states and another four countries either having applied or preparing the applications for membership.

With many of the EU's new member countries having seen rising standards of living, more regard for human rights, and more stable democratic institutions, enlargement indeed seems to be one of the most successful EU policy instruments. Critics of the EU's enlargement policy, however, warn that this conclusion may be flawed. They point to the difficulties that enlargement has posed to the EU's decision-making system, with an increasing number of states making the finding of consensus increasingly difficult (Preston, 1995). They also point out that the impact of enlargement on the accession countries may not have been as benign as emphasized by the enlargement optimists (Bohle, 2006). For some accession countries, it may have been better if they had themselves decided (based on broad societal support) to pursue certain economic and social reforms rather than having these reforms forced upon them from the

outside. Absent EU membership, they may also have had greater flex-
ibility to pursue autonomous economic policies more in line with their
domestic needs. The controversy is of outmost importance for the future
of the EU, not least as a result of Turkey's membership application.

In this volume, Rachel Epstein and Christopher J. Bickerton engage
in this debate. Epstein stresses the beneficial effects of enlargement on
the accession countries – according to her, it enhanced the security of
these countries, reinforced democracy, and created wealth. Bickerton
disagrees. In his view, the EU's expansion to the east depoliticized these
countries' transition to democracy and by doing so degraded political
life. Their debate is complemented by Chapter 2, which looks at the
impact of enlargement on decision making in the EU and Chapter 9
that discusses the EU's ability to stimulate economic growth by way of
cohesion funds.

13.1 The benefits of EU enlargement: stability, democracy and prosperity

Rachel Epstein

European Union enlargement to ten post-communist countries is the single most important development in erasing an east–west divide on the continent that had long predated the Cold War. To be sure, EU enlargement has had its flaws, both in process and outcomes. But the overwhelming weight of the evidence suggests that for central and eastern Europe (CEE), enlargement has enhanced security, reinforced democracy, and created wealth.

Enhancing security

Central and eastern Europe has always been geopolitically unstable. The Allies emerging from the Second World War divided Europe into two separate spheres. The Soviet Union was allowed to claim a significant buffer zone of 'satellite states', including the entire region that we now refer to as CEE. These 'satellites' would not only have regimes friendly to the USSR, but they would also be forced to undergo wholesale social transformation to ensure ideological consistency between the newly founded, so-called 'People's Democracies' of CEE and the Soviet Union. Included in the transformation were communist party takeovers of entire political systems between 1945 and 1948, authoritarian rule thereafter, collectivization in agriculture, and the nationalization of most property and industry (Rothschild and Wingfield, 2000).

The Western Allies allowed the Soviet Union to consolidate a sphere of influence under state socialist authoritarianism in part because of the massive – some would say heroic – efforts of the USSR during the Second World War. Indeed, without the enormous commitment required of Germany's Nazis on the Eastern Front, it is not clear the Allies could have defeated the Axis in the west and in the Pacific. But there is another reason for the Iron Curtain's particular configuration. And that is the division of Europe that is much deeper and older – in developmental, political and even psychological terms (Brenner, 1989; Wolff, 1994). Whether it was Stalin and Churchill negotiating the 'Percentages Agreement' in 1944 or the Allies constructing the post-war order at Potsdam in 1945, it was as if these victors were looking at a much older map of Europe in which a centuries-old developmental divergence marked a logical division of Europe – the eastern half, of which the west was not willing to defend (Bunce, 2000: 212–13). Western perceptions of eastern 'backwardness' help explain why the Allies ultimately relinquished Poland, Czechoslovakia, and Hungary despite the former two countries' longstanding formal ties to the Western Allies and the latter's uncertain status after the war. The Soviet Union, it turns out, was not committed to asserting hegemony over Hungary after the war, but ultimately did so when its political interventions there went unchallenged by the United States.

To the extent, then, that the Cold War division of Europe reflected much older understandings of what belonged to the west and what belonged to the east, the post-communist enlargement of the EU promises to undermine that earlier understanding and make CEE a much safer place to live. By giving CEE states a voice in the world's most powerful regional institution and through CEE's own embrace of the political and economic integration that EU membership requires, enlargement has shifted expectations of what constitutes 'Europe'. Expanding the definition of 'Europe' to include the experiences of post-communist states puts CEE out of reach of eastern aggression in a way the region has never been before. If the EU's power to shift expectations about such grand themes as 'what belongs to the west' seems far-fetched, it is worth remembering that the original impetus behind post-war European integration was precisely about shifting expectations. In that case, however, the organizing principle of the European Coal and Steel Community (ECSC) in 1952 was to make war between Germany and France not only impossible, but also 'unthinkable'.

Reinforcing democracy

If European integration has, from the outset, been about changing the European political context from one in which war had been commonplace to one in which war was unthinkable, European integration, and subsequently, enlargement, has also aspired to be about consolidating democracy. The common market for coal and steel had the practical effect of rechanneling German power through a supranational authority. By controlling the major inputs of war, the ECSC prevented German politicians from mobilizing political support around economic nationalism – in stark contrast to the inter-war period (Tooze, 2006). Greece had been a military dictatorship before joining in 1981. Similarly, both Spain and Portugal had been authoritarian before they became members in 1986. All three experienced early versions of European 'conditionality' in the sense that in order to join, they had to fulfil more than just the basic requirements of democratic governance.

The post-communist enlargements have put democratic aspirations at the centre of the EU's agenda. Starting with the Copenhagen Criteria in 1993, democracy, the rule of law, the protection of human rights, in addition to the economic criteria, were put forth as clear conditions that post-communist countries would have to meet in order to join. As in earlier enlargements, however, it is not easy to state definitively that it was the EU that made the difference between democracy on the one hand and authoritarianism on the other. That caveat notwithstanding, some evidence from the post-communist period and the democratizing effects of the EU can be brought to bear.

The existence of the EU, its policy of enlargement, and its monitoring practices in all likelihood did consolidate democracy in Romania and Bulgaria. Romania had no opposition movement to speak of under communism, so in the transition it was operatives from within the former dictatorial regime that orchestrated the ouster of President Nicolae Ceaușescu. When the same personnel took power through elections, they took the country in a decidedly 'illiberal' direction, limiting media freedoms, undermining the opposition (sometimes through violent means), and resorting to ethno-nationalist mobilization to build political support. Bulgaria did have an array of opposition groups that united in the transition and they did have some early electoral success. But in that country too, it was the former communists, re-named the Bulgarian Socialist Party, who dominated politics in the first seven years. And they, like their Romanian counterparts, were less than fully committed to the range of democratic practices that the EU ultimately insisted on. In both cases, the EU provided a clear alternative to both the political and economic programmes of the dominant communist successor parties, and in so doing, also helped mobilize opposition parties in both countries with EU-reform based platforms (Vachudova, 2005).

Slovakia is a third post-communist case in which EU pressure in the run-up to enlargement consolidated democracy. Both before and following Czechoslovakia's break-up at the beginning of 1993, nationalist elements under Vladimir Mečiar's leadership sought to centralize power, restrict the free flow of information and intimidate the opposition. Because of what appeared to be creeping authoritarianism, Slovakia was increasingly isolated internationally. The country risked falling irrevocably behind in the processes of both EU and the North Atlantic Treaty Organization's (NATO) enlargements. International opprobrium put pressure on Mečiar's coalition and provided the organizing basis for the opposition. Mečiar's party still won the most votes in the 1998 elections, but a new and pro-western coalition formed the government and thereafter embarked on a reform programme consistent with EU membership criteria (Kopstein and Reilly, 2003: 144–6). Democratic reforms concerning minority rights were also strengthened by EU conditionality in the Baltic States (Kelley, 2004).

Poland, Hungary and the Czech Republic are widely believed to be countries that would have been strongly democratic regardless of EU enlargement. This may be true, though it is also worth noting that only Czechoslovakia had any more than a very brief experiment with limited democracy in the inter-war period. We also do not know what toll a policy of EU exclusion would have had on these small, weak states that had repeatedly suffered invasion, occupation and massive loss of life. Admittedly, Ukraine, Georgia and Belarus are not perfectly comparable cases because of their recent histories as Soviet republics rather than as, at least nominally, independent nation-states. On the other hand, it is clear that whereas the EU has liberated Poland, Hungary and the Czech Republic from perennial and over-riding concerns about their power positions in the international system, a security deficit still plagues Ukraine, Georgia and Belarus – and their politics show it. Thus while the former three dedicate their energies to internal matters in ways largely consistent with EU norms, the latter three have been prone to centralizing authority (Ukraine) if not outright authoritarianism (Belarus) or military conflict (Georgia). Indeed, there is no post-communist country that has not been admitted to the EU that is more democratic than those within the EU's ranks. Again caution is warranted because it could be that the EU only admits those countries that are strongly democratic. Weighing the evidence, however, the EU has admitted several borderline cases in which democracy absent EU conditionality and membership was hardly a foregone conclusion.

A serious objection to the argument that the EU has consolidated democracy in post-communist countries is that much about the EU's process is in fact undemocratic. It is certainly true that the *acquis communautaire* is an enormous and non-negotiable body of law that candidate countries must take on in order to join. In everything from fisheries to central bank law, much policy that would normally be the domain of domestic debate is already decided. It may even be argued that the EU's top-down method of legal harmonization leaves little to the democratic process that in theory the EU, at least as stated in the Copenhagen criteria, champions.

Two arguments in the EU's defence come to mind. First, the EU's democratic credentials are at least in part supported by the fact that candidate countries have all wanted to join and so have voluntarily signed up for the rigorous accession process. The Copenhagen criteria, the *acquis*, and even the monitoring process that began with *Agenda 2000* in 1997 and the Regular Reports on each country's progress toward accession thereafter have been transparent pieces of the 2004 and 2007 enlargements that post-communist countries could have rejected – but at the cost of EU membership. It is therefore difficult to argue that the EU imposed anything on CEE.

Second, with regard to the claim that the EU's accession process takes issues off the table that should otherwise be the subject of domestic debate, this is true. But it is not true to an extent that seriously undermines democratic process in CEE states because there are still myriad issues on which the EU does not have established law and does not even have a firm opinion. So for example, the use of partially privatized pension schemes in CEE did not originate with the EU and has been an important distributional debate for some years in CEE (Orenstein, 2008). The EU also does not impinge on how education or health systems are organized. The welfare state, its scope and mission, have been left to member states to negotiate – this is as true in CEE as in the older 15 members. Moreover, although it was not the EU's preference, several of the post-communist candidates, later members, have even debated issues that were ostensibly dictated by the EU – including, for example, central bank independence. There has also been considerable room for domestic debate on monetary policy more generally. For although CEE states agreed to join the eurozone eventually, there is no fixed time-line in which they must do so. This has left CEE considerable latitude concerning policies that affect inflation, debts, deficits, interest rates and employment (Epstein and Johnson, 2010).

The aforementioned agenda is a crowded one, even given the 80,000 pages of law that CEE states had to adopt outright. It is therefore unlikely that symbolic politics in the form of ethno-nationalist mobilization or lustration have taken on a bigger role in CEE than they would have in the absence of enlargement. Symbolic politics are everywhere part of the democratic mix. If anything, the EU (with NATO's help) probably dampened the salience of symbolic politics by requiring that all aspiring members have good relations with their neighbours (Epstein, 2008). In addition, the absence of a membership perspective in the Balkans in the 1990s did little to subdue symbolic politics there.

Creating wealth

By joining the EU, CEE states gained access to a large and wealthy market, EU structural funds for economic development, and the Common Agricultural Policy (CAP) to protect their farmers. For those that have not yet done so, CEE states also have the option ultimately of joining the eurozone as a means of eliminating exchange rate risk, reducing transaction costs and thereby encouraging still more international economic exchange (by 2011, Slovenia, Slovakia and Estonia were the only post-communist states to have adopted the euro).

Economic growth in CEE has outpaced that of the west in recent years. CEE wages are rising and consumer access to goods and services is vastly greater than was ever possible under communism. In some sense, though, these material improvements in CEE were to be expected. Post-communist states started out, after all, with very low unit labour costs. Trade arrangements with the EU and later EU membership would, of course, lead to at least an initially impressive boost in output. Their proximity to western Europe, very competitive wages and production costs, and relatively high levels of education have also made the CEE states a magnet for foreign investment, which has accelerated capital accumulation and upgraded technology (EBRD, 2011).

But while the CEE growth model appeared impressive at least until the financial crisis that began in 2008, there is also little doubt that the region faces serious challenges going forward. As CEE wages have risen and some degree of price equalization across western and eastern economies has taken hold, CEE's earlier competitive edge will likely deteriorate. In addition, the financial crisis revealed that CEE's heavy dependence on foreign capital (most of the region's banks are foreign-owned, see Epstein, 2008) contributed to severe asset bubbles and foreign currency borrowing. With domestic demand likely to be weak in the years to come, it will be more imperative than ever to promote exports – but under conditions less auspicious than a decade ago.

Economic challenges within the EU notwithstanding, it is clear that economic opportunities are enhanced through membership, rather than diminished. In addition to the aid and CAP funds coming from the EU, post-communist members, even those still outside the euro, have likely enjoyed lower borrowing costs than they would have in the absence of membership. Inflation has also been brought under control. Membership has boosted investor confidence. International travel and working and studying abroad have been greatly eased by enlargement. The EU and CEE might have achieved most of these economic outcomes just by extending the market, foregoing the rigors of enlargement. That this more 'minimalist' vision of post-Cold War integration did not prevail is a credit to European leaders, who seem finally on the verge of obliterating an east–west divide that had defined the continent for far too long. Enlargement has conferred not just market access to CEE states, but more importantly, institutional power through EU structures. Such power and inclusion represent an enormous improvement upon any prior geostrategic arrangement the peoples of CEE have faced.

13.2 EU enlargement: a critique

Christopher J. Bickerton

Expansion has always been a part of European integration: from the inclusion of the British, Irish and Danes in 1973 through to the Iberian expansion in 1986 (Portugal and Spain; Greece joined in 1982) to the Scandinavian expansion in 1995 (Sweden and Finland). This ongoing expansion has been controversial. Twice over in the 1960s, General de Gaulle vetoed British membership of the EC, at least partly because he felt it would entrench US influence and power over western Europe. Others, not least the President of the European Commission, José-Manuel Barroso, have seen in the ever-expanding EU the birth of a European empire (Leca, 2009; Zielonka, 2006).

This contribution will focus on the most recent wave of enlargement: the 'big bang' of 2004. This saw the entry of ten new member states into the EU, eight of whom were former members of the eastern bloc. This was the largest single expansion and it has transformed the EU institutionally and ideologically. Celebrated as the realization of the dream of a united Europe, the EU's 2004 expansion was used to rejuvenate a flagging political project. Faced with an unprecedented political mobilization against the EU, most evident in the negative referendums on the EU Constitution in 2005 in France and the Netherlands, the EU and its member states hoped enlargement would serve as a source of political renewal. As one of its proponents put it, 'we may haggle and barter in Brussels, but it may be that it is in Istanbul that we shall write the next chapter in the European story' (Patten, 2005: 149).

Since those heady days of the mid-2000s, the EU's expansion has hit hard times. Croatia is likely to join soon, as is Iceland, but no other country is close to membership. Negotiations with the rest of the Balkans are slow and Turkey is losing interest in joining a club that keeps raising the bar to membership. Some welcome this 'enlargement fatigue', arguing that institutionally the EU cannot manage any new members. In particular, they point to Turkey, arguing that such a large country will only generate budgetary and labour mobility problems. Behind this endorsement of 'enlargement fatigue' is an ugly chauvinism: the difficulties of institutional adaptation serve as a façade behind which lurk cultural prejudices and fears.

This text will not criticize enlargement because of what the new members have done to the EU. In fact, it may be that new members have injected some life into an otherwise moribund Union. Rather, this contribution will criticize enlargement for what the EU has done to its new member states. Enlargement has consolidated two negative trends in eastern European political life: the rise of illiberal populist-style politics and technocracy. Additionally, the enlargement process can be criticized for the EU's narcissism: as a policy, it has been driven more by the EU's concerns about itself, its identity and its future, than by any concern with improving conditions of life in candidate countries. In this sense, enlargement has not effaced the old east–west divide. As in previous eras, eastern Europe remains the terrain upon which western Europe pursues its own concerns and desires.

Expansion into eastern Europe

The expansion of the EU into eastern Europe began in the early 1990s when European leaders, as a result of public and institutional pressures, offered eastern European governments the prospect of membership. Reticence and ad hocery were key features of the early years of the enlargement process. By the end of the 1990s, the question was no longer if but when and how many: would all candidate states join at the same time, or would they join one-by-one, or in groups? In the end, the enlargement process took just over ten years: from the elaboration of the membership criteria in 1993 to the entry of ten candidate states into the Union in 2004.

The problem of enlargement lies in this decade-long process of externally directed political, social and economic transformation. Of course, the trajectory of eastern European states since 1989 cannot all be attributed to the accession process to the EU. Indigenous developments are probably most important and they determined the manner in which astern European societies would interact with the EU (Bickerton, 2009). However, the accession process consolidated two negative features of the transition process: the technocratic manner in which transition was conducted and the undermining of the main institutions of democratic representation in eastern Europe. This latter feature lies behind a rise in populism in eastern Europe and the instability of its political life after 2004.

Depoliticizing transition

Whilst there was strong support for some of the more radical measures introduced after the collapse of Soviet rule in eastern Europe, there was also a good deal of discontent. After all, an entire way of life was being dismantled, to be replaced with an alternative that embraced wealth creation but ushered in great inequality and insecurity. Eastern European elites, cognizant of the demands they were making on their own populations, were careful to yoke these changes to the EU enlargement process. Transition was lifted from the realm of choice into the realm of necessity by virtue of its place in the reforms demanded by the European Commission of all candidate states. There was no point therefore in debating the ins and outs of the transition to capitalism: it had to be this way if countries were to join the EU club.

Transition, and all its attendant effects, was experienced as a technical necessity. It took the form of implementing rules and regulations emanating from Brussels rather than that of political choices made by elected representatives and – ultimately – made by the people themselves. Whilst this made life easier for political elites in candidate states and for the negotiators in the European Commission (why present your demands in the form of political choices when you can present them as inevitable, beyond the pale of debate?), it slowly severed domestic societies from their own political representatives. Accession became an executive-dominated affair, justified in the language of experts, far removed from the daily lives of people in eastern Europe. Support for enlargement in candidate states was therefore essentially a matter of faith rather than a conscious political choice. It is worth noting that this legalizing of public policy choices is not only a feature of enlargement: the Single Market itself has been built and enforced via the legal judgments of the European Court of Justice.

Degrading national political life

The consequences of this for the political institutions of candidate states were significant. In the early days of the post-1989 period, parliaments were held up as the main institution embodying the new democratic era. Hungarian political scientist, Attila Agh, called them 'governing parliaments' (1999: 89). This did not last: as the enlargement process picked up pace, power shifted from parliaments to executives. Slowly, within candidate states 'islands of excellence' emerged, tasked with managing the implementation of EU laws (Grabbe, 2001: 1017). The result was that on the side of candidate states, negotiations were conducted by a small team, backed up by extensive administrative support but shorn of any real relationship to either the legislature or society at large. In what way could these negotiation teams properly articulate and defend the national interest when their claims to being representative were so weak?

The role of national legislatures was essentially to rubber stamp EU laws. Scholars studying enlargement at the time remarked that the deliberative culture associated with well-functioning parliaments was being lost. Political parties also followed suit. For all the political debates that were being conducted at the time, one issue that was firmly off the agenda was that of enlargement itself. It was, as Grzymala-Busse and Innes put it, a 'valence issue', meaning that it was something all parties agreed on and chose not to discuss (2003: 64). Since enlargement included within its remit most of the major policy issues of the time, the political sphere itself was stripped of much of its content. As Ivan Krastev has put it, the result was a growing sense of powerless *vis-à-vis* politics: people were able to change governments but not to change policies (2007: 59).

Over time, this process transformed the nature of political contestation in candidate states. Political scientists in the region have noted a collapse in the liberal consensus of the 1990s and the rise of illiberal politics (Ost, 2005). As anger and frustration about the changes being made were unable to express themselves in an open debate about the merits of transition, they were channeled back into society itself. From witch hunts driven by virulent anti-communists in Poland to attacks on Roma communities in Hungary, attention focused on the identity of groups rather than the right or wrongs of government policies. Enlargement thus consolidated a sense of political powerlessness and disenchantment that was strong already at the end of the 1980s. As one author recounts, in Estonia people began to see the EU in the same way as they had seen the USSR: a powerful but distant body, imposing laws upon them that they would outwardly accept but would resist in practice (Raik, 2004). Raik describes this as the strategy of 'double-think': doing one thing but thinking something quite different. A similar point was made in a study of local and regional elites in Hungary, Estonia and Slovenia: 'local elites are highly adept at window-dressing and paying lip service while doing the opposite or at least the minimum'. 'Non-fulfillment' of EU directives, these authors concluded, 'or poor fulfillment, is, after all, a classic 'weapon of the weak' strategy of resistance as well as a sign of alienation from a decision-making process elsewhere' (Hughes *et al.*, 2002: 356).

This sense of alienation helps us understand the trajectory taken by enlargement since 2004. A reason given for 'enlargement fatigue' is that some new member states have proven themselves unable to properly implement European laws. This has been particularly acute in the two members that joined in 2006: Romania and Bulgaria. Regularly castigated for being unwilling to crack-down on corruption, some within the EU are saying that these countries should not have joined when they did. Future enlargements will be conditional upon evidence of *actual* implementation of laws, not just the promise of implementation. Of course, one of the reasons why laws can be so difficult to implement is that local actors do not believe in them. Unless laws are considered legitimate, it is unlikely they will be properly implemented. Legitimacy demands more than just an acceptance by political elites; it also rests upon a broader, social consensus.

Narcissus EU

A second problem with enlargement has been its internal orientation. Fêted as a major peace-building initiative for the EU, enlargement was adopted by governments and civil society groups as a model for how to democratize weak states and how to re-build post-conflict societies. The European Stability Initiative, a pro-enlargement think tank focusing on the Balkans, called this 'member state building': building states through the accession process. For all the hubris, in practice, the enlargement process has often been more about the EU than about exporting democracy to others. Justifications of enlargement have corresponded to the EU's own anxieties and doubts about the vitality of its political project. In the debate about Turkish membership, for instance, supporters and critics differ principally in terms of their attitudes towards European identity: some think Turkey will corrupt its Christian heritage; others think it will inject new life into its multicultural model. Still others stress the material gains for the EU in terms of expanding and deepening the European Single Market.

For candidate states, this suggests they are the terrain upon which the travails of European identity-building and integration are played out. That leaves them hostage to fortune: tidal changes in political sentiment within the EU can keep them firmly in the cold, as is presently the case with Turkey and countries in the Balkans. From this vantage point, enlargement is not an objective, meritocratic process. It is capricious and subjective, and for a country attached to its own independence and autonomy, a rather humiliating affair.

Conclusion

Far from being the success story much vaunted by its supporters, the EU's expansion has negatively impacted upon the political life of new member states. Justified as a way of stabilizing new democracies, enlargement eviscerated much of the political debate in candidate states and it has juridified political choices in ways that pushed critics to the margins of public life. Unable to directly contest the policy choices being made, anger and frustration ineEastern Europe has been channelled into illiberal directions. Technocracy and populism are the true legacies of enlargement. Yet, lest new member states feel too hard done by, they can comfort themselves with the thought that now at least they look just like their western counterparts. Technocracy and populism dominate the politics of western European states too, and thus enlargement has brought about a kind of united Europe but not the one imagined by its ideologues.

Chapter 14

Towards a Common European Army?

Editors' introduction

In April 2011, Libya, one of the many countries in the Arab world that witnessed protests against decades of oppression during this so-called 'Arab spring', descended into bloody chaos as aging dictator Muammar al-Quaddafi clung to power with the help of his well-equipped army. Immediately, intense debates erupted in EU member states on whether the EU could stand by idly as many people were massacred in its immediate neighbourhood while exerting their democratic rights. In the end, France and Britain were at the forefront of the countries that actively intervened with their militaries whereas countries such as Germany and Poland refused to participate. Once more, a common security and defence policy of the Europeans seemed to be more of a fata morgana *than a real prospect.*

While few would argue against the idea that more cooperation in the area of security and defence policies is a desirable end, scepticism has accompanied the idea since its first manifestations, such as the doomed European Defence Community of the early 1950s, the rather ineffectual European Political Cooperation (EPC) of the 1970s or the widely ridiculed response of the EU to the breakdown of Yugoslavia in the 1990s. This disaster, however, and the end of the Cold War have led to the formal integration of a Common Foreign and Security Policy (CFSP) into the European treaties as pillar two of the Maastricht Treaty. Following an important Franco-British understanding at St Malo in 1998, a formalized European Security and Defence Policy (ESDP)supplemented CFSP and was added to the treaties in 2001, if only after long and intense debates.

Ambitious goals regarding forces and capabilities were formulated. As of this writing (September 2011), the EU has pursued 25 military and civilian missions. In December 2003, the EU formulated its first European Security Strategy, modelled after the regular American practice of summing up the challenges and responses of US defence policy to a changing security environment in a comprehensive document. However,

218

pervasive doubts remained concerning, for instance, the lack of credible capabilities given shrinking defence spending in Europe, technological limitations, divergent strategic outlooks and cultures among EU member states, fears of decoupling from and duplication of NATO. In a famous book, US political analyst Robert Kagan drew a sharp dichotomy between a US comfortable with the use of force, and a Europe which is essentially mired in a culture which prevents the development of real military capabilities (Kagan, 2003). Renamed Common Security and Defence Policy (CSDP) *in the Lisbon Treaty, the EU's efforts at creating credible structures in this area continue to face challenges from many sceptics, not least from member state governments which are hesitant to transfer decision-making power in defence matters to the EU.*

Hanna Ojanen and Anand Menon continue this debate on the pro and cons of CSDP. Hanna Ojanen, a Finnish national who has worked in Swedish and Finnish think-tanks on EU defence policies, maintains that these policies should not be judged only for their specific contribution to Europe's security but also for various other functions they serve. Anand Menon from the University of Birmingham (UK) says that the CSDP failed in its ambitions. EU member states rather decline together than muster the effort to pull together. Their arguments also bear on other important themes in this volume, for example the question of the efficiency of EU policies (Chapter 2) and the controversy overwhether the EU acts as normative power (Chapter 12).

14.1 Defence integration in the EU: a successful vision

Hanna Ojanen

A good part of the literature on CSDP is pessimistic about the potential of a common European security and defence policy to become a reality one day. Many are worried about the consequences should CSDP emerge against all odds. These doubts originate from the idea that security and defence are the policy fields closest to the core of national sovereignty, fields in which states would never totally relinquish their decision-making rights. The continued dissonance of views and the vitality of various national discourses on security and defence policy would seem to confirm this. According to these sceptics, any agreement on common policies or steps ahead in defence integration will be frail and merely exist on paper. Member states will always continue to defend the priority of their national interests in this area.

It is true that there remains a considerable degree of ambiguity over CSDP which opens up the possibility for the member states to at least seemingly pursue independent policies of their own. Even the Lisbon Treaty refers to the specificities of certain member countries' policies and to the important role played by other organizations in the field, notably NATO. When looking at what CSDP consists of in concrete terms, it is, however, easy to list a set of structures and policies that are already in place: the European Defence Agency, the European Security Strategy, the European External Action Service (EEAS), the solidarity and mutual defence clauses in the Lisbon Treaty, and the 20 plus crisis management operations that the EU has carried out since 2003. Here, too, the critics would first see what is missing, the empty spots. The operations have been rather small and it has been difficult to gather enough capabilities. It has been hard to get the member states to invest more, be it in terms of increasing the number of police officers in joint operations or increasing defence budgets. The institutions of CSDP are still in their infancy and have not proven that they work. Some would say that they are rather dysfunctional. From this many would conclude that CSDP has not meant much in practice at all (for example, Menon, 2009).

Even those who agree that CSDP does have an impact, often claim that this impact is mostly negative. It is seen as a challenge to NATO or even as a liability to the security of the member states (see, for example, in Howorth and Keeler, 2003). The EU allegedly duplicates NATO's functions, causing unnecessary spending and inefficiency, while being an unreliable alternative to existing structures, not really able to take over important tasks, neither from NATO, nor from the member states.

These critics suffer from three fallacies. First, there is the lure of numbers. Big numbers are not always the right solution, whether one tries to solve a crisis by augmenting the number of troops in action or spends more money on defence technologies. Second, there is the lure of being able to tell a story, to make the development seem logical by proposing one aim to the whole process. As I will demonstrate, CSDP has many goals, and not all of them are related to military issues *per se*. Third, there is the lure of time. Why would CSDP simply be about replicating the past, trying to achieve what others have achieved previously? CSDP cannot be reduced to yet another chapter in a story already written about the development of defence capabilities or capabilities for external action and intervention. There are a multitude of interpretations of CSDP, of why it is needed or is important.

To start with, different member states all have their specific reasons for signing on to and benefiting from it. CSDP serves their interests – but also those of a variety of other actors, not only the member states and not of *all* at *all* times, but rather of *most* and for *most* of the time. It is this very multitude that constitutes a firmer basis for CSDP to work than if it was based on one view only. When we look for an already visible impact of CSDP, we see it not only on the member states but also on other organizations, notably NATO. In the long run, it could potentially open up a totally new way of looking at security and defence policy through changing the locus and mode of decision making on security and defence, including an increase in parliamentary accountability.

Drivers and interests behind CSDP

The existence of CSDP cannot really be explained in ordinary terms of converging interests, even less so in terms of responding to a shared security threat. There is no external threat that would compel the member states to cooperate, nor is there a lack of existing arrangements for cooperation in the field. Still, defence integration has started to grow. Why? It is important to stress that the drivers of CSDP are not necessarily those that one would first think about. They are not the same as for security and defence cooperation traditionally. In traditional terms, cooperation between states in security and defence develops because of shared security concerns. For a military alliance to form, there needs to be a common enemy. In the case of CSDP, the basic driver is not a common enemy but something else (see also, for example, Smith, 2003 and Howorth, 2007: 52–7). The end of the Cold War, the internal logic of integration in Europe, and the creation of new norms, notably those concerning sovereignty are all factors that paved the way for CSDP.

If we look at the member states, we find that different countries benefit from CSDP in very different ways. While Germany might appreciate the added legitimacy the shared framework gives, the United Kingdom has seen in CSDP a way of strengthening its position in the EU, and for a country like Finland, CSDP is seen to strengthen national security in a rather tangible way given its close proximity to Russia. Smaller groups of member states within the EU have also been instrumental in taking new steps together in integration, first among themselves and then drawing with them a growing number of followers. An important example would be the Saint-Malo summit between France and Great Britain in December 1998 that soon led to Union-wide steps forward in defining the stages to reach an autonomous military capacity for the Union. The Lisbon Treaty opens new possibilities for this kind of development within security and defence: new core groups could emerge through the scheme of permanent structured cooperation.

States outside of the Union do have the possibility to play a role, be it furthering or hampering CSDP, and the United States, to take the most obvious example, has in an interesting way moved from opposing the creation of CSDP to formally welcoming the EU's greater self-reliance and thus a more even burden sharing (Howorth, 2007: 137) It is also important to look at the role of different EU institutions that see their own position within the Union enhanced by getting a voice, even in this relatively new but growing field.

Not only EU institutions, but the European defence industry has a big stake in CSDP. Perhaps surprisingly, even other organizations in the field of security may have an interest in a stronger CSDP. NATO and the UN are examples of organizations, which have a shared interest in getting the EU to play a more active role: the EU more than any other organization can make its members comply and deliver. External expectations constitute a fundamental motivation for the development of CSDP: the EU is expected to act in crises, because of its good image and acceptability internationally, or because 'all others' are already there. Finally, the actors are about to include, one could argue, even EU citizens as well as the European Parliament. Particularly the establishment of the EEAS seems to have opened a door for these newcomers: should they see their interests served by CSDP, they, too, could at least occasionally turn into its proponents.

CSDP has for the most part been of low practical consequence for EU citizens in general. It has not had budgetary consequences that a European tax-payer would directly feel. It has not been an issue of political debate, neither at the national nor European (parliamentary) level. It has not led to significant loss of life bound to lead to serious questioning. With the EEAS, however, one already sees budgetary discussions becoming more central. The European Parliament takes a role in the building-up and, eventually, also in the control of its functioning. European citizens may also start to notice the EU's external role more, having access to EU delegations around the world. These may provide help in an emergency situation. National diplomats, therefore, get the possibility to join the proponents of integrative efforts if they feel they benefit from the new career possibilities offered in the European diplomatic service – in a similar way to that which their counterparts in national armed forces and defence administrations already see in European military structures.

This kind of development is slow. Yet, having several drivers makes the process more stable. Thus, CSDP cannot be explained by traditional security political calculations. It develops for other reasons, internal and external, and in interaction with other actors. And, it is also about the internal development of the Union, the hybrid that it is with its state-like and organization-like features.

Impact of CSDP on other organizations and on member states

CSDP might well require that we adopt a different perspective altogether, as Smith (2003) points out: not looking at the lacunae of, for example, European identity as hindrance to its development, and not expecting a security policy to emerge that is of a similar kind as the security policies of states. Looking only at these impedes one from seeing that CSDP actually is consequential, both internally and externally. Internally, as Smith would point out, it is a feature of the EU's internal governance system and contributes to the safeguarding and protecting of the integration process as such. Externally, it is part of broader systems of European or global governance, whereby the EU is a contributor to a broader world order as well as a provider of European regional governance.

CSDP is consequential also for other organizations. When looking at the relations between the EU and NATO, or also between the EU and the UN, the importance of the EU for both is evident (see more in Ojanen, 2011a). NATO's new Strategic Concept from 2010 is particularly telling on this. Under the title 'Partnerships', it devotes considerable space to the EU, which it characterizes as 'a unique and essential partner for NATO'. NATO recognizes the importance of a stronger and more capable European defence and welcomes the entry into force of the Lisbon Treaty which is seen to provide a framework for further strengthening the EU's capacities to address common security challenges. There emerges a 'strategic partnership' between NATO and the EU that NATO would like to be strengthened in many tangible ways to get help in overcoming its own internal divisions. CSDP has also clearly inspired NATO when it comes to civilian crisis management, and the new consultative way in which the 2010 Strategic Concept was prepared.

Similarly for the UN, the EU, with its increasingly clear role in security, may be an indispensable ally because of its command over a large part of the UN's peace support resources, but also in sustaining multi-lateralism and international order. It can be a partner, but also a rival, a challenger, not willing to be dependent on UN mandates but having the possibility even to act alone if necessary.

When looking at the member states, the impact of CSDP is evident as well. Behind the evident first layer of influence in defence spending, planning and operations, one can see a deeper level where the EU and CSDP are transforming the state, altering in a fundamental way how the essential elements of a state, territory, citizens, and security functions, are seen – by making the external borders shared and dissolving the internal ones, but also by making the member state consider as its own a territory much wider than the traditional national one. In all, the EU becomes an influential actor in the framing of both the internal and the external security of its member states (Ojanen, 2011b).

What is particularly striking is the way supranationalism comes in. Decision making still remains for the main part strictly intergovernmental; qualified majority voting is possible only in matters of implementation. The struggle against single member states' solo politics is a challenge, too. Yet, the Commission and the European Parliament are indeed getting a say – as would be the case in the other policy realms of the Union.

Wagner (2003) argues that while the Common Foreign and Security Policy as such would tend to remain intergovernmental – it does not need strong institutions to work – the possibility of using qualified majority voting does make CFSP more efficient. It is, however, above all, that CSDP might be conducive to supranationalism because of the nature of the substance itself: security and defence being more likely to raise public awareness and consequently political pressure than matters of ordinary foreign policy.

Indeed, during the negotiations on the EEAS, the European Parliament also showed a new face. It pushed through considerable changes using its budgetary powers: budget control in the EEAS also implies control over its activities even when it comes to defence, a field where the EP is formally not competent at all. Regular question time and consultations prior to approval of strategies and mandates also strengthen the position of the EP. The traditional consultative role of the EP seems thus to become also participatory, if not even one revealing some co-leadership aspirations, even though the EP does not have a say over long-term policy objectives or priorities. Democratic legitimacy, therefore, forms the basis for its aspirations towards such a role in EU decision making. Interestingly, the EP might here be seeking, and eventually accumulating, powers that do not exist at the national level – if we think back to the specific features of security and defence and how little they have in many countries been a topic of parliamentary scrutiny or public debate. The CSDP, thus, has the potential of making security and defence policy more democratic (see also Kietz and von Ondarza, 2010).

When it comes to the consequences of CSDP for states outside the Union, the picture is interesting. For EU accession candidates, CSDP has direct relevance as conformity with the EU's policies is required from them. For Turkey, CSDP could also be a way of contributing to the Union before actual accession. Among the big outsiders, CSDP is of growing importance particularly for the United States as a way to decrease the need for American presence in Europe. At the same time, outsiders may themselves actively try to downplay CSDP, portray it in a certain way, or purposefully ignore it and keep turning to the member states instead. These, in turn, might be flattered and, therefore, play along; in the long run, their capacities to act alone are, however, utterly limited. The efforts at downplaying CSDP might be a sign of it becoming increasingly consequential.

Conclusion

CSDP is working on a practical day-to-day level of security and defence integration. It has mattered in different ways for different member countries: as a provider of legitimacy, leadership, and security. In the future, it will matter increasingly in defence planning, defence expenditure, but also in the joint monitoring of air space, sea and borders. But it is also working on another level. It changes national debates on security and defence by highlighting the need for comparison across states and by introducing elements of a joint scrutiny on what the real security and defence needs in today's world are. National policies no longer exist in a vacuum. It also doubles citizens' stakes in these debates by offering a new European arena. The predominance of pessimistic views, therefore, is not so much a reflection of objective shortcomings of CSDP, but rather a result of the fact that it lacks outspoken proponents, a firm representative with the will and power to promote it and answer the criticisms pouring over it. In cases such as Libya in 2011, there is also need for a better articulation of how CSDP relates to EU's other external relations policies and tools.

14.2 Flattering to deceive: the Common Security and Defence Policy

Anand Menon

On 3–4 December 1998, at the picturesque French seaside resort of Saint Malo, Tony Blair and Jacques Chirac concluded that the 'European Union needs to be in a position to play its full role on the international stage' (British–French Summit, 1998). To that end, they declared, 'the Union must have the capacity for autonomous action, backed up by credible military forces, the means to decide to use them and a readiness to do so, in order to respond to international crises'. Thus were laid the foundations for what was to become the Common Security and Defence Policy (CSDP).

The rationale for CSDP lay in a perceived need to improve the Union's ability to respond to security crises. Dismay at its failure to halt conflict in the Balkans carried over to the Saint Malo meeting. And it was reinforced thereafter by frustration that a sex scandal in the United States could stymie western responses to the unfolding drama in Kosovo. Consequently, British and French political leaders saw CSDP as a means to enable Europeans to act more decisively. In London, such concerns were exacerbated by fears that European weakness might lead to American disillusionment with, and conceivably even disengagement from, NATO.

CSDP spawned intense debate. On the one hand, official statements of intent were bullish. The Headline Goal 2010, approved by the European Council in June 2004, declared boldly that the 'European Union is a global actor, ready to share in the responsibility for global security' (General Affairs and External Relations Council, 2004). On the other, critics expressed concern at attempts to equip the Union with the instruments of 'hard power.' They issued dire warnings lest an increasing emphasis on military power undermine the Union's ability to wield other, 'softer,' of influence (Sangiovanni, 2003: 200–1).

Both camps, however, made a fundamental mistake in basing their analyses on what proved to be an erroneous assumption: that the EU's stated ambitions represented an accurate guide to future action. The fundamental weakness of CSDP has not been to skew the nature of EU external policies towards an emphasis on military force. Rather, it has been a failure to live up to ambitious claims that the Union was about to become an effective international security actor.

Substantive shortcomings

It would, of course, be unfair to describe CSDP as a failure *tout court*. After all, it does provide the EU with a policy instrument previously lacking from its repertoire. The Union had previously been criticized for 'a disproportionately heavy focus on economics, human rights and democratization to the neglect of diplomatic conflict prevention measures that seek to significantly alter the political dynamics of an emerging conflict' (International Crisis Group, 2001: ii). And the twenty plus CSDP operations carried out to date have undoubtedly exerted a positive impact on the ground. EU (and NATO) interventions in Macedonia, for instance, quite possibly helped avert civil conflict. The peace brokered in Aceh has held, while a report by the highly respected charity Oxfam acknowledged that an CSDP mission in Chad 'has made many civilians feel safer through its activities, which include patrolling known dangerous routes, destroying unexploded ordnance, making contact with local leaders, and positioning itself defensively around civilians during rebel and government fighting' (Oxfam, 2008: 13).

Yet such achievements mask a reality of significant shortcomings. Whilst enthusiasts have compared the EU's activism favourably with the single mission launched by NATO this century, such analyses overlook profound differences in scale. EU military interventions in particular have been highly limited in scope (particularly in comparison to the massive NATO deployment in Afghanistan). One particularly trenchant critique describes CSDP missions to date as 'small, lacking in ambition and strategically irrelevant' (Korski and Gowan, 2009: 11). Moreover, the Union has been quite prepared to let others do the heavy lifting for it. A significant proportion of its military operations have either followed, or accompanied, action on the ground by other institutions (NATO troops preceded those of the EU in both Macedonia and Bosnia, whilst the Union operated alongside UN forces in Congo).

Certainly, the Union has declared success following each of its CSDP missions. Yet this is largely explicable in terms of the limited mandates adopted in the first place. Getting EU personnel in and out of an unstable theatre is one thing. Bringing about stability is quite another. Numerous CSDP interventions have signally failed to resolve the real problems on the ground. Thus, EU intervention addressed 'only the consequence and not the issues underlying the conflict in Chad' (Secretary General of the United Nations, 2008: §52). Operation Artemis, deployed to the Democratic Republic of Congo in 2003, was the object of much hostile comment from humanitarian groups, for being 'totally insufficient' to meet the challenges on ground, because of its limited scope in terms of both space and time (International Crisis Group, 2006).

This track record of rapid, small interventions declared successful whilst leaving conditions on the ground largely unaltered raises the suspicion that CSDP missions can be designed with an eye as much on their implications for the Union itself as for the host state. Such suspicions are merely heightened by the apparent belief on the part of some that CSDP is as much about 'completing' European integration as it is about promoting security. As former French Foreign Minister Dominique de Villepin put it in his BBC Dimbleby Lecture in October 2003: 'There will be no Europe without a European Defence' (Villepin, 2003).

A desire to strengthen integration is not, however, an adequate rationale for military intervention. Whether conceived of to test European capabilities, or to illustrate that the EU does indeed have the capacity to act, operations can appear tokenistic. Observers voiced their suspicion that the first CSDP mission to be deployed to Africa was conceived for purely political or cosmetic reasons – in order to show the EU could act rather than to solve problems on the ground (Haine and Giegerich,

2006). Moreover there are reasons to doubt the practical value of EU participation alongside a NATO mission and multinational 'Combined Task Force 150' in the struggle against Somali pirates (Korski and Gowan, 2009: 35).

If the history of EU missions is one of limited objectives met by limited deployments that reflect limited ambitions, the picture in terms of capability developments is, if anything, bleaker still. CSDP was, from the first moment of its inception seen by some as a tool for enhancing member states' military capabilities. Admittedly, it has spawned a bewildering variety of initiatives. These have ranged from the so-called Helsinki Headline Goal of December 1999, which set ambitious capabilities targets for member states, to annual capabilities pledging conferences, to the November 2001 Capabilities Improvement Conference, itself leading to the creation of the European Capabilities Action Plan of December 2001 – drawn up to deal with numerous shortfalls *vis-à-vis* the original Helsinki targets. In December 2003, member states created the so-called Capability Development Mechanism, whilst the following June saw the unveiling of a brand new Capabilities Plan in the form of the Headline Goal 2010. The following month, the member states created the European Defence Agency to assist them in meeting their objective of capabilities improvements, while 2006 witnessed the drafting of a 'Long-Term Vision' for capability needs.

A parallel process was launched on the civilian side. The Helsinki meeting that produced the Headline Goal also gave birth to a Civilian Crisis Management action plan; at Lisbon in March 2000 a Committee for Civilian Crisis Management was set up; the following June, the Feira Council adopted its four priority areas as the basis of Civilian Crisis Management. In May 2002, a Rule of Law Commitment Conference in Brussels saw member states commit civilian personnel for crisis management operations. In November 2004 a Civilian Capabilities Commitment Conference was held; in December 2004 a Civilian Headline Goal 2008 was drawn up; in November 2005, the first Civilian Capabilities Improvement Conference was held and, in 2008, a new Civilian Headline Goal was unveiled.

It is possible that EU requirements may have helped drive forward some national defence reform processes and the development of new capabilities. Certainly, most member states are taking steps to enhance their force-projection capabilities (International Institute for Strategic Studies, 2008).

Yet significant substantive improvements have been slow to materialize. In comparison to the roughly 6,000 EU troops deployed in 2008, the African Union fielded more than 30,000, and the UN 75,000, while the NATO force in Afghanistan then numbered around 130,000 (Toje,

2008: 12). In a coruscating critique, the former head of the European Defence Agency baldly characterized as a 'failure' attempts to enhance European capabilities (Witney, 2008: 30). A recent report comments that 'institutional initiatives have generated flurries of bureaucratic activity, but achieved limited results' (International Institute for Strategic Studies, 2008: 29). And this while targets are shifted at will. As the former EDA chief has put it, from Helsinki to the Headline Goal 2010, 'the goalposts were not so much moved as dismantled altogether' (Witney, 2008: 30). In sum, it is hard not to agree with the conclusion reached by a report for the European Council on Foreign Relations that member states 'have proved no slouches when it comes to delivering on paper' (Korski and Gowan, 2009: 43). Real progress, meanwhile, remains distinctly limited.

Partly, the capabilities problem is one of spending. In 2005, Europe was the only region in the world where military spending decreased – by some 1.7 per cent. Defence spending by European NATO members fell by 35 per cent between 1985 and 1995 (International Institute for Strategic Studies, 2008: 94). More recently, large scale defence cuts (amounting, in the case of Germany, to some €8 billion by 2014) have led American and NATO officials to express concern that Europeans will no longer be able to contribute effectively to western defence efforts. The disparities between member states, moreover, are huge: France and the UK make up 45 per cent of total EU defence spending; they, along with Cyprus, Bulgaria and Greece are the only member states to spend over the 2 per cent of GDP that NATO has deemed a minimum requirement.

Yet insufficient funding is not the main problem. After all, in 2006, member states together spent the equivalent of 60 per cent of the total US defence budget – almost a quarter of global defence spending. The fact is that defence budgets are frequently badly spent. Despite the Cold War having ended almost two decades ago, European armed forces still own 10,000 main battle tanks and 2,500 combat aircraft (Witney, 2008: 30). And despite large manpower budgets – the 27 member states had almost 2 million active service personnel on their books in 2006 – only 30 per cent of these can actually operate outside European territory because of legal restrictions or inadequate training. Finally, inefficiencies result from the fragmentation of the European defence market. Several small national defence industries producing similar hardware for several small national militaries is a recipe for duplication and waste. The resultant capabilities shortfalls have had practical implications. Two months after the deployment of a mission to Macedonia, in 2003, the Union reported a 30 per cent personnel shortfall (Korski and Gowan, 2009: 22), whilst a shortage of trainers has also plagued the EU Police Mission in Afghanistan.

Perhaps most strikingly and most significantly, chronic shortages of airlift capacity continue to bedevil operational capacity. The EU deployment to Chad had to be delayed by six months because of a failure to locate 16 helicopters and 10 transport aircraft. Meanwhile the long-term solution to such shortfalls – the Airbus A400M – has been the victim of repeated and prolonged delays, with the first deliveries now not expected until 2012 at the earliest (*Financial Times*, 13 January 2009). Hardly a glowing endorsement of a policy explicitly intended to address capability shortfalls.

Conclusion

The ambitions of CSDP were, broadly, twofold: improving the Union's ability to intervene in international security affairs, and enhancing European capabilities for such interventions. It has, to a greater or lesser extent, failed on both counts. In terms of the capacity to intervene, it is undeniable that a certain measure of success has been achieved. The European Union is now capable of acting in a way that it was not, prior to the creation of CSDP. And whilst, in the words of senior EU official Robert Cooper, it has not saved the world, it has, undeniably, saved lives.

This being said, however, the most striking feature of the first ten years of EU defence policy is how limited interventions have been. Granted, something might be better than nothing, but that something represents little to show for a decade of work and of hugely ambitious rhetoric.

When it comes to capabilities, the picture is clearer still. A central rationale for the creation of an EU defence competence was that this might serve to spur member states into action to address fundamental capability shortfalls. This has not occurred. Indeed, in what is perhaps the most damning critique of CSDP imaginable, one observer has noted that 'the problem of insufficient European military capacity is arguably more acute than at the time when President Jacques Chirac and Prime Minister Tony Blair met [at Saint Malo]' (Toje, 2008: 19).

If proof were needed of the disappointing nature of progress to date, one need look no further than the Anglo-French summit held in London in November 2010. Just as at Saint Malo more than ten years earlier, a British Prime Minister and a French President met to discuss increasing pressure on their respective defence policies. Again, as at Saint Malo, they decided that enhanced cooperation was a logical way to mitigate such pressures. Yet, in stark contrast to the conclusions drawn by Tony Blair and Jacques Chirac, ten years of CSDP convinced David Cameron and Nicolas Sarkozy that EU defence collaboration is not the way to improve capabilities. CSDP is barely mentioned in a summit communiqué that focuses on the need for bilateral cooperation.

British and French scepticism about CSDP was based partly on frustration with the apparent inability of their partners to invest more in capabilities. Partly, too, it stemmed from an unwillingness on the part of both governments to allow defence integration within EU institutional structures to impinge too closely on a crucial area of national sovereignty. Herein lies a fundamental problem confronting the Union's defence policy ambitions. Whilst collective action might represent the only means by which Europe can contribute effectively to international security affairs, member states may yet prefer autonomous decline.

(The author wishes to gratefully acknowledge the invaluable support provided by ESRC standard grant RES-062-23-2717. For a longer and more detailed presentation of the arguments of this contribution, see Menon, forthcoming.)

Conclusion

Andreas Dür

While the chapters for this book were written, the EU's most important project for the last twenty years, Economic and Monetary Union, was under vicious attack from financial markets as a result of the sovereign debt crises of several member countries. Many observers see this as an existential crisis for the EU. The *Financial Times*, for example, commented that a disintegration of the eurozone could pose 'a threat to the EU itself' (Rachman, 2011). Even French President Nicolas Sarkozy stated that 'Allowing the destruction of the euro is to take the risk of the destruction of Europe.' He continued that this would lead to the 'resurgence of conflict and division on our continent' (*Financial Times*, 2011). Other observers expect that the euro crisis will eventually strengthen the EU. They point out that crises have frequently boosted European integration as only they make member countries willing to give up sovereignty and agree to further integration.

Although overshadowed by the euro crisis, other controversies on European integration continue. In the first address by a President of the European Council before the United Nations General Assembly, Hermann van Rompuy stressed the EU's (positive) role in international affairs (van Rompuy, 2011b). He mentioned the EU's role as the largest donor of development aid, its peacekeeping missions, its cooperative stance in international negotiations in areas, such as, climate change and trade, and its mediation in international conflicts. Not all observers agree with this benign assessment. The EU still is a military dwarf compared to the US, partly because military spending is low in the EU's nation states and partly because national military efforts are often not coordinated across the EU. But more astonishingly, for a long time, the EU was unable to take a common position on the revolutions that swept across the Middle East as part of the 'Arab spring' in 2011. Germany abstained in the vote on a United Nations resolution allowing military intervention in Libya that had been pushed by fellow EU members France and Great Britain. In the case of Syria, Italy objected to an EU oil import embargo for a long time. That the self-proclaimed 'normative power' EU was unable to react to political unrest in its direct neighbourhood casts some doubt on van Rompuy's assessment.

Neither do all observers agree that when the EU actually has influence on world affairs, that this influence is necessarily benign. Back in 2007, the *Wall Street Journal* attacked the EU's 'regulatory imperialism'

(*Wall Street Journal*, 2007). It argued that the EU used its attractive internal market to impose its rules on global business. The inference of its criticism was that these rules were not fair, but 'unapologetically to the benefit of [the EU's] own industry.' The 2011 squabble about the application of the EU's emissions trading system (a measure intended to reduce carbon dioxide emissions and thereby to soften the impact of climate change) to non-European airlines further contributed to this feeling of EU imperialism. Others point out that the EU's policies in the areas of climate change and environmental and consumer protection more generally benefit all countries. A 'Green Europe' that takes climate change seriously and helps curtail global emissions of greenhouse gases produces a global public good.

The purpose of the present volume has been to stake out these and other important debates and to offer an outline of the opposing points of view: do we see a renationalization of competencies and/or weakening of the EU's supranational institutions? How democratic is the EU? Is the European Court of Justice too powerful? How much money should the EU spend on agricultural and cohesion policy? How much influence do interest groups have on the EU's foreign economic policies? And should new member countries, especially Turkey, be admitted to the EU? These are just some of the questions that we have tackled in the previous chapters. While we could not address all issues that are currently debated in the EU (for example, some aspects of the Schengen Agreement that eliminated border controls among signatories have been hotly discussed), the chapters depict the fault lines that shape academic and real-world debates about the EU and its policies.

Several general lessons emerge from the preceding fourteen controversies. First, the existence of these debates clearly is an indication of the complexity of the social world that we inhabit. This complexity makes it difficult to come to clear-cut conclusions that can guide policy making. Nevertheless, on most of these controversies we observe a narrowing of positions over time: each controversy started out with positions that were very far apart. The debate between intergovernmentalists and supranationalists is a case in point. Up into the 1990s the debate was largely cast in 'either/or' terms. Intergovernmentalists stressed that member states were dominant and supranational institutions nothing more than a commitment device to ensure cooperation in the long term (Moravcsik, 1998). Supranationalists, by contrast, highlighted the important role that supranational actors, especially Jacques Delors as President of the European Commission, played in getting member states to agree to the Single Market Programme and the common currency (Sandholtz and Stone Sweet, 1998). As the texts in this volume show, the debate between intergovernmentalists and supranationalists has become much more nuanced, with the former accepting that the Commission's and the European Parliament's power are here to stay and the latter recognizing the strong role that member states play in at least some policy fields.

Second, taking a position on one debate seems to a large extent to determine which position one takes on another debate. Those that criticize the EU's political efficiency also tend to stress the EU's democratic deficit. And those that stress the important role that supranational institutions play in the EU also see the EU more capable of acting coherently in new fields, such as security and defence policy and to keep interest groups at arm's length. Related to this is the fact that the long-standing theories of European integration, intergovernmentalism and supranationalism, continue to be of relevance to many of the debates. The strength of these theories is that they inspire positions across many of the questions that the process of European integration poses. Many of these debates also have a normative underpinning. The stark question the EU poses is whether democratic decision making should remain firmly attached to the national level or whether nations should work towards global institutions which effectively govern above the nation-state and are able to overcome the narrow nationalism which has plagued the world for centuries.

Finally, we observe interdependence between major debates in the real world and scholarly controversies. Both eurosceptics and europhiles can find support for some of their positions in academic arguments. Influence also seems to go in both directions. For example, the democratic deficit debate has partly originated with, and partly been adopted by, eurosceptics. The EU's democratic deficit is one of only three substantive points that the eurosceptic party group in the European Parliament, Europe of Freedom and Democracy, could agree upon (Europe of Freedom and Democracy, 2009). Academic debates also played a role in the campaigns that surrounded the referenda on major EU treaty revisions in countries such as Denmark, France, Ireland, and the Netherlands.

So what will the future of the EU look like? The contributions offer a wide variety of responses, ranging from a move towards an intergovernmental forum that only coordinates cross-border externalities to a much more integrated entity with citizens that share a common identity. In fact, however, most contributions are not as far apart. Most recognize that the EU has gone through crises before without withering away. From the empty chair crisis in 1965, when France failed to attend meetings of the Council of Ministers, to the French 'No' to the Constitutional Treaty in 2005, the EU has weathered too many storms to be written off easily. Even the end of the Cold War, which signified a major structural change in the international system and which had been seen as creating the danger of armed warfare in Europe (Mearsheimer, 1990), did not undermine the EU's foundations. In analogy to the young shepherd who shouted 'wolf' too often in Aesop's fables, the end of the EU has been predicted too often to be credible at this time. Neither would enlargement to include Turkey signify the end of the EU, as predicted in 2002 by the then President of the Convention on the Future of Europe that drafted the failed Constitutional Treaty, Valéry Giscard d'Estaing (Castle, 2002).

Most contributors therefore agree that there are few viable alternatives to continued integration, and that some EU policies require reform but no revolution. The prediction that the EU will continue to exist, but that its institutional set-up and policy outputs will remain the subject of controversy and 'contentious politics' (for this term, see Paterson, *et al.*, 2010) thus seems to be a safe bet. As this volume has shown, controversies on the future of European integration have been here for a long time and will most probably persist beyond the current crisis.

Bibliography

Abromeit, H. (1998) *Democracy in Europe: Legitimising Politics in a Non-State Polity* (New York: Berghahn).

Adler, E. and Crawford, B. (2006) 'Normative power: The European Practice of Region-Building and the Case of the Euro-Mediterranean Partnership', in E. Adler, F. Bicchi, B. Crawford and R. Del Sarto (eds), *The Convergence of Civilizations: Constructing a Mediterranean Region* (Toronto: University of Toronto Press): 3–47.

Adler, E., Bicchi, F., Crawford, B. and Del Sarto, R. (eds) (2006) *The Convergence of Civilizations: Constructing a Mediterranean Region* (Toronto: University of Toronto Press).

Aggestam, L. (2008) 'Introduction: Ethical Power Europe?', *International Affairs* 84(1): 1–11.

Agh, A. (1999) 'Europeanisation of Policymaking in East Central Europe: The Hungarian Approach to EU Accession', *Journal of European Public Policy* 6(5): 839–54.

Alesina, A., Ardagna, S. and Galasso, V. (2010) 'The Euro and Structural Reforms', in A. Alesina and F. Giavazzi (eds), *Europe and the Euro* (Chicago: University of Chicago Press): 57–93.

Alter, K. J. (2006) 'Delegation to International Courts and the Limits of Re-contracting Power', in D. Hawkins, D. A. Lake, D. Nielson and M. J. Tierney (eds), *Delegation and Agency in International Organizations* (Cambridge: Cambridge University Press).

Alter, K. J. (2009) *The European Court's Political Power: Selected Essays* (Oxford: Oxford University Press).

Amstrong, K.A. (2010) *Governing social inclusion. Europeanization through policy coordination* (Oxford: Oxford University Press).

Anderson, P. (2009) *The Old New World* (London: Verso).

Ansell, C. and Vogel, D. (eds) (2006) *What's the Beef? The Contested Governance of European Food Governance* (Boston, MA: MIT Press).

Asher, A. (2005) 'A Paradise on the Oder? Ethnicity, Europeanization, and the EU referendum in a Polish-German Border City', *City & Society* 17:127–52.

Bach, D. and Newman, A. (2007) 'The European Regulatory State and Global Public Policy: Micro-institutions, Macro-influence', *Journal of European Public Policy*, 14(6): 827–46.

Bache, I. and George, S. (2006) *Politics in the European Union,* 2nd ed, (Oxford: Oxford University Press).

Banks, M. (2011) 'MEPs in Fresh Appeal to Abolish Strasbourg Seat', *The Parliament*, 9 June, http://www.theparliament.com/latest-news/article/newsarticle/meps-is-fresh-appeal-to-abolish-strasbourg-seat/.

Barca, F. (2009) 'An Agenda for a Reformed Cohesion Policy: A Place-Based Approach to Meeting European Union Challenges and Expectations', (Brussels: European Commission).

Bartolini, S. (2006) *Restructuring Europe: Centre Formation, System Building, and Political Structuring between the Nation State and the European Union* (Oxford: Oxford University Press).

Bauer, R.A., De Sola Pool, I. and Dexter, L.A. (1972) *American Business and Public Policy: The Politics of Foreign Trade* (New York: Atherton Press).

Beach, D. (2005) *The Dynamics of European Integration* (Basingstoke: Palgrave Macmillan).

Bellamy, R. (2010) 'Democracy without emocracy? Can the EU's democratic "outputs" be separated from the democratic "inputs" provided by competitive parties and majority rule?', *Journal of European Public Policy* 17 (1): 2–19.

Bickerton, C. (2009) 'From Brezhnev to Brussels: Transformations of Sovereignty in Eastern Europe', *International Politics* 46: 732–52.

Bickerton, C. (2011) 'Legitimacy Through Norms: The Political Limits to Europe's Normative Power', in R. Whitman (ed.), *Normative Power Europe: Empirical and Theoretical Perspectives* (Basingstoke: Palgrave Macmillan): 25–42.

Billig, M. (1995) *Banal Nationalism* (London: Sage).

Birchfield, Vicki (2011) 'The EU's Development Policy: Empirical Evidence of 'Normative Power Europe'?', in R. Whitman (ed.), *Normative Power Europe: Empirical and Theoretical Perspectives* (Basingstoke: Palgrave): 140–59.

Björkdahl, A. (2011) 'Building Peace: Normative and Military Power in EU Peace Operations', in R. Whitman (ed.), *Normative Power Europe: Empirical and Theoretical Perspectives* (Basingstoke: Palgrave Macmillan): 103–25.

Bohle, D. (2006) 'Neoliberal hegemony, transnational capital and the terms of the EU's eastward expansion', *Capital & Class* 30(1): 57–86.

Bohman, J. (2007) 'Democratizing the Transnational Polity, the European Union and the Presuppositions of Democracy How to Reconstitute Democracy in Europe? Proceedings from the Recon Opening Conference', in E.-O. Eriksen and J.-E. Fossum, *How to Reconstitute Democracy in Europe? Proceedings from the Recon Opening Conference* (Oslo: Recon/ARENA): 65–89.

Bonaglia, F., Goldstein, A. and Petito, F. (2006) 'Values in European Union Development Cooperation Policy', in S. Lucarelli and I. Manners (eds), *Values and Principles in European Union Foreign Policy* (London: Routledge): 162–84.

Bonino, E. (2007) 'It is Time to Act as One', *European Union: The Next Fifty Years, Financial Times*, 9 November, http://europa.eu/50/news/views/071109_en.htm.

Bouwen, P. (2002) 'Corporate lobbying in the European Union: The logic of access', *Journal of European Public Policy* 9(3): 365–90.

Brenner, R. (1989) 'Economic Backwardness in Eastern Europe in Light of Developments in the West', in D. Chirot (ed.), *The Origins of Backwardness in Eastern Europe* (Berkeley: University of California Press): 15–52.

Bretherton, C. and Vogler, J. (2006) *The European Union as Global Actor* (London: Routledge).

British–French Summit (1998) 'Joint Declaration on European Defence', Saint-Malo, France, 3–4 December.

Browne, A. and Persson, M. (2011) *The Case for European Localism* (Open Europe).

Brubaker, R. and Cooper, F. (2000) 'Beyond "Identity"', *Theory and Society* 29(1): 1–47.

Bruter, M. (2005) *Citizens of Europe? The Emergence of a Mass European Identity* (Basingstoke: Palgrave Macmillan).

Buch-Hansen, H. and Wigger, A. (2011) *The Politics of European Competition Regulation: A Critical Political Economy Perspective* (London: Routledge).

Buck, T. (2007) 'Dream of MIFID Harmony at Risk', *Financial Times*, 21 February.

Buckley, J. and Howarth, D. (2011) 'Internal market: regulating the so-called "Vultures of Capitalism"', *Journal of Common Market Studies* 49 (Annual Review): 123–43.

Budka, H. (2011) 'Editorial: The European Response to BSE', *EFSA Journal* 9(9).

Bull, H. (1982) 'Civilian Power Europe: A Contradiction in Terms?', *Journal of Common Market Studies* 21(2): 149–82.

Bunce, V. (2000) 'The Historical Origins of the East-West Divide: Civil-Society, Political Society, and Democracy in Europe', in N. Bermeo and P. Nord (eds), *Civil Society before Democracy* (Lanham: Rowman & Littlefield): 209–36.

Burley, A.-M. and Mattli, W. (1993) 'Europe before the Court: A political theory of legal integration', *International Organization* 47: 41–76.

Cappelen, A., Castellacci, F., Fagerberg, J. and Verspagen, B. (2003) 'The Impact of EU regional support on growth and convergence in the European Union', *JCMS: Journal of Common Market Studies* 41(4): 621–44.

Carrubba, C., Gabel, M. and Hankla, C. (2008) 'Judicial behavior under political constraints: Evidence from the ECJ', *American Political Science Review* 102(4): 435–52.

Carta, C. (2012) *The European Union Diplomatic Service: Ideas, Preferences and Identities* (Oxford: Routledge).

Castle, S. (2002) 'Giscard Predicts "End of EU" if Turkey Joins', *The Independent*, 9 November.

Christiansen, T. and Reh, C. (2009) *Constitutionalizing the European Union* (Basingstoke: Palgrave Macmillan).

Cichowski, R. (1998) 'Integrating the environment: The European Court and the construction of supranational policy', *Journal of European Public Policy* 5: 387–405.

Cichowski, R. (2004) 'Women's rights, the European Court and supranational constitutionalism', *Law and Society Review* 38(3): 489–512.

Cichowski, R. (2007) *The European Court and Civil Society* (Cambridge: Cambridge University Press).

Cini, M. and Perez-Solorzano Borragan, N. (eds) (2009) *European Union Politics*, 3rd edn (Oxford: Oxford University Press).

Coen, D. and Richardson, J. (eds) (2009) *Lobbying the European Union: Institutions, Actors, and Issues* (Oxford: Oxford University Press).

Cohen, B. (2000) 'Beyond EMU: The Problem of Sustainability', in B. Eichengreen and J. Frieden (eds), *The Political Economy of European Monetary Unification* (Boulder: Westview Press): 179–204.

Commission (2011), Civil Service, 'Who We Are', available at http://ec.europa.eu/civil_service/about/who/index_en.htm.

Commission of the European Communities (1998) 'Financial Services: Building a Framework for Action', Communication of the Commission, Brussels.

Commission of the European Communities (1999) 'Financial Services: Implementing the Framework for Financial Markets: Action Plan', Communication of the Commission, COM (1999)232, 11 May, Brussels.

Conceição-Heldt, E.da (2004) *The Common Fisheries Policy in the European Union: a Study in Integrative and Distributive Bargaining* (London: Routledge).

Conceição-Heldt, E.da (2011) *Negotiating Trade Liberalization at the WTO: Domestic Politics and Bargaining Dynamics* (Basingstoke: Palgrave Macmillan).

'Consolidated Version of the Treaty on the Functioning of the European Union' (2010) *Official Journal of the European Union*, C83/47, 30 March.

Corporate Europe Observatory and India FDI Watch (2010) *Trade Invaders: How Big Business Is Driving the EU-India Free Trade Negotiations.*

Costa v ENEL (1964), *Costa v Ente Nazionale per L'Energia Elettrica (ENEL)*, ECJ Case 6/64, [1964] ECR 585.

Court of Auditors (2004) 'Special Report No 14/2003 on the Measurement of Farm Incomes by the Commission Article 33(1) of the EEC Treaty together with the Commission's Replies', *Official Journal of the European Union* (2004/C 45/01).

Cowles, M. G. (2001) 'The Transatlantic Business Dialogue and Domestic Business-Government Relations', in M. G. Cowles, J. Caporaso, and T. Risse (eds), *Transforming Europe: Europeanization and Domestic Political Change* (Ithaca: Cornell University Press): 159–79.

Craig, P. (2010) *The Lisbon Treaty: Law, Politics, and Treaty Reform* (Oxford: Oxford University Press).

Cram, L. (2012) 'Does the EU need a navel? Implicit and explicit identification with the European Union', *Journal of Common Market Studies* 50(1): 71–86.

Crawford, C. (2009) 'European Foreign Policy vs the Iron Laws of Physics', 15 November, http://charlescrawford.biz/blog/european-foreign-policy-v-the-iron-laws-of-physics (accessed 15 December, 2011).

Daugbjerg, C. and Swinbank, A. (2007) 'The politics of CAP reform: trade negotiations, institutional settings and blame avoidance', *Journal of Common Market Studies* 45(1): 1–2.

De Bièvre, D. and Dür, A. (2005) 'Constituency interests and delegation in European and American trade policy', *Comparative Political Studies* 38(10): 1271–96.

De Burca, G. (2010) 'The European Court and the International Legal Order after Kadi', *Harvard International Law Journal* 51 (1): 1–49.

De Burca, G. (2011) 'Roads not taken: the EU as a global human rights actor', *American Journal of International Law* 105: 649–93.

De Witte, B. (2011) 'The European Treaty Amendment for the Creation of a Financial Stability Mechanism', SIEPS (Swedish Institute for European Policy Studies), European Policy Analysis, June, Issue 6: 1–8.

Der Spiegel (2010) 'The EU has No vision of Where We are Heading', *Der Spiegel*, 9 February.

DeSoucey, M. (2010) 'Gastronationalism: food traditions and authenticity politics in the European Union', *American Sociological Review* 75(3): 432–55.

Deutscher Bundestag (2005) 'Schriftliche Fragen mit den in der Woche vom 2 Mai 2005 eingegangenen Antworten der Bundesregierung', Drucksache 15/5434.

Die Welt (2012), Österreich profitiert am meisten vom Euro', 10 January; http://www.welt.de/wirtschaft/article13806244/Oesterreich-profitiert-am-meisten-vom-Euro.html (accessed 11 January, 2012).

Diez, T. and Pace, M. (2011) 'Normative Power Europe and Conflict Transformation', in R. Whitman (ed.), *Normative Power Europe: Empirical and Theoretical Perspectives* (Basingstoke: Palgrave): 210–55.

Dinan, D. (2010) *Ever Closer Union: An Introduction to European Integration*, 4th edn (Basingstoke: Palgrave Macmillan).

Document (1973) 'Document on the European Identity', published by the Nine Foreign Ministers (Copenhagen, 14 December 1973), http://aei.pitt.edu/4545/1/epc_identity_doc.pdf (last accessed 25 January, 2012)..

Duchêne, F. (1972) 'Europe's Role in World Peace', in: R. Mayne (ed.), *Europe Tomorrow: Sixteen Europeans Look Ahead* (London: Fontana): 32–47.

Duchesne, S. (2008) 'Waiting for a European identity ... reflections on the process of identification with Europe', *Perspectives on European Politics and Society* 9(4): 397–410.

Duchesne, S. (2010) 'L'identité européenne, entre science politique et science fiction' *Politique Européenne* 30 (Winter), 7–16.

Duchesne, S., Haegel, F., Frazer, E., Van Ingelgom, V., Garcia, G. and Frognier, A.-P. (2010) 'Europe between Integration and Globalisation: Social Differences and National Frames in the Analysis of Focus Groups Conducted in France, Francophone Belgium and the UK', *Politique Européenne* 30 (Winter): 67–106.

Duke, S. (2005) 'The Linchpin COPS: Assessing the Workings and Institutional Relations of the Political and Security Committee', *EIPA Working Paper*.

Dür, A. (2007) 'EU trade policy as protection for exporters: the agreements with Mexico and Chile', *Journal of Common Market Studies* 45(4): 833–55.

Dür, A. (2008) 'Bringing economic interests back into the study of EU trade policy making', *British Journal of Politics and International Relations* 10(1): 27–45.

Dür, A. (2010) *Protection for Exporters: Power and Discrimination in Transatlantic Trade Relations, 1930–2010* (Ithaca: Cornell University Press).

Dür, A. (2011) 'Fortress Europe or open door Europe? The external impact of the EU's Single Market in financial services', *Journal of European Public Policy* 18(5): 619–35.

Dür, A. (2012) 'The EU's Foreign Economic Policy: Limits to Delegation', in J. Richardson (ed.), *Constructing a Policy-making State? Policy Dynamics in the European Union* (Oxford: Oxford University Press).

Dür, A. and D. De Bièvre (2007) 'Inclusion without Influence? NGOs in European Trade Policy', *Journal of Public Policy* 27(1): 79–101.

Dyson, K. (ed.) (2008) *The Euro at Ten: Convergence, Europeanization and State Power* (Oxford: Oxford University Press).

Dyson, K. and Featherstone, K. (1999) *The Road to Maastricht: Negotiating Economic and Monetary Union* (Oxford: Oxford University Press).

ECJ (1978) *Amministrazione delle Finanze dello Stato v Simmenthal SpA (II)*, ECJ Case 106/77, [1978] ECR 629.

ECJ (2007) *Laval un Partneri Ltd v Svenska Byggnadsarbetareförbundet...* (Case C-341/05) Judgment of the Court (Grand Chamber) of 18 December 2007 ECR 2007: I-11767.

ECJ (2011) *Association belge des Consommateurs Test-Achats ASBL v Conseil des ministres*, 1 March 2011 (Case C/236/09).

Egan, M. P., Nugent N., and Paterson, W.E. (2010) *Research Agendas in EU Studies: Stalking the Elephant* (New York: Palgrave Macmillan).

Ehrlich, S. (2009) 'How common is the Common External Tariff? Domestic influences on European Union trade policy', *European Union Politics* 10(1): 115–41.

Eichengreen, B. (2010) 'The Breakup of the Euro Area', in A. Alesina and F. Giavazzi (eds), *Europe and the Euro* (Chicago: University of Chicago Press): 11–51.

Elsig, M. (2007) 'The EU's choice of regulatory venues for trade negotiations: aA tale of agency power?', *Journal of Common Market Studies* 45(4): 927–48.

Emmanouilidis, J. A. (2011) 'The Leitmotiv of a Global Europe', in L. Tsoukalis and J. A. Emmanouilidis (eds), *The Delphic Oracle on Europe: Is There a Future for the European Union?* (Oxford: Oxford University Press): 181–201.

Enderlein, H. and Verdun, A. (2009) 'EMU's teenage challenge: shat have we learned and can we predict from political science?', *Journal of European Public Policy* 16(4): 490–507.

Epstein, R. A. (2008) *In Pursuit of Liberalism: International Institutions in Postcommunist Europe* (Baltimore, MD: Johns Hopkins University Press).

Epstein, R. A. and Johnson, J. (2010) 'Uneven integration: Economic and Monetary Union in Central and Eastern Europe', *Journal of Common Market Studies* 48(5): 1235–58.

ESS (2003) 'A Secure Europe in a Better World. European Security Strategy' (Brussels: EU Institute for Security Studies).

Eurobarometer (1990) 'Public Opinion in the European Community', Standard Eurobarometer 33, Spring 1990.

Eurobarometer (2004) 'Public Opinion in the European Union', Standard Eurobarometer 61, Spring 2004.

Eurobarometer (2007) 'Public Opinion in the European Union', Standard Eurobarometer 68, Autumn 2007.

Eurobarometer (2010a) 'National and European Identity', Eurobarometer 73.3.

Eurobarometer (2010b) 'European Citizenship – Cross-Border Mobility: Aggregate Report August 2010', Survey co-ordinated by the European Commission's Directorate-General for Communication (DG COMM).

Eurobarometer (2010c) 'Europeans, Agriculture and the Common Agricultural Policy', Special Eurobarometer: 336.

Eurobarometer (2011) 'Public Opinion in the European Union', Standard Eurobarometer 75, Spring 2011.

Europe of Freedom and Democracy (2009) Charter. http://www.efdgroup.eu/index.php/about-us/who-we-are/charter.html.

EBRD (European Bank for Reconstruction and Development) (2011) *Transition Report 2010: Recovery and Reform* (London: EBRD).

European Commission (1973) 'Report on the Regional Problems in the Enlarged Community (Thomson report)' (Brussels: European Commission).

European Commission (1999) 'The Fifteen at the WTO: a Stronger, More United Voice', http://ec.europa.eu/agriculture/ (last accessed 8 May 2008).

European Commission (2007) *Single Market in Financial Services Progress Report 2006* (Brussels: European Commission).

European Commission (2009) 'Report from the Commission – 27th Annual Report on Monitoring the Application of EU Law', Brussels, 1.10.2010, COM(2010) 538 Final.

European Commission (2010a) 'Ex Post Evaluation of cohesion policy programmes 2000-06 co-financed by the ERDF (Objective 1 & 2)' (Brussels: European Commission).

European Commission (2010b) 'Investing in Europe's future, Fifth Report on Economic, Social and Territorial Cohesion' (Brussels: European Commission).

European Council (2011) *The European Council in 2010* (Luxembourg: Publications Office of the European Union).

Favell, A. (2007) *Eurostars and Eurocities: Free Moving Urban Professionals in an Integrating Europe* (London: Blackwell).

Featherstone, K. (2011) 'The Greek sovereign debt crisis and EMU: a failing state in a skewed regime', *JCMS: Journal of Common Market Studies* 49(2): 193–217.

Feldstein M. (1997a) 'The political economy of the European Monetary Union', *Journal of Economic* Perspectives 11 (4).

Feldstein, M. (1997b) 'EMU and international conflict', *Foreign Affairs* 76(6).

Feldstein, M. (2012), 'The failure of the euro', *Foreign Affairs*, January/February.

Fierke, K. and Wiener, A. (2009) 'Constructing Institutional Interest: EU and NATO Enlargement', in F. Schimmelfennig and U. Sedelmeier (eds), *The Politics of European Union Enlargement* (Routledge): 99–119.

Financial Times (2006) 'Largest EU States Will Work Together on Crime' (J. Burns), 27 October.

Financial Times (2007) 'Commissioner Attacks EU Fisheries Policies', 19 February.

Financial Times (2011) 'French Warning to Euro Summit', 18 October.

Finke, D., König Th., Proksch S.-O. and Tsebelis, G. (2012) *Reforming the European Union: Realizing the Impossible* (Princeton: Princeton University Press).

Fischer-Boel, M. (2007), 'The Future of Rural Regions', Speech given at the informal Agriculture Council, Mainz, 22 May.

Fligstein, N. (2008) *Euroclash: The EU, European Identity, and the Future of Europe* (Oxford: Oxford University Press).

Føllesdal, A. and Hix, S. (2006) 'Why there is a democratic deficit in the European Union, s response to Majone and Moravcsik', *JCMS: Journal of Common Market Studies* 44(3): 533–62.

Forsyth, D. and Notermans, T. (eds) (1997) *Regime Changes* (Berghahn: Providence).

Franchino, F. (2007) *The Powers of the Union: Delegation in the EU* (Cambridge: Cambridge University Press).

Franchino, F. and Rahming, A. J. (2003) 'Biased Ministers, inefficiency, and control in distributive policies: sn application to the EU Fisheries Policy', *European Union Politics* 4(1): 11–36.

Friedrich, C. J. (1954) 'Introduction: The Background of These Studies and the Development of the Draft Constitution', in R. Bowie and C. Friedrich (eds) *Studies in Federalism* (Boston: Little Brown): xxv–xlii.

Gadinis, S. (2008) 'The politics of competition in international financial regulation', *Harvard International Law Journal*, 49(2): 447–507.

Garrett, G. (1992) 'International cooperation and institutional choice: The European Union's internal market', *International Organization* 46(2): 533–60.

Garzon, I. (2007) *Reforming the Common Agricultural Policy: History of a Paradigm Change* (London:Palgrave).

Gaxie, D., Hubé, N., de Lassalle, M. and Rowell, J. (2010) *L'Europe des Européens – Enquête comparative sur les perceptions de l'Europe* (Paris: Economica).

General Affairs and External Relations Council (2004) 'Headline Goal 2010', 17 May, http://ue.eu.int/uedocs/cmsUpload/2010%20Headline%20Goal.pdf (last accessed: 4 March 2012).

Geppert, K. and Stephan, A. (2008) 'Regional disparities in the European Union: convergence and agglomeration', *Papers in Regional Science* 87(2): 193–217.

Gerlach, C. (2006) 'Does business really run EU trade policy? Observations about EU trade policy lobbying', *Politics* 26(3): 176–83.

Gerrits, A. (ed.) (2009) *Normative Power Europe in a Changing World: A Discussion* (The Hague: Netherlands Institute of International Relations Clingendael).

Gerston, L. N. (2006) *American Federalism: A Concise Introduction* (Armonk, NY: M.E. Sharpe).

Gillingham, J. (2003) *European Integration, 1950-2003: Superstate or New Market Economy?* (Cambridge: Cambridge University Press).

Gillingham, J. (2005) 'Europe at the Tipping Point', Telders Lecture, Leiden NL, March.

Gillingham, J. (2006a) *Design for a New Europe* (New York: Cambridge University Press).

Gillingham, J. (2006b) 'Redesigning Europe', St. Stephen's Club, London, 13 February.

Goldsmith, J. and Posner, E. (2009). 'Does Europe Believe in International Law?', *Wall Street Journal*, 25 November: A15.

Goodhart, C. (2009), 'Procyclicality and Financial Regulation', Banco de España, *Estabilidad Financiera*, No. 16: 10–20.

Góra, M. and Mach, Z. (eds) (2010) 'Collective Identity and Democracy. The Impact of EU Enlargement', *ARENA Report* 4(10); *RECON Report* 12 (Oslo).

Gottwald, J.-C. (2010) *Regulierung der Finanzmärkte in der EU. Möglichkeiten und Grenzen der politischen Gestaltung dynamischer Märkte im europäischen Mehr-Ebenen-System* (Baden-Baden: Nomos).

Gowan, R. and Brantner, F. (2008) *A Global Force for Human Rights? An Audit of European Power at the UN* (London: European Council on Foreign Relations).

Grabbe, H. (2001) 'How does Europeanization affect CEE governance? Conditionality, diffusion and diversity', *Journal of European Public Policy* 8(6): 1013–32.

Greenwood, J. (2011) *Interest Representation in the European Union* (Basingstoke: Palgrave Macmillan).

Grosche, G. and Puetter, U. (2008) 'Preparing the Economic and Financial Committee and the Economic Policy Committee for enlargement', *Journal of European Integration* 30(4): 529–45.

Grugel, J. (2004) 'New regionalism and modes of governance – comparing US and EU strategies in Latin America', *European Journal of International Relations* 10(4): 603–26.

Grzymala-Busse, A. and Innes, A. (2003) 'Great expectations: The EU and Domestic Political Competition in East Central Europe', *East European Politics and Societies* 17: 64–73.

Guéguen, Daniel (2010) *Comitology: Hijacking European Power?* (Brussels: European Training Institute).

Haas, E. B. (1958) *The Uniting of Europe: Political, Social, and Economic Forces 1950–1957* (London: Stevens & Sons Limited).

Habermas, J. (1996) *Between Facts and Norms* (Cambridge: Polity).

Hafner-Burton, E. M. (2009) *Forced to Be Good: Why Trade Agreements Boost Human Rights* (Ithaca: Cornell University Press).

Haine, J.-Y.and Giegerich, B. (2006) 'In Congo, a Cosmetic EU Pperation', *International Herald Tribune*, 12 June.

Hayes-Renshaw, F. and Wallace, H. (2006) *The Council of Ministers* (Basingstoke: Palgrave Macmillan).

Heipertz, M. and Verdun, A. (2010) *Ruling Europe: The Politics of the Stability and Growth Pact* (Cambridge: Cambridge University Press).

Hix, S. (2008) *What's Wrong with the European Union and How to Fix It* (Cambridge: Polity).

Hix, S. and Høyland, B. (2011) *The Political System of the European Union,* 3rd edn (Basingstoke: Palgrave Macmillan).

Hix, S., Noury, A.G. and Roland, G. (2007) *Democratic Politics in the European Parliament* (Cambridge University Press).

Hodson, D. (2011) 'The EU economy: the eurozone in 2010', *Journal of Common Market Studies* 49 (Annual Review): 231–49.

Hoffmann, S. (1966) 'Obstinate or obsolete? The fate of the nation state and the case of western Europe', *Daedalus* 95(3): 862–916.

Hooghe, L. (1996) *Cohesion policy and European Integration: Bbuilding Multi-level Governance* (Oxford: Oxford University Press).

Hope, K., Murphy, M. and Tett, G. (2010) 'Athenian Arrangers', *Financial Times,* 17 February.

Horvath, A. (2008) 'From Policy to Politics? Informal Practices within the Social Protection Committtee after the Enlargement', *Journal of European Integration* 30(4): 545–61.

House of Commons Library (2010) 'How Much Legislation Comes from Europe?', Research Paper 10/62.

House of Lords (2006) 'European Union – Fortieth Report', European Union Committee.

House of Lords (2008) *The Future of EU Regional Policy,* European Union Committee, Nineteenth Report of Session 2007-08, HL paper 141 (London: TSO).

Howarth, D. and Loedel, P. (2005) *The European Central Bank: The New European Leviathan* (Basingstoke: Palgrave Macmillan).

Howorth, J. (2007) *Security and Defence Policy in the European Union* (Basingstoke and New York: Palgrave Macmillan).

Howorth, J. and Keeler J. (eds) (2003) *Defending Europe: the EU, NATO and the Quest for European Autonomy* (New York: Palgrave Macmillan).

Hughes, J., Sassen, G. and Gordon, C. (2002) 'Saying "Maybe" to the Return to Europe', *European Union Politics* 3(3): 327–55.

Ilzkovitz, F., Dierx, A., Kovacs, V. and Sousa, N. (2007) 'Steps towards a Deeper Economic Integration: The Internal Market in the 21st Century', *European Economy – Economic Papers,* 271, January, Directorate-General for Economic Affairs.

International Crisis Group (2001) *EU Crisis Response Capability: Institutions and Processes for Conflict Prevention and Management* (Brussels: ICG).

International Crisis Group (2006) *Congo Crisis: Military Intervention in Ituri* (Brussels: ICG).

International Institute for Strategic Studies (2008) *European Military Capabilities: Building Armed Forces for Modern Operations* (London: IISS).

Janning, J. (1996) 'A German Europe – a European Germany. On the debate over Germany's Foreign Policy', *International Affairs* 72(1): 33–41.

Joerges, C. (2011) 'A New Type of Conflicts Law as the Legal Paradigm of the Postnational Constellation', in C. Joerges and J. Falke (eds), *Karl Polanyi, Globalisation and the Potential of Law in Transnational Markets* (Portland: Hart Publishing): 465–501.

Joerges, C. and Neyer, J. (1997) 'Transforming strategic interaction into deliberative problem-solving: European comitology in the foodstuffs sector', *Journal of European Public Policy* 4(4): 609–25.

Johnson, S. and Kwak, J. (2010) *13 Bankers: The Wall Street Takeover and the Next Financial Meltdown* (New York: Pantheon).

Jones, A. and Clark, J.R. (2001) *The Modalities of European Union Governance: New Institutionalist Explanations of Agri-Environment Policy* (Oxford: Oxford University Press).

Jones, E. (2008) *Economic Adjustment and Political Transformation in Small States* (Oxford: Oxford University Press).

Jones, E. (2011) 'The Eurobond: Proposals, Comments, and Speeches', Johns Hopkins University, Bologna Centre, mimeo; http://www.jhubc.it/facultypages/ejones/Eurobond.pdf.

Judge, D. and Earnshaw, D. (2008) *The European Parliament*, 2nd edn (Basingstoke: Palgrave Macmillan).

Juncker, J. C. (2008) Transcription du discours lors de la Journée de deuil national (Volkstrauertag), Bundestag, Berlin, available at http://www.gouvernement.lu/salle_presse/discours/premier_ministre/2008/11-novembre/16-juncker/index.html.

Juncos, A. (2011) 'Power Discourses and Power Practices: The EU's Role as a Normative Power in Bosnia', in R. Whitman (ed), *Normative Power Europe: Empirical and Theoretical Perspectives* (Basingstoke: Palgrave Macmillan): 83–99.

Kadi (2008) *Kadi v Council of the European Union,* Decision of 3 September 2008 (Case C-402/05 P), decided along with *Al Barakaat International Foundation v Council* (C-415/05 P), ECR I6351.

Kagan, R. (2002) 'Power and weakness,' *Policy Review* 113 (June/July): 3–28.

Kagan, R. (2003) *Paradise and Power: America and Europe in the New World Order* (London: Atlantic Books).

Kelemen, D. (2010) *Eurolegalism: The Rise of Adversarial Legalism in the European Union* (Cambridge: Harvard University Press).

Kelemen, D. (2011) 'Political Foundations of Judicial Independence in the European Union', Paper for European Union Studies Convention, 23 February (Boston, MA).

Kelemen, D. and Vogel, D. (2009) 'Trading places: the role of the United States and the European Union in international environmental politics', *Comparative Political Studies* 43(4): 427–56.

Kelley, J. (2004) *Ethnic Politics in Europe: The Power of Norms and Incentives* (Princeton: Princeton University Press).

Kietz, D. and von Ondarza, N. (2010) 'Parliamentary dawn. The new self-confidence of the European Parliament', *Stiftung Wissenschaft und Politik Comments* (20) August.

Knudsen, A.-C. L. (2009) *Farmers on Welfare: The Making of Europe's Common Agricultural Policy* (Ithaca: Cornell University Press).

Kohli, M. (2000) 'The battlegrounds of European identity', *European Societies* 2(2).

Kopstein, J. and Reilly, D. A. (2003) 'Postcommunist Spaces: A Political Geography Approach to Explaining Postcommunist Outcomes', in G. Ekiert and S.E. Hanson (eds), *Capitalism and Democracy in Central and Eastern Europe: Assessing the Legacy of Communist Rule* (New York: Cambridge University Press): 120–56.

Korski, D. and Gowan, R. (2009) *Can the EU Rebuild Failing States? A Review of Europe's Civilian Capacities* (London: European Council on Foreign Relations).

Krastev, I. (2007) 'The strange death of the liberal consensus', *Journal of Democracy* 18(4): 56–63.

Kutas, G., Lindberg, C. and Steenblik, R. (2007) 'Biofuels – At What Cost? Government Support for Ethanol and Biodiesel in the European Union', The Global Subsidies Initiative of the International Institute for Sustainable Development (Geneva).

Lacroix, J. and Nicolaïdis, K. (2010) *European Stories: Intellectual Debates on Europe in National Contexts* (Oxford: Oxford University Press).

Laïdi, Z. (2008a) *Norms over Force: The Enigma of European Power* (Basingstoke: Palgrave Macmillan).

Laïdi, Z. (ed.) (2008b) *EU Foreign Policy in a Globalized World: Normative Power and Social Preferences* (London: Routledge).

Lamfalussy, A. (2001) 'Final Report of the Committee of Wise Men on the Regulation of European Securities Markets', 15 February, http://ec.europa.eu/internal_market/securities/docs/lamfalussy/wisemen/final-report-wise-men_en.pdf, (last accessed 29 October 2010).

Lascoumbes, P. and Le Galès, P. (2007) 'Introduction: Understanding Public Policy through its Instruments. From the Nature of Instruments to the Sociology of Public Policy Instrumentation', *Governance: An International Journal of Policy, Administration, and Institutions* (20): 1–21.

Le Monde (2010) 'Edouard Balladur: L'Europe à 27 est vouée à l'échec', 25 September .

Le Soir (2011) 'Steven Vanackere critique Catherine Ashton', 4 May.

Leca, J. (2009) '"The Empire Strikes Back!" an uncanny view of the European Union', *Government and Opposition* 45(2): 208–93.

Lequesne, C. (2000) 'Quota hopping: the Common Fisheries Policy between states and markets', *Journal of Common Market Studies* 38(5): 779–93.

Levine, C. (2007) 'A market Turned Upside Down', *Wall Street and Technology* 25(2) (February): 27f.

Liebert, U. (2001) 'Constructing Monetary Union: Euro-Scepticism, and the Emerging European Public Space', in B. Strath and L. Magnusson (eds), *From the Werner Plan to European Monetary Union: Towards a Political Economy for Europe* (Brussels: Peter Lang).

Liebert, U. (ed.) (2007) 'Europe in contention. Debating the Constitutional Treaty', *Special Issue of Perspectives on European Politics and Society* 8(3).

Liebert, U. (2010) 'Contentious European Democracy: National Intellectuals in Transnational Debates', in J. Lacroix and K. Nicolaïdis (eds), *European*

Stories. Intellectual Debates on Europe in National Contexts (Oxford: Oxford University Press): 50–76.

Liebert, U. and Trenz, H.-J. (eds) (2010) *The New Politics of European Civil Society* (London: Routledge).

Lightfoot, S. and Burchell, J. (2004) 'Green hope or greenwash? The actions of the European Union at the World Summit on Sustainable Development', *Global Environmental Change* 14(4): 337–44.

Lightfoot, S. and Burchell, J. (2005) 'The European Union and the World Summit on Sustainable Development: Normative Power Europe in Action?', *Journal of Common Market Studies* 43(1): 75–95.

Lindberg, L. and Scheingold, S. (1970) *Europe's Would-be Polity* (Upper Saddle River, NJ: Prentice Hall).

Lindseth, P. L. (2010) *Power and Legitimacy: Reconciling Europe and the Nation-State* (Oxford, New York: Oxford University Press).

Lister, F. K. (1996) *The European Union, the United Nations, and the Revival of Confederal Governance* (Westport, CT: Greenwood).

Lord, C. (2004) *A Democratic Audit of the European Union* (Basingstoke: Palgrave Macmillan).

Lord, C. (2011) 'Polecats, lions and foxes: Coasian bargaining theory and attempts to legitimate the Union as a constrained form of political power', *European Political Science Review* 3(1): 83–102.

Lucarelli, S. (ed.) (2007) *Values and Principles in European Union Foreign Policy* (London: Routledge).

Lucarelli, S. and Manners, I. (eds) (2006) *Values and Principles in Eruopean Foreign Policy*, (London and New York: Routledge).

Maduro, M. P. (1998) *We the court: the European Court of Justice and the European Economic Constitution : a critical reading of Article 30 of the EC Treaty* (Oxford: Hart Publishers).

Majone, G. (1998) 'Europe's "democratic deficit": the question of standards,' *European Law Journal* 4(1): 5–28.

Majone, G. (2005) *Dilemmas of European Integration: The Ambiguities and Pitfalls of Integration by Stealth* (Oxford: Oxford University Press).

Majone, G. (2009) *Europe as the Would-be World Power: The EU at Fifty* (Cambridge: Cambridge University Press).

Majone, G. (2011) 'Political and Normative Limits to Piecemeal Integration Rethinking the European Project After the Crisis of Monetary Union', Keynote Lecture at RECON Concluding Conference, Oslo, 24–26 November.

Manners, I. (2002) 'Normative Power Europe: a contradiction in terms?', *Journal of Common Market Studies* 40(2): 235–58.

Manners, I. (ed) (2010) 'Normative Power', Virtual Special Issue of *Journal of European Public Policy*, http://www.tandf.co.uk/journals/access/rjpp.pdf.

Marks, G., Hooghe, L. and Blank, K. (1996) 'European integration from the 1980s: state-centric v. multi-level governance', *Journal of Common Market Studies* 34(3): 341–78.

Martin, M. (2011) 'Human Security and the Search for a Normative Narrative', in R. Whitman (ed.), *Normative Power Europe: Empirical and Theoretical Perspectives* (Basingstoke: Palgrave Macmillan): 187–209.

McCormick, J. (2010) *Europeanism* (Oxford: Oxford University Press).

McCormick, J. (2011a), *European Union Politics* (Basingstoke: Palgrave Macmillan).

McCormick, J. (2011b) *Understanding the European Union,* 5th edn (Basingstoke: Palgrave Macmillan).

McGowan, L. (2010) *The Antitrust Revolution in Europe: Exploring the European Commission's Cartel Policy* (Aldershot: Edward Elgar).

Mearsheimer, J. J. (1990) 'Back to the future: instability in Europe after the Cold War', *International Security* 15(1): 5–56.

Meinhof, U. H. (2004) 'Europe Viewed from Below: Agents, Victims, and the Threat of the Other', in R. K. Herrmann, T. Risse and M. B. Brewer (eds), *Transnational Identities: Becoming European in the EU* (Oxford: Rowman & Littlefield).

Menon, A. (2009) 'Empowering Paradise? The ESDP at Ten', *International Affairs* 85(2): 227–46.

Menon, A. (forthcoming) 'Defence Policy', in E. Jones, A. Menon and S. Weatherill (eds), *The Oxford Handbook of the European Union* (Oxford: Oxford University Press).

Merkel, A. (2010) Speech at the occasion of the opening of the 61st Academic Year of the College of Europe, 2 November, Bruges.

Meunier, S. (2005) *Trading Voices: The European Union in International Commercial Negotiations* (Princeton: Princeton University Press).

Meunier, S. and Nicolaïdis, K. (2006) 'The European Union as a conflicted trade power', *Journal of European Public Policy* 13(6): 906–25.

Milward, A. (1993) *The European Rescue of the Nation State* (London: Routledge).

Moloney, N. (2008) *European Securities Regulation,* 2nd edn (London/New York: Oxford University Press).

Monnet, J. (1978) *Memoirs* (Garden City, NY: Doubleday).

Moravcsik, A. (1993) 'Preferences and Power in the European Community: A Liberal Intergovernmentalist Approach', *Journal of Common Market Studies* 31(4): 473–524.

Moravcsik, A. (1998) *The Choice for Europe: Social Purpose and State Power from Messina to Maastricht* (Ithaca: Cornell University Press).

Moravcsik, A. (2002) 'In defence of the "democratic deficit": reassessing legitimacy in the European Union', *Journal of Common Market Studies* 40(4): 603–24.

Moravcsik, A. (2010) 'The Foreign Policy of the European Union: Assessing Results, Ushering in a New Era', panel discussion, The Brookings Institution, EU-2010/04/08. www.brookings.edu/~/media/Files/events/2010/0408_european_union/20100408_european_union.pdf.

Mügge, D. (2010) *Widen the Market, Narrow the Competition. Banker interests in the making of a European capital market* (Colchester: ECPR Press).

Mügge, D., Blom, J. and Underhill, G. (2010) 'Whither Global Financial Governance after the Crisis?' in G. Underhill, J. Blom and D. Mügge (eds), *Global Financial Integration Thirty Years On: From Reform to Crisis* (Cambridge: Cambridge University Press): 304–15.

Mundell, R. (1961) 'A theory of optimum currency areas', *American Economic Review* 51(4).

Murkens, J. E. K. (2009) 'Countering Anti-constitutional Argument: The Reasons for the European Court of Justice's Decision in Kadi and Al Barakaat', in C. Barnard and O. Odudu (eds), *Cambridge Yearbook of European Legal Studies 2008–2009* (Oxford: Hart Publishing): 15–52.

Nedergaard, P. (2006) 'The 2003 Reform of the Common Agricultural Policy: against all odds or rational explanations?', *Journal of European Integration* 28(3): 203–24.

Nicolaïdis, K. (2003) 'The New Constitution as European Demoi-cracy?', *Critical Review of Social and Political Philosophy* 7(1): 76–93.

Noelle-Neumann, E. (1984) *The Spiral of Silence: Public Opinion – Our Social Skin* (Chicago: UCP).

Nugent, N. (2010) *Government and Politics of the European Union*, 7th edn (Basingstoke: Palgrave Macmillan).

Nye, J. (2002) *The Paradox of American Power: Why the World's Only Superpower Can't Go It Alone* (Oxford: Oxford University Press).

Oersted Nielsen, H., Branth Pedersen, A. and Christensen, T. (2009) 'Environmentally sustainable agriculture and future developments of the CAP', *Journal of European Integration* 31(3): 369–87.

Official Journal of the European Union (2008) Judgment of the Court (Grand Chamber) of 26 February 2008, 12 April 2008: C 92/3.

Ojanen, H. (2011a) 'The EU as a Security Actor: In and With the UN and NATO', in D. Bourantonis, and S.Blavoukos (eds), *The EU Presence in International Organisations* (Abingdon, Oxon and New York: Routledge).

Ojanen, H. (2011b) 'European Defence: Functional Transformation Under Way', in M. Foucault, B. Irondelle and F. Mérand (eds), *European Security Since the Fall of the Berlin Wall* (Toronto: University of Toronto Press).

Open Europe (2009) *Out of Control? Measuring a Decade of EU Regulation* (London: Open Europe).

Open Europe (2010) *Still Out of Control? Measuring Eleven Years of EU Regulation* (London: Open Europe).

Orbie, J. (2011) 'Promoting Labour Standards Through Trade: Normative Power or Regulatory State Europe?', in R. Whitman (ed), *Normative Power Europe: Empirical and Theoretical Perspectives* (Basingstoke: Palgrave Macmillan): 160–83.

Orenstein, M. A. (2008) 'Out-liberalizing the EU: Pension Privatization in Central and Eastern Europe', *Journal of European Public Policy* 15(6): 899–917.

OECD (Organisation for Economic Co-operation and Development) (2010) *Agricultural Policies in the OECD Countries at a Glance* (Paris: OECD).

Ost, D. (2005) *The Defeat of Solidarity: Anger and Politics in Postcommunist Europe* (Ithaca, NY: Cornell University Press).

Oxfam (2003) *EU Hypocrisy Unmasked: Why EU Trade Policy Hurts Development* (Brussels: Oxfam).

Oxfam (2008) *Mission Incomplete: Why Civilians remain at risk in Eastern Chad* (Oxford: Oxfam).

Paterson, W.E., Nugent, N. and Egan, M.P. (2010) 'Hastening Slowly: European Studies – Between Reinvention and Continuing Fragmentation', in M.P. Egan, N. Nugent and W.E. Paterson (eds) *Research Agenda in EU Studies: Stalking the Elephant* (Basingstoke: Palgrave Macmillan): 398–419.

Patten, C. (2005) *Not Quite the Diplomat: Home Truths about World Affairs* (London: Penguin).

Payne, D. C. (2000) 'Policy-making in nested institutions: explaining the conservation failure of the EU's Common Fisheries Policy', *Journal of Common Market Studies* 38(2): 303–24.

Peterson, J. (2008) 'José Manuel Barroso: Political Scientist, ECPR Member', *European Political Science* 7: 64–77.

Piris, J.-C. (2010) *The Lisbon Treaty: A Legal and Political Analysis* (Cambridge: Cambridge University Press).

Pochet, P. (2004) 'The Nature of the Open Method of Co-ordination', in R. Salais and R. Villeneuve (eds), *Europe and the Politics of Capabilities* (Cambridge: Cambridge University Press): 185–201.

Poehl, O. (2010) 'Bailout Plan is All About "Rescuing Banks and Rich Greeks"', Spiegel-online, 18 May.

Polenske, K. (2007) *The Economic Geography of Innovation* (Cambridge: Cambridge University Press).

Pollack, M. A. and Shaffer, G. C. (2009) *When Cooperation Fails: The Global Law and Politics of Genetically Modified Organisms* (New York: Oxford University Press).

Posner, E. (2009) 'Making rules for global finance: transatlantic regulatory cooperation at the turn of the millennium', *International Organization*, 63 (4): 665–99.

Posner, E. (2010) 'Is a European Approach to Financial Regulation Emerging from the Crisis?', in E. Helleiner, S. Pagliari and H. Zimmermann (eds), *Global Finance in Crisis. The Politics of International Regulatory Change* (Milton Park, New York: Routledge): 108–20.

Posner, E. and Véron, N. (2010) 'The EU and Financial Regulation: Power without Purpose?', *Journal of European Public Policy* 17(3): 400–15.

Preston, C. (1995) 'Obstacles to EU enlargement: the classical community method and the prospects for a wider Europe', *Journal of Common Market Studies* 33(3): 451–63.

Puetter, U. (2006) *The Eurogroup: How a Secretive Circle of Finance Ministers Shape European Economic Governance* (Manchester: Manchester University Press).

Puetter, U. (2012) 'Europe's Deliberative Intergovernmentalism – the Role of the Council and European Council in EU Economic Governance', *Journal of European Public Policy* 19(2).

Quaglia, L. (2008) 'Financial Sector Committee Governance in the European Union', *Journal of European Integration*, 30(4): 563–78.

Quaglia, L. (2010) *Governing Financial Services in the European Union* (London: Routledge).

Rachman, G. (2006) 'How the Square Mile Fell Out of Love with Brussels', *Financial Times,* 12 December.

Rachman, G. (2011) 'Financial Services: Building a Framework of Action', Communication of the Commission, Brussels

Raik, K. (2004) 'EU Accession of Central and Eastern European Countries: democracy and Integration as Conflicting Logics', *East European Politics and Societies* 18(4): 567–94.

Rawls, J. (1993) *Political Liberalism* (New York: Columbia University Press).

Richmond, O., Björkdahl, A., and Kappler, S. (2011) 'The Emerging EU Peacebuilding Framework: Confirming or Transcending Liberal Peacebuilding?', *Cambridge Review of International Studies* 24(3): 449–69.

Rieger, E. (2005) 'Agricultural Policy: Constrained Reforms', in: H. Wallace, W. Wallace and M.A. Pollack (eds), *Policy-Making in the European Union*, 5th edn (Oxford: Oxford University Press): 161–90.

Risse, T. (2010) *A Community of Europeans? Transnational Identities and Public Spheres* (Ithaca: Cornell University Press).

Romp, W. and De Haan, J. (2007) 'Public Capital and Economic Growth: A Critical Survey', *Perspektiven der Wirtschaftspolitik* 8 (S1): 6–52.

Rothschild, J. and Wingfield, N. (2000) *Return to Diversity: A Political History of East Central Europe since World War II* (Oxford: Oxford University Press).

Saad, L. (2011) 'Americans Express Historic Negativity Toward U.S. Government', http://www.gallup.com/poll/149678/Americans-Express-Historic-Negativity-Toward-Government.aspx.

Sabel, C. and Zeitlin, J. (2007) 'Learning from Difference: the New Architecture of Experimentalist Governance in the European Union', *European Governance Papers* (EuroGov).

Sadeh, T. (2006a) 'Adjusting to EMU: electoral, partisan and fiscal cycles', *European Union Politics* 7 (3): 347–72.

Sadeh, T. (2006b) *Sustaining European Monetary Union: Confronting the Cost of Diversity* (Boulder: Lynne Rienner).

Sadeh, T. (2009) 'EMU's diverging micro foundations – a study of governments' preferences and the sustainability of EMU', *Journal of European Public Policy* 16(4): 545–63.

Sandholtz, W. and Stone Sweet, A. (eds) (1998) *European Integration and Supranational Governance* (Oxford: Oxford University Press).

Sandholtz, W. and Zysman, J. (1989) '1992: Recasting the European bargain', *World Politics* 42(4): 95–128.

Sangiovanni, M. E. (2003) 'Why a Common Security and Defence Policy is bad for Europe', *Survival* 45(3): 193–206.

Scharpf, F. (1988) 'The Joint-decision trap: lessons from German Federalism and European integration', *Public Administration* 66: 239–78.

Scharpf, F. (1999) *Governing in Europe: Effective and Democratic?* (Oxford: Oxford University Press).

Scharpf, F. (2009) 'Legitimacy in the Multilevel European Polity', *European Political Science Review* 1(2): 173–204.

Scheipers, S. and Sicurelli, D. (2007) 'Normative Power Europe: a credible utopia', *Journal of Common Market Studies* 45(2): 435–57.

Scheipers, S. and Sicurelli, D. (2008) 'Empowering Africa: Normative Power in EU-Africa Relations', *Journal of European Public Policy* 15(4): 607–23.

Schiek, D., Liebert, U. and Schneider, H. (eds) (2011) *European Economic and Social Constitutionalism after the Treaty of Lisbon* (Cambridge: Cambridge University Press).

Schimmelfenning, F. (2011) 'How substantial Is substance? Concluding reflections on the study of substance in EU democracy promotion', *European Foreign Affairs Review* 16 (special issue): 727–34.

Schimmelfennig, F. and Sedelmeier, U. (2005) 'Conclusions: The Impact of the EU on the Accession Countries', in F. Schimmelfennig and U. Sedelmeier (eds), *The Europeanization of Central and Eastern Europe* (Ithaca: Cornell University Press): 210–28.

Schimmelfennig, F. and Sedelmeier, U. (eds) (2009) *The Politics of European Union Enlargement* (London: Routledge).

Schmidt, V.A. (2011) 'Saving the euro will mean worse trouble for Europe', *Foreign Affairs*, 28 November.

Secretary General of the United Nations (2008) Report of the Secretary General on the United Nations Mission in the Central African Republic and Chad.

Sheehan, J. (2008) *Where Have All the Soldiers Gone? The Transformation of Modern Europe* (New York: Houghton Mifflin).

Shore, C. (2000) *Building Europe: the Cultural Politics of European Integration* (London: Routledge).

Siedentop, L. (2000) *Democracy in Europe* (London: Allen Lane).

Sindicato (1998), Case C-303/98, Sindicato de Médicos de Asistencia Pública (SiMAP) v. Conselleria de Sanidad y Consumo de la Generalidad Valenciana.

Singer, D. (2004) 'Capital rules: the domestic politics of international regulatory harmonization', *International Organization*, 58(3): 531–65.

Sjursen, H. (ed.) (2006) *Civilian or Military Power? The European Union at a Crossroads* (London: Routledge).

Smith, K. E. (2001) 'The EU, Human Rights, and Relations with Third Countries: "Foreign Policy" with an Ethical Dimension?' in K. E. Smith and M. Light (eds), *Ethics and Foreign Policy* (New York: Cambridge University Press): 185–204.

Smith, M. (2003) 'The Framing of European Foreign and Security Policy: Towards a Post-modern Policy Framework?', *Journal of European Public Policy* 10(4): 556–75.

Smith, M. (2011) 'The European Union, the United States and Global Public Goods: Competing Models or Two Sides of the Same Coin?', in R. Whitman (ed.) *Normative Power Europe: Empirical and Theoretical Perspectives* (Basingstoke: Palgrave Macmillan): 126–38.

Statistisches Bundesamt (2011), *Fast 10 Jahre Euro – Preisentwicklung vor und nach der Bargeldumstellung,* Dezember (Wiesbaden: Statistisches Bundesamt).

Stein, E. (1981) 'Lawyers, judges and the making of a transnational constitution', *American Journal of International Law* 75(1): 1–27.

Stone, A. (1995) 'Governing with Judges: the New Constitutionalism', in J. Hayward and E. Page (eds), *Governing the New Europe* (Durham: Duke University Press).

Stone Sweet, A. (2004) *The Judicial Construction of Europe* (Oxford: Oxford University Press).

Stone Sweet, A. (2010) 'The European Court of Justice and the judicialisation of EU governance', *Living Reviews in EU Governance* 5(2).

Stone Sweet, A. and Brunell, T. (1998) 'Constructing a supranational constitution: dispute resolution and governance in the European Community', *American Political Science Review* 92: 63–81.

Stråth, B. (2002) 'A European identity: to the historical limits of a concept', *European Journal of Social Theory* 5(4).

Stråth, B. (ed.) (2010) *Europe and the Other and Europe as the Other*, 4th edn (Brussels: Peter Lang).

Süddeutsche Zeitung (2006) 'Der Kommissar ist nur ein Hausbesetzer', 4 October.

Swinbank, A. and Daugbjerg, C. (2006) 'The 2003 CAP Reform: Accommodating WTO Pressures', *Comparative European Politics* 4(1): 47–64.

Tallberg, J. (2008) 'Bargaining power in the European Council', *Journal of Common Market Studies* 46(3): 685–708.

Tallberg, J., Beach, D., Naurin D. and Tiilikainen T. (2011) *Makten i Europa* (Stockholm: SNS Förlag).

The Economist (2011) 'The Euro Area's Flagging Economy: The Shadow of Recession', *The Economist* 400 (8752), 24–30 September: 89.

The Economist (2011), 'Germany's Debt Brake: Tie Your Hands, Please', 10 December.

The Parliament (2011) 'MEPs Urge Member States to Halt "Misuse" of EU Arrest Warrant', 12 April.

The Telegraph (2010) 'Whatever Germany Does, the Euro as We Know it is Dead', *The Telegraph*, Monday 29 August, http://www.telegraph.co.uk/finance/comment/jeffrandall/7746806/Whatever-Germany-does-the-euro-as-we-know-it-is-dead.html.

Thomson, R. (2011) *Resolving Controversy in the European Union: Legislative Decision-Making Before and After Enlargement* (Cambridge: Cambridge University Press).

Tocci, N. (ed.) (2008) *Who is a Normative Foreign Policy Actor? The European Union and Its Global Partners* (Brussels: CEPS).

Tocci, N. and Manners, I. (2008) 'Comparing Normativity in Foreign Policy: China, India, the EU, the US and Russia' in N. Tocci (ed), *Who is a Normative Foreign Policy Actor?: The European Union and Its Global Partners* (Brussels: CEPS): 300–29.

Toje, A. (2008) *The EU, NATO and European Defence :- A Slow Train Coming* (Paris: EU Institute for Security Studies).

Tooze, A. (2006) *The Wages of Destruction: The Making and Breaking of the Nazi Economy* (Harmondsworth: Penguin Books).

Torres, F., Verdun, A. and Zimmermann, H. (eds) (2006) *EMU Rules: The Political and Economic Consequences of European Monetary Integration* (Baden-Baden: NOMOS).

'Treaty Establishing the European Economic Community' (1957), in *Treaties Establishing the European Communities. Treaties Amending these Treaties* (Luxembourg: Office of Official Publications of the European Communities, 1987).

Trubek, D.M. and Mosher, J.S. (2003) 'New Governance, Employment Policy, and the European Social Model', in J. Zeitlin and D.M. Trubek (eds), *Governing Work and Welfare in a New Economy: European and American Experiments* (Oxford: Oxford University Press): 33–58.

Tsoukalis, L. (1977) *The Politics and Economics of European Monetary Integration* (London: George Allen and Unwin).

Vachudova, M. A. (2005) *Europe Undivided: Democracy, Leverage and Integration after Communism* (Oxford: Oxford University Press).

van den Hoven, A. (2004) 'Assuming leadership in multilateral economic institutions: The EU's 'development round' discourse and strategy', *West European Politics* 27(2): 256–83.

Van Gend en Loos (1962), *Van Gend en Loos v Nederlandse Administratie Belastingen*, ECJ Case 26/62, [1963] ECR 1.

van Pottelsbergh de la Potterie, B. (2008) 'Europe's Rand D: missing the wrong targets', *Intereconomics,* July/August.

Van Raepenbusch, S. (2004) *Droit institutionnel de l'Union* (Brussels: De Bock and Larcier).

van Rompuy, H. (2011a) 'European Economic Governance and the New Institutional Balance', Speech at the 10th anniversary of the Association of Former Members of the European Parliament, Brussels, 4 May.

van Rompuy, H. (2011b) Address by Herman van Rompuy, President of the European Council, 66th United Nations General Assembly General Debate, http://www.consilium.europa.eu/uedocs/cms_data/docs/pressdata/en/ec/124714.pdf.

Verdun, A. (1996) 'An "Asymmetrical" Economic and Monetary Union in the EU: Perceptions of Monetary Authorities and Social Partners', *Journal of European Integration* 20(1): 59–81.

Verdun, A. (2000) *European Responses to Globalization and Financial Market Integration, Perceptions of EMU in Britain, France and Germany* (New York: St Martin's Press).

Verdun, A. and Christiansen, T. (2000) 'Policy-making, Institution-building and European Monetary Union: Dilemmas of Legitimating European Integration', in C. Crouch (ed.), *After the Euro: Shaping Institutions for Governance in the Wake of European Monetary Union* (Oxford: Oxford University Press): 162–78.

Villepin, D. de (2003), Annual BBC Dimbleby Lecture; available at: http://news.bbc.co.uk/2/hi/europe/3207948.stm (last accessed 25 January 2012).

von Weizsäcker, J. and Delpla, J. (2011) 'Eurobonds: The Blue Bond Concept and its Implications', 21 March, www.bruegel.org/publications/publication-detail/publication/509-eurobonds-the-blue-bond-concept-and-its-implications/.

Wagner, W. (2003) 'Why the EU's Common Foreign and Security Policy will Remain Intergovernmental: A Rationalist Institutional Choice Analysis of European Crisis Management Policy', *Journal of European Public Policy* 10(4): 576–95.

Wall Street Journal (2007) 'European Imperialism', *Wall Street Journal*, 31 October.

Wallace, H., Pollack, M. and Young, A. (eds) (2010) *Policy-Making in the European Union,* 6th edn (Oxford: Oxford University Press).

Webber, C. (2010) 'Normative Power or Economic Powerhouse? The State of Military and Dual-Use Item Regulation in the European Union,' unpublished paper, Temple University.

Weber, E. (1976) *Peasants into Frenchmen: The Modernization of Rural France, 1870–1914* (Stanford: Stanford University Press)

Weiler, J. (1991) 'The transformation of Europe', *Yale Law Journal* 100(8): 2403–73.

Weiler, J. (1995) 'Does Europe need a constitution? reflections on demos, telos and the German Maastricht decision', *European Law Journal* 1(3): 219–58.

Werner, P. (1970) 'Report to the Council and the Commission on the Realisation by Stages of Economic and Monetary Union in the Community (Werner Report)', Brussels.

White, J. (2011) *Political Allegiance after European Integration* (Basingstoke: Palgrave Macmillan).

White, J. (forthcoming) 'Community, transnationalism and the left–right metaphor', *European Journal of Social Theory*.

Whitman, R. (ed.) (2011) *Normative Power Europe: Empirical and Theoretical Perspectives* (Basingstoke: Palgrave Macmillan).

Whitman, R. and Nicolaïdis, K. (eds) (forthcoming) 'European Union and normative power: Assessing the Decade', Special Issue of *Cooperation and Conflict*.

Witney, N. (2008) *Re-energising Europe's Security and Defence Policy* (London: European Council on Foreign Relations).

Wolff, L. (1994) *Inventing Eastern Europe: The Map of Civilization on the Mind of the Enlightenment* (Stanford, CA: Stanford University Press).

Woll, C. (2008) *Firm Interests: How Governments Shape Business Lobbying on Global Trade* (Ithaca, NY: Cornell University Press).

Woll, C. (2009) 'Trade Policy Lobbying in the European Union: Who Captures Whom?', in D. Coen and J. Richardson (eds), *Lobbying in the European Union: Institutions, Actors and Issues* (Oxford: Oxford University Press): 277–97.

Yesilada, B. A. and Wood, D. M. (2010) *The Emerging European Union,* 5th edn (London: Pearson Education).

Young, A. (2004) 'The incidental fortress: the Single European Market and world trade', *Journal of Common Market Studies* 42(2): 393–414.

Zielonka, J. (2006) *Europe as Empire: The Nature of the Enlarged European Union* (Oxford: Oxford University Press).

Zimmermann, H. (2007) 'Realist power Europe? The EU in the negotiations about China's and Russia's WTO accession', *Journal of Common Market Studies* 45(4): 813–32.

Zimmermann, H. (2012) 'Getting Real? The International Role of the Euro after the Financial Crisis', in: A. Cafruny and H. Schwartz (eds), *The Permanent Crisis? Yearbook of International Political Economy* 18 (Lynne Rienner: Boulder) (forthcoming).

Zürn, M. and Checkel, J. T. (2005) 'Getting socialized to build bridges: constructivism and rationalism, Europe and the nation-state', *International Organization* 59(4): 1045–79.

Index